THE
DESIGN
LAB GALERIE
KREO

With contributions by

Clémence and Didier Krzentowski

Virgil Abloh
Johanna Agerman Ross
Barber & Osgerby
François Bauchet
Ronan & Erwan Bouroullec
Marcel Brient
Pierre Charpin
Alex Coles
Front Design
Naoto Fukasawa
Donatien Grau
Konstantin Grcic
Jaime Hayon
Guillaume Houzé
Hella Jongerius
Bertrand Lavier
Jasper Morrison
Marc Newson
Marco Romanelli
Christian Schlatter
Muller Van Severen
Jerszy Seymour
Brynjar Sigurðarson
Studio Wieki Somers

THE DESIGN LAB

GALERIE KREO

Edited by Clément Dirié

Flammarion

CONTENTS

9 THE INTERVIEW
A CONVERSATION WITH CLÉMENCE AND DIDIER KRZENTOWSKI

31 THE YEARBOOK
EXHIBITIONS 1999–2019, PARIS AND LONDON

283 THE COMPANIONS
EIGHT INFORMED PERSPECTIVES ON GALERIE KREO

325 THE DESIGNERS' WORLD
CARTE BLANCHE FOR NINETEEN DESIGNERS

361 A CHRONOLOGY OF CONTEMPORARY DESIGN
GALERIE KREO: A MAJOR PLAYER IN THE 2000S AND 2010S

Published on the occasion of Galerie kreo's twentieth anniversary, this book retraces the innovative activities of this lab dedicated to contemporary design. It features an interview with its founders, Clémence and Didier Krzentowski, essays by those who have accompanied Galerie kreo on its adventure, original contributions from the designers, and a chronology connecting the activities of the gallery's designers with the world of contemporary design. The core of this publication is The Yearbook, i.e. all the exhibitions "made in kreo," organized since 1999, in Paris and, since 2014, in London. For it, we have chosen to reproduce, as far as possible, photographs, documents, and texts contemporary with their exhibitions. Fourteen collectors close to Galerie kreo also testify to their relationship with the designers they met there.

Since 2010, I have collaborated with Galerie kreo on the publication of books and other writing. Immersing myself in the archives, evoking the origins and contexts of the exhibitions with their designers, and realizing the uniqueness of each of them, as well as the coherence of Clémence and Didier Krzentowski's vision of design, have been a source of intellectual pleasure—a wonderful combination of words—which, I'm convinced, will be repeated again and again on the occasion of each new exhibition.

Clément Dirié

This interview purposely focuses on a few key moments in the history of Galerie kreo and of its founders, providing a context for the subsequent sections in this volume. The Yearbook and The Companions, in particular, address at greater length some of the subjects touched on here.

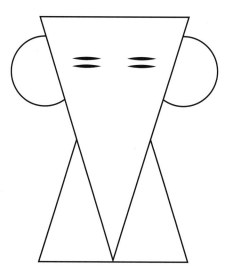

THE INTERVIEW

A CONVERSATION WITH CLÉMENCE AND DIDIER KRZENTOWSKI

THE KREO ADVENTURE: AN ONGOING PASSION

Clément Dirié   It's June 5, 2019. As I've been pursuing my discoveries in the gallery archives, we've put off this interview for several weeks. Once the idea for this publication came to us in November 2018, knowing you had a mass of documents concerning almost all of your exhibitions was both encouraging and exciting. It meant that, instead of having to reconstruct the kreo story *a posteriori*, we were going to be able to base it on documents, texts, and photographs from the time, as in the Yearbook. And this morning, on the occasion of our first interview, I looked up the date of the opening of your launch exhibition on rue Louise Weiss, where the gallery was located from 1999 to 2008. The date was June 5, 1999! Twenty years ago to the day. No reader will believe us, but it's true. Do you remember that day and that debut exhibition?

Didier Krzentowski   Of course! I also remember the background to it and all the luck that led to us opening a gallery. Together with Clémence, we had founded Agence kreo in 1992, and seven years later I was getting a little tired of it. After enthusiastic beginnings, we realized that carrying out really interesting projects was becoming more and more complicated.

    The only way to get it to work was to talk directly to CEOs and share our creative vision with them, but "marketing and communication" departments were gaining a hold and becoming a drag on creativity. Though many splendid projects did see the light of day in the 1990s, it was starting to get us down.

    One evening in 1999 I forgot my cellphone on rue Louise Weiss after visiting a few exhibitions. That part of the 13th *arrondissement* was then beginning to take off and become a hub for contemporary art in Paris. So, the next day, I went to pick it up at Audiernes, the bistro on the street and our HQ in those years. I had a coffee there with the gallery owners Jennifer Flay and Emmanuel Perrotin, who informed me, "You, who love design, there's 45m² [480 sq. ft.] free just opposite. You could do something with it." I discussed it with Clémence and we got going right away.

Clémence Krzentowski   Didier called me up and said, "Are you sitting down? What do you think about opening a place to show duplicates from our collection?" I have to say that at that time he was spending more and more time in galleries and flea markets!

D.K. So the first exhibition featured "duplicates" from my own collection: notably pieces by Joe Colombo, Verner Panton, Pierre Paulin, and Gino Sarfatti. Our location on rue Louise Weiss, where contemporary art galleries were beginning to attract an informed audience, helped us a lot. From the opening there were a lot of people and all the visitors seemed very interested in seeing furniture—this was unusual for the time. As I had been collecting contemporary art and photography since the 1980s, I had many friends in the art world. All these people came to say hi. This first experience confirmed our belief that we might try to do something around design—even though there were not, as yet any, very precise plans.

C.D. Do you recall the reactions of the earliest visitors?

D.K. The reaction was generally good, but we knew that there would be a lot of work to do, informing and persuading.

One thing I do remember is my own reaction on visiting the exhibition *Passions privées: Collections particulières d'art moderne et contemporain en France*, organized by Suzanne Pagé in 1995 at the Musée d'Art Moderne de la Ville de Paris. We contributed items from my photography collection: Cindy Sherman, Nan Goldin, Louise Lawler—contemporary photography formed one of my earliest collections. Later, we lent our dining-room furniture to the Maison Rouge for their inaugural

Clémence and Didier
Krzentowski at home,
Paris, 2017

Pages 14–15
At Clémence and
Didier Krzentowski's
home, Paris, 2019

exhibition, *L'intime, le collectionneur derrière la porte* in 2004. When they called us up to arrange its return, I didn't want it back in the house. We'd shifted everything around! In short, at *Passions privées* I was a bit shocked to see that in three-quarters of the collectors' homes there were sublime paintings (impressionist, modern, contemporary) often accompanied by mediocre, even dreadful furniture.

Besides, things were able to get moving quickly because we had already forged strong links with many of the most talented designers of the time thanks to the industrial projects we had undertaken within Agence kreo.

As soon as I told them about our gallery project, they voiced their interest immediately. Without blowing our own horn, between 1999 and 2001 we exhibited new pieces by Ron Arad, François Bauchet, Ronan & Erwan Bouroullec, Pierre Charpin, Alessandro Mendini, Jasper Morrison, Marc Newson, Martin Szekely, and Maarten Van Severen. What a list! It was often one of their first exhibitions in galleries, or in France, or else their career debut.

C.K. After a few shows with historic pieces, we very quickly opted for production and started in 2000. We realized that we would rather produce and curate new pieces than show old ones. This desire was also widely shared by the designers. At that time only a handful of producers gave them any real freedom to think up particular pieces. And the latter were more products to project an image, rather than mass-produced. In addition, marketing was beginning to take over, leaving very little room for designers. Hence their desire, if they wanted to do research, to enter a new system—that of the gallery.

C.D. What was on offer in Paris in terms of contemporary design at that time, at the beginning of the 2000s?

D.K. In my opinion, just one name and one gallery really stood out, around which all the others orbited: Pierre Staudenmeyer (1952–2007) and his gallery, Néotù.[1] Pierre invented a modern model for the contemporary design gallery. He showed a lot of contemporary design in the 1980s and 1990s, allowing many designers to express themselves and exhibit. By the end of the 1990s, he was shifting back to vintage design. It has to be said that production

costs for contemporary design are significant. When we organized Marc Newson's first exhibition in 2000, he warned us it would be very expensive. He was right. Obviously, it was much cheaper than today, but still. Nevertheless, we managed it because rent was low, our team was small, and we knew we were breaking new ground. It was very exciting.

Shortly before opening the gallery we had also gained some experience with exhibitions. At the end of the 1990s we were close to groups like Olivier Zahm and his magazine *Purple*, with whom we organized a Martin Szekely show in 1999. The same is true of the Radi Designers, with whom we collaborated on an exhibition at the Fondation Cartier pour l'Art Contemporain organized by Hervé Chandès that same year. When the foundation was in Jouy-en-Josas, that is, until 1994, the furniture and office fittings were signed François Bauchet. Marie-Claude Beaud, its then director, was really interested in contemporary design. So at the time in Paris there was a cluster of people curious about developments in that area: critics, journalists, a few collectors, a few museum curators—more curators in contemporary art than in design, for that matter. So, thanks to and together with them, we were able to float a few ideas before opening the Galerie kreo.

C.K. I can't say if the late 1990s was a good time to open a design gallery, but what I can say is that we were really lucky. We had the impression we were the only ones who cared, but that wasn't the case. From the very first exhibitions there was a great deal of interest—despite our small-sized location. A lot of people wanted to get a feel for what we were doing. They were curious and brought a positive energy, a desire to encounter new things and learn about them. Collectors of contemporary art who had never looked at furniture before began to show an interest in it. So, this allowed us to quickly raise funds to finance our research. The sale of one exhibition made it possible to put on the next. To us, all this seemed quite routine. Looking back though, we benefited from some really favorable conditions. On the one hand, you had designers who wanted to get involved in this type of research and, on the other, collectors interested in it and ready to buy. An ideal combination. That's what allowed us to grow and create a close-knit family, respectful of one another. This energy still flows. I felt it again at our inaugural

exhibition on rue Dauphine in September 2008, for which each designer conceived a really important piece, and more recently at the party and show for our twentieth anniversary.

C.D. When you think back to the opening in 1999, could you have imagined where you would be today?

D.K. Of course not! First of all, if we are talking about location and space, a long chain of events brought us to rue Dauphine. Our site at 11, rue Louise Weiss soon proved to be too small. In 2001, we moved to another space on rue Duchefdelaville, with an annex on rue Zadkine. But planning for two venues is complicated. When contemporary art galleries began abandoning the 13th *arrondissement* in the mid-2000s, we started thinking about where to go next. Fabienne Leclerc from the In Situ gallery told us about a wonderful space next to her new gallery on rue du Pont de Lodi. I went to see it but I didn't think I could even cover the rent: the place was huge. It used to be a nightclub called Ruby's Club. We were lucky—the owner made us a reasonable offer.

Good fortune also smiled on us when it came to opening a gallery in London in 2014. Clémence and I were in a taxi in New York when a friend called us to ask if we knew anyone who might want to take over a vacant space in Mayfair. We thought about it for ten minutes and then snapped it up.

As for the Paris gallery, I have to say we're very glad to be in this neighborhood. Fabienne's space on rue du Pont de Lodi used to be the Galerie de Paris, Éric Fabre's gallery in the 1980s and 1990s, where I met many friends and artists, and artist friends, such as Bertrand Lavier. Today, the space is run by Kamel Mennour, with whom we celebrated our tenth anniversary in 2009 and our twenty years in 2019. I like all these interconnections. It's the same with designers. It's good to recall how we've gathered around the gallery, a family of designers, and that they almost all know each other; that some are friends, that others collaborate on projects or exhibitions; that our young designers have sometimes studied and worked with those we've been representing since they started out.

C.K. Honestly, we could never have dreamed we would be here today. At first, it was Didier who really pushed for the gallery. Agence kreo was starting to go well,

but there were the "complications" Didier mentioned earlier. So we started by exhibiting pieces from our collection, as at that time the idea of producing did not come into our mind at all. Our model remained the same as the classic gallery we knew with Néotù and contemporary art galleries: a system of buying and selling, or sale or return, but no production. In retrospect, I find it intriguing how we started production so quickly. There were several reasons for this, but the need to control quality was probably the main one. If you don't produce your own pieces, then you depend on someone else and that can become really tedious. If you have high standards, if you want to oversee the whole production chain and understand why there is a problem, why this material behaves in such and such way, why lead times are so long, etc., it's better to manage production yourself. It's no picnic every day, far from it, but it allows you to track things and keep people on their toes. Following some unsatisfactory experiences with our early exhibitions, we realized it would be much better if we managed our own production. I haven't changed my mind. The first pieces we produced and exhibited were by Pierre Charpin, in January 2000.

C.D. How did it all work out, in terms of trajectory? For many, Galerie kreo—and I'm not the only one to say this—is one of the major players in contemporary design worldwide.

D.K. I'd say the main thing's been a change in scale. I'm not sure that today we could hold the kind of exhibitions we used to on rue Louise Weiss. Or rather we'd do it differently. To host Jerszy Seymour and his exhibition *Lowlife* in 2003 was a crazy risk. Production was really expensive; the pieces were huge; polyurethane is impossible to sell as it's toxic! But it was important to do it to show the potential and freedom of contemporary design. Between 1999 and 2009, things followed on quite naturally, expanding and developing steadily. Today, the whole environment's changed and the economy of production too. Obviously, there's also internationalization, the most visible facet of which, for us, is our participation in design fairs and at the sectors dedicated to design at contemporary art fairs: FIAC and PAD in Paris, Design Miami and Design Miami/Basel founded by our friend Craig

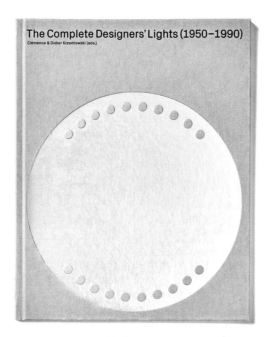

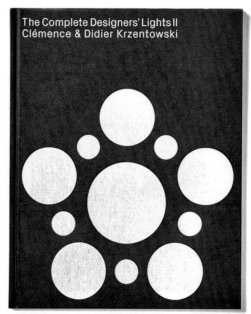

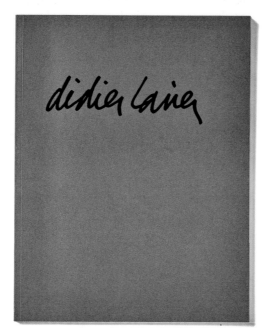

Covers of books published by Galerie kreo: *The Complete Designers' Lights*, first and second editions, coedited by JRP|Ringier, Zurich, 2011 and 2014; *Didier Lavier*, 2017; *Opération Contact: Jean-Michel Sanejouand à la Galerie kreo*, 2018

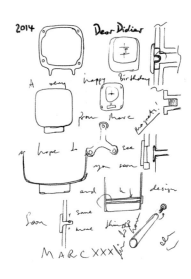

Drawings and sketches by Brynjar Sigurðarson, Konstantin Grcic, Ronan Bouroullec, Alessandro Mendini, Marcel Brient, Marc Newson, Dominique Perrault, and Hella Jongerius

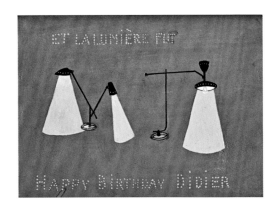

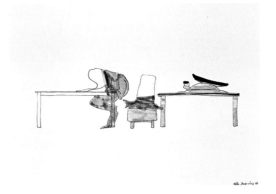

Robins, Tefaf Maastricht and Tefaf New York, PAD in London, and many others. Since 2011 we've participated in six or seven design fairs a year. As all professionals say, this has changed our business a lot, a development accompanied by both positive and negative aspects.

One crucial fact to bear in mind—one which has a marked impact on the gallery's schedule and activities—is the practice of the creators with whom we work. All of them also work mainly for industry and major producers, such as Alessi, Apple, Artek, Fritz Hansen, Hay, Ikea, Magis, Samsung, Vitra, etc. Every year, or very regularly, in April, they unveil their projects during Milan Design Week, an essential date in the international design calendar. All year round they are constantly battling with deadlines relating to the development, presentation, and marketing of products: lamps, vases, chairs, TVs, carpets, etc. It's incredibly time-consuming. That suits me just fine because, for me, a designer is above all an industrial designer: he or she has to grapple with the question of use and form for the greatest number and this, in turn, adds to what he or she offers the gallery. But this comes at a cost: we very often find ourselves waiting for an exhibition. The research and production phases can take several months, a year or so, or even several years. Of course, this is something we understand and we are happy to put up with, because we only want to show fully realized projects. It seems natural to us that a designer needs time and freedom to develop a project, but that's an essential difference with how contemporary art galleries operate.

The first time I asked Konstantin Grcic to put on a show, we had to wait six years! Sometimes these gaps in our exhibition schedule can become a problem. When you have to hold off for several years before showing a new project by one of your designers it can be a bit tricky in terms of communication and follow-through with collectors, institutions, and magazines. But that's the way it is and we adapt to it perfectly.

C.D. The solo exhibition forms the heart of Galerie kreo's DNA. While preparing this book, and meeting your designers and design lovers, something that regularly came up was your unique way of treating the gallery space as somewhere to hold exhibitions that make a statement. The fact you've had a strong and coherent graphic identity for twenty years, as well as your long-term relationships with writers, such as Johanna Agerman Ross, Alex Coles, Pierre Doze, Donatien Grau, Christian Schlatter—and I include myself in the list—reinforces this. Where did it come from, this desire you've had from the outset to think in terms of an exhibition, rather than just a "showroom"?

D.K. It emerged very quickly, at our first exhibition, which, it must be said, did look like a showroom of vintage 1950s design trying to pass for an exhibition. Going to contemporary art galleries certainly influenced my desire to present real exhibitions and not just a mishmash of pieces. It was probably also due to our move into contemporary design happening so quickly. To pick up what Clémence was saying, I didn't find it rewarding, interesting, or fun to do "showroom" displays and just showcase vintage stuff. As a collector of design, I love hunting down, spotting, and buying things. If I could purchase something every day, I would. When you are developing your collection and you can add more pieces—that's my famous metaphor of the jigsaw puzzle all my friends have heard—that's great. On the other hand, to run a gallery I believe you need a completely different approach—at least we did. It's no fun just buying pieces and immediately setting off to sell them on. You wait for a customer but you've nothing to say. Holding a contemporary design exhibition, on the other hand, is exciting because you feel that it's part of history, that you're trying to second guess the future. You produce advanced pieces, you take risks. Some pieces that we've produced and exhibited are now part of the history of design and form. It's fantastic to have contributed to this to the best of our abilities, and I reckon designers are happy to have Galerie kreo as a space for freedom, a laboratory that allows them to put things into development that they couldn't produce industrially. Galerie kreo is first and foremost a research laboratory for designers. We want them to be able to develop their thinking. There are therefore no constraints on them: neither financial, nor in terms of deadlines, dimensions, materials, techniques. This research can also be theoretical in the sense that the pieces produced may sometimes dispense with function.

C.D. I'd like to do a recap on "kreo before kreo" and in particular your experience at Agence kreo. But first of all, a simple question, since the history of the Galerie kreo is also the story of your relationship, how did you meet?

C.K. Through mutual friends in late 1985, before the Albertville 1992 Winter Olympic Games venture we worked on in the late 1980s and early 1990s. Didier was a member of the Games bid committee with Jean-Claude Killy. I was on the organizing team. Our first joint professional project was Agence kreo, which we launched in the wake of the Games.

D.K. That's what sparked the whole kreo adventure. In 1992, Clémence was emerging from her experience at the Albertville Olympic Games. For my part, I'd just left the Killy company, in which my family had been associated with Jean-Claude Killy and where I ran communications and then commercial development. I think that, unconsciously, the Killy era left its stamp on me. For that firm, which produced ski clothing and accessories, the question of the effectiveness of an object and of practical demands was obviously central. Studying design, you quickly realize that the two areas in which the most research and innovation are done are the Army and sports. Two sectors where you have no choice but to be the best technically—in other areas, marketing and the desirability of a product are sometimes more important than efficiency.

C.K. On my side, I grew up in a very traditional setting, surrounded by replica Louis XVI rather than contemporary design. I simply had the feeling that my horizon lay ahead of me, that something in stark contrast to my family background was going to happen that would spur me on. This was design. I worked on a number of projects within the organization for the Albertville Olympic Games and one of the last briefs I had was the responsibility for the route to be taken by the flame. That was my first contact with design: we'd asked Philippe Starck to design the torch. The organizers, Jean-Claude Killy and Michel Barnier, wanted the Games to be "exemplary and creative." That appears self-evident today, but it was far from the case at the time. Before Philippe Decouflé designed the fantastic opening ceremony at the Albertville Olympic Games, the tradition was more like a military marchpast. Our entire organization was entirely open to the contemporary, to the creative. The medals had been created by Lalique: it was the first time they hadn't been produced according to the classical system. When Philippe Starck designed the torch, he was the first designer to be commissioned to do so. For the 2012 Summer Olympic Games in London, the torch was designed by Edward Barber and Jay Osgerby, both of whom we represent.

C.D. Why did you think of Philippe Starck?

C.K. He was clearly *the* French icon of the time, in the early 1990s. We wanted to represent France, with a name known abroad. Philippe was won over by the project. He threw himself into it. The torch appears on the back cover of the most authoritative book on him. The whole Games experience remains a highpoint of my career.

Agence kreo's basic idea was to present companies with designers who are not actual industrial designers but creators with something important to contribute to industrial projects. In short: to convince large companies to take on Marc Newson and Ronan & Erwan Bouroullec rather than a specialized agency. Starting out really galvanized us, though it was hard because we spent our time trying to convince decision-makers that designers who had never designed products in their field of activity might offer something novel, thanks to their fresh perspective. Still, we were lucky enough to meet a few major business leaders who were also real product people, who loved getting products up and running and who shared our outlook. We didn't have a model as such, but we were inspired somewhat by sports agents who help athletes in their careers. We thought we could do the same for designers. Moreover, we'd seen that at that time they rarely worked for industry, except perhaps Philippe Starck. There was really something to develop there.

D.K. It was a period of triumph and disappointment. We learned that it was really hard to shake things up. It's complicated because when you invent new shapes, expressions, or uses, the eye has to get used to them. This is why standardization and repetition is the rule in the industrial field and in communication. Agencies often offer customers what they already know they want. Looking at bank logos, you soon see that three quarters of them look the same. When you put something different forward, decision-makers become skeptical, distrustful. Bringing them round takes a colossal amount of work.

C.D. Still, you've had some incredible successes.

D.K. That's true. The first of these was the Soleil decanter developed for Ricard by Élisabeth Garouste and Mattia Bonetti. That was one of our earliest projects. Another crucial success was the Perrier glass designed by Martin Szekely. More than twenty-five million have been manufactured since 1996. On a completely different scale, I'm also thinking of the Montpellier tramway project, for which Garouste and Bonetti worked on both the interior and the exterior—a global vision that was very rare at that time. These experiences provided the real theoretical foundation, in terms of both image and contacts, for building up strong relationships with designers.

C.K. With Ricard, it was a long-term collaboration. It began with the decanter and lasted about ten years. More than fifteen designers have worked on Ricard projects. No one believed in the decanter at first, but it became a real hit. The whole process was exciting. We'd conducted studies with café owners. Naturally, there was Élisabeth and Mattia's beautiful design, a wonderfully evocative sun, but it was also a masterly technical tour de force that fulfilled the requirements of bar owners as regards storage space and other constraints. When it came out, it made quite a splash. It was the first time a brand had turned to a designer to remodel a catering article that no one had bothered with before. The idea was to completely reshape a consumer environment, from the very first contact with the customer. And you can still see these products in cafés thirty years later!

C.D. How long did you carry on doing this kind of work?

C.K. Until about 2005. Mainly so we could finish off projects with clients we wanted to accompany to the end. Since the gallery opened in 1999, a system of osmosis has sprung up, gradually becoming more active. It was clearly more exciting to do experiments in the free-and-easy playground of the gallery than to continue to try to satisfy increasingly unfeasible specifications. It's also a question of the era. Nowadays there's much less demand for creative design from manufacturers than in the past. From the 1950s to the 1970s there was an explosion in creativity in every field and the designer held a special place. He was often close to industry heads, who understood his approach and his utility. From the 1980s—and this has accelerated going forward— the designer began to lose his privileged position in favor of more closely supervised structures. Also, the product has been eclipsed by the drive for profitability. Marketing goes from strength to strength. Quantitative and qualitative studies are commissioned. The freedom left to creators is shrinking. Every creative person needs to be able to experiment, to research, and this research no longer has any place in industry. On the other hand, today it is sometimes possible for industry to take up a project we've developed in the gallery, as was the case with Ronan & Erwan Bouroullec's *Lianes*, shown in 2010 and subsequently manufactured by Flos.

Top
Soleil decanter designed by Élisabeth Garouste and Mattia Bonetti for Ricard, project directed by Agence kreo, 1994

Bottom
Love Seat designed by Martin Szekely for MK2 Cinéma, project directed by Agence kreo, 2003

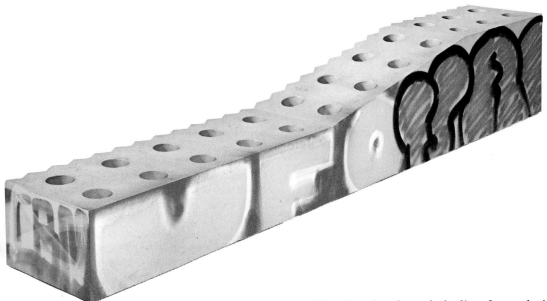

Virgil Abloh

Top: UFO Bench, from the
Efflorescence collection, 2019.
Concrete and resin, hand-
painted graffiti by the designer,
h. 1 ft. 8 in. × w. 10 ft. × d. 1 ft.
5 ½ in. (h. 51 × w. 307.5 ×
d. 46.1 cm). Unique piece.
Bottom, left: Acid Chair, from
the Efflorescence collection,
2019. Concrete and resin,
hand-painted graffiti by the
designer, h. 33 ½ × w. 16 ×
d. 20 in. (h. 85 × w. 41 ×
d. 51.1 cm). Unique piece.
Bottom, right: IBM Chair, from
the Efflorescence collection,
2019. Concrete and resin,
hand-painted graffiti by the
designer, h. 33 ½ × w. 16 ×
d. 20 in (h. 85 × w. 41 ×
d. 51.1 cm). Unique piece.

"The pieces designed by Virgil Abloh
express (the aspirations of our) his
time. It is no longer a question of 'high'
and 'low,' of legitimacy, of avant-garde,
or of being an outsider. It is a question
of producing an interactive design,
where the dialogue between the
producer and the user is horizontal,
where past references are filtered by
the experience of a present that
questions future uses. Here, the
heritage of brutalism, its forms and
ideas, are literally perforated, extruded
to serve as a pedestal for the creative
expression of the street. As Virgil
Abloh indicates, 'it's about constructing
a language that adverts to the norm
that both a purist and a tourist alike
can comprehend,' and use."
Clément Dirié, June 2019

C.D. Glancing through the list of your designers since
you started out, we noticed the existence of
successive "generations," which, of course, overlap
depending on affinities between individuals. There
are the designers with whom you worked at Agence
kreo and with whom you continued to work
afterwards: François Bauchet, Ronan & Erwan
Bouroullec, Pierre Charpin, Élisabeth Garouste and
Mattia Bonetti, Marc Newson, Martin Szekely. There
are designers already active in the 1980s, discovered
and/or exhibited by Pierre Staudenmeyer, and who
pursue their career with you, such as Jasper
Morrison and Olivier Gagnère. There are those who
arrived in the 2000s, like Hella Jongerius and Jerszy
Seymour; those who arrived around the time of your
tenth anniversary, like François Azambourg, David
Dubois, Front Design, Konstantin Grcic, and Wieki
Somers. And finallly, those who have arrived more
recently, such as Virgil Abloh, Jaime Hayon, and
Brynjar Sigurðarson. And I've left out some. How
would you define each of them? What might they
have in common?

D.K. My main criterion is surprise. I get interested in
something and take a closer look when I don't
understand it right away. We have to be astonished
by a piece, because it is astonishment that generates
the need for possession that is so dear to us as
collectors and to those who come to the gallery.
That's what just happened with Virgil Abloh. Every
year I receive a lot of proposals from designers or
creative people in other disciplines who want to do
design. I reject most of them. But when Virgil came
to show us his projects, I was intrigued and our

collaboration began. He's offering something I've never seen before.

I'm convinced that all the designers we work with bring something different, each in their own way. Ron Arad and Marc Newson immediately brought about formal and material innovations. When I saw Ronan & Erwan Bouroullec's *Lit clos* at the VIA (Valorisation de l'innovation dans l'ameublement), it opened up the possibility of micro-architectures in design—a vein they're still pursuing today. When I discovered Droog Design and Hella Jongerius, I became interested in what they were doing because it didn't look like anything I knew. I could say the same of all our designers.

C.K. The designers we deal with all have an individual and uncompromising style. They are all engaged in a kind of never-ending, personal quest. The significant financial investment the gallery makes in each project means that we work with a limited number of designers. Over these twenty years, a kind of "family" of about twenty people has formed with whom we remain in almost constant contact. With them, we keep thinking things through and have almost daily discussions.

C.D. How do you get to meet the designers?

D.K. It often happens via a designer who draws our attention to a colleague. When we started out there were very few designers who fitted in with our way of thinking. The milieu was quite small, and you got to know everyone pretty quickly. We show French, English, German, and Spanish designers, but also Italians, like Alessandro Mendini and Andrea Branzi, and Japanese, such as Naoto Fukasawa. Group shows also allow us to test out collaborations, to start a conversation with a designer and see how we might collaborate and move forward together, or we might invite a figure such as Andrée Putman, simply for the pleasure of doing something together. There are also twentieth-century designers like Ettore Sottsass, who I'd have adored to work with. He left an undeniable mark on the history of design. We produced few pieces with him. I'd have loved to have done more. And of course, if I were thirty years younger, I'd have worked with Gino Sarfatti!

C.D. He's a kind of paragon for you, isn't he?

D.K. Absolutely. He sets up his own company, produces two or three models that sell well and the money he earns from these sales is pumped back into research. That's a great business model.

C.D. To return to the development of the gallery, how do you view the evolution of contemporary design since 1999 in terms of visibility, the technical possibilities, and its social and cultural relevance?

D.K. To my mind, the great changes have been in technology. Over the past twenty years, I've had the opportunity of witnessing technological advances that make it possible to produce pieces that were previously unthinkable. In visual terms, the current era is probably less receptive to our "aesthetics" than a few years ago. We live in a decorative, much less conceptual age. This is undoubtedly linked to the political, economic, and cultural environment. Often, in times of crisis, there's a preference for the lavish, the opulent—probably to counterbalance the zeitgeist. Nevertheless, we continue working as before, with the same rigor. I'm sure it's tough for young designers starting out today, having to deal with this decorative, exuberant, ornamental overkill. This is probably why I don't meet many young designers who could join the gallery today. But I'm sure they exist. It'll come.

C.D. I now have some "technical" questions that are also important. They define the kreo model. For example, how many pieces do you produce a year?

C.K. We produce between fifty and sixty different pieces a year. This is a very large number, even if, in the end, not all the pieces are shown. Even major furniture companies don't produce as many, chiefly due to the cost of developing molds. Moreover, the crucial aspect of this type of research is the time it takes for a project to come to fruition. From the initial sketches to the presentation of a piece, each project takes, on average, two and a half years.

C.D. Do you have a specific network of manufacturers?

C.K. Absolutely. Our goal is to make the optimum piece. The gallery's investment in the finest craftsmen and manufacturers is therefore of paramount importance. After twenty years in the business,

we have built up a solid network of partners and specialists in various materials (wood, metal, resin, carbon, marble, etc.), located all over the world.

C.D. In most cases your editions are limited to twelve. Why did you choose this system?

D.K. In our eyes, we're pioneers in offering limited edition design pieces. The reason's very simple. We began collecting contemporary art in the 1980s. At that time, in photography and sculpture, the principle of a limited edition of twelve already existed, in that case 8 copies + 2 prototypes + 2 artist's proofs. We simply duplicated the principle in the field of design and it has proved a good system.

C.D. And what about the name? How did you choose it?

D.K. Very simply. We were looking for a short name that was available, a name that would evoke the act of creating and be understandable in every language. I opened an Esperanto dictionary and found this word: "*kreo*," which means "creation." I immediately liked it because it alluded to research and yet added something poetic. And the fact that it sounded like the beginning of my surname finally convinced us.

C.D. I'd now like to turn to two people close to you, two friends who occupy a special place in your private and professional lives. First, Marcel Brient.

D.K. Marcel has been key to the gallery. He's not only a significant and knowledgeable collector who has acquired many pieces from our designers, he is above all a friend who has urged me to take risks, to try out things, to question our own stance. From the early beginnings of the gallery, we called on critics and journalists—not only those in design—to write about the exhibitions and the designers. That's something Marcel particularly encouraged us to do.
        I met Marcel at the time of *Passions privées,* at which he also exhibited. Four years later, he walked into the gallery on rue Louise Weiss and asked me what I was doing. He was interested in this new contemporary design gallery opening and he came back and began to buy. Marcel is one of the few people who helped the gallery to gain a great deal of freedom very quickly. It was therefore a real pleasure to organize two exhibitions together in 2012

and 2013, as a material expression of a dialogue that is still ongoing. We are very touched that he has agreed to participate in this book.

C.D. Let us turn now to Azzedine Alaïa.

C.K. Meeting Azzedine was one of the most important encounters of my life. He was curiosity personified, living life to the full, with an extraordinary eye. It was like in some love story: we met, we fell for one another, we stayed together. Everything in this book owes him so much. For Didier, talking with Azzedine fed his ideas—talking about design and also about more strategic issues, such as the growth of the gallery, what choices to make or not, communication. He was as kind as he could have possibly been with us and, as well as that, he helped us, guided us, accompanied us, and kept an eye on the designers' work.

We also did a few projects together. When we organized the *Around the Neck* jewelry exhibition in 2012, Azzedine immediately proposed that we exhibit a dress he'd designed for Tina Turner's first European tour, all covered in beads. For the same exhibition Marcel had also very generously lent us a work by Mike Kelley composed of costume jewelry. Another project we collaborated on was for the London Design Museum, which devoted a retrospective to Azzedine in 2018—an exhibition he'd been working on before his death in November 2017. As it's not an easy space to exhibit in, he'd asked five people to design screens to give the exhibition a sense of pace and enhance visitor circulation. Alongside Christoph von Weyhe and Kris Ruhs, he chose Ronan & Erwan Bouroullec, Konstantin Grcic, and Marc Newson. Of course, the screens were designed to harmonize completely with the creations on show. All these pieces are both very characteristic of their output and at the same time extremely respectful of Azzedine's work, which they all admire. The exhibition was so successful because there was really this idea of a dialogue between the disciplines. With Azzedine, nothing was ever completely fixed; for him, everything is open, things talk to each other. Fashion relates to the world and to other areas of art. This perspective gave us food for thought.

I think the world of fashion has finally realized that he was right, in a way. For years, there was this very clear pattern of intense production, of frenetic pace. He protected the most essential thing: his absolute freedom to do exactly what he wanted, when he wanted. It was not always easy, but, thanks to it, his work will endure.

C.D. It would be remiss of me not to mention your own outfits. As I've also had the opportunity of seeing you setting up at fairs and exhibitions, I must be one of the few people in recent years to have seen you in jeans.

C.K. I was waiting for this. However hard it may be to believe today, before meeting Azzedine I never wore a skirt. I always wore trousers. I started wearing skirts because of him.

D.K. We met Azzedine through Marc Newson. We had a lot in common, especially a passion for collecting. In 2005, we interviewed one another, each of us explaining how we began collecting. When Azzedine was a child living in Tunisia, his grandfather, who worked at the immigration service, often left him with the girl who made passports and ID cards, on days when Azzedine didn't have school. She would take three portraits: one for the ID, another for the State, and a third to be kept just in case. He started a collection of these third photographs, classifying them by face for five years. He'd built up his own collection.

C.D. You, too, caught the collecting bug while still a child.

D.K. Yes. First, Easter eggs, then blotters we used to get at the pharmacy, then odd-shaped key-rings, advertising watches. Any kind of thing. Later, Rolexes. I had a very nice collection I sold in the 1980s. My fun comes not from buying in a traditional shop, but from embarking on a collection when the things don't have much value, which was the case with Rolex when I was collecting them.

C.D. What about design?

D.K. I think it was Néotù that set things in motion. We began to go there a lot after we moved into our new apartment thirty years ago. After Killy's was sold, I was able to start buying designer pieces from Pierre Staudenmeyer.

Top
Views of the exhibition
*Azzedine Alaïa:
The Couturier*, Design
Museum, London,
2018, with the
specially commissioned
screens by Marc
Newson (left) and
Konstantin Grcic
(right)

Center, left
View of the exhibition
*Aujourd'hui plus qu'hier
et moins que demain*
dedicated to the
Clémence and Didier
Krzentowski design
collection, Galerie des
Galeries, Galeries
Lafayette, Paris,
spring 2009

Center, right
Galerie kreo booth,
Design Miami/Basel,
Basel, June 2002
Exhibition view

Bottom
Galerie kreo à Monaco,
Galerie Art & Rapy,
Monaco, April–May
2012

C.K. When we moved in together we thought we'd choose everything in tandem, and not take anything from our previous apartments. We naturally turned up at Néotù and Didier became a close friend of Pierre's. One of the first pieces we bought was, I believe, a Jasper Morrison desk.

D.K. I embarked on my first design collection during the same years, first focusing on Pierre Paulin, his furniture and lighting. Then I started a collection of lamps that's still ongoing. Initially, I'd thought of chairs, but when I saw the collection assembled by Vitra and its president, Rolf Felhbaum, I immediately realized I'd never be able to catch up. So I turned to lamps; nobody bothered with them at the time. Recently, I've started assembling a new collection that epitomizes the origins of design—flint handaxes.

C.D. Can you talk a bit more about the lamp collection, which is probably the most impressive ever assembled?[2]

D.K. I collect mainly French and Italian lighting, with a few outliers, including the Scandinavian designers Arne Jacobsen and Tapio Wirkkala. I range from the early 1950s to the mid-1980s and up to Matteo Thun's creations in 1985–86. Then, with a few exceptions, I jump straight to contemporary, especially pieces we've produced with Galerie kreo. The core of my collection and my most abiding passion focuses, as you know, on Gino Sarfatti. I love everything he did! I especially like the fact that, from the 1950s onwards, he treated every new bulb as an "industrial craftsman" would, to create from it a lamp *a minima*. In his interview with Jean-François Grunfeld for the catalog to the exhibition *Lumières, je pense à vous* at the Centre Pompidou in 1985, he said, "But I've never been interested in form, except in the form of the bulb, for which I have to create a terminal, a support. We really don't need to have so many lamps. We need one lamp, a new lamp, if we have a new bulb, then yes." For me, Gino Sarfatti represents the epitome of the pioneer. His main characteristic is his desire to rationalize production, as his way of naming his models makes clear. The lights are classified by number: 100 for wall lights, 500 for table lamps, 1000 for standards, 2000 for chandeliers, 3000 for ceiling lights. He never uses the term "lamp," he says "lighting fixture." During

his life he brought out more than six hundred, always with that technical and saleable quality, a fusion of elegance and innovation. In the pantheon of lighting designers, we might also mention Pierre Guariche, Serge Mouille, Pierre Paulin, the Castiglionis, Joe Colombo. And I'm surely forgetting some.

For my collection I started out with a specific template: the *Repertorio 1950–1980*, published by Mondadori in 1985—that is, the Italian design bible, for every type of furniture. In a way, that's the framework of my "puzzle." One of my goals was to collect every lamp reproduced in it. I've almost got there. Assembling a lighting collection also means amassing a collection of books on lamps in order to find models, collections, and other information. Another criterion that's really important to me is innovation: I am interested in any light that bears the stamp of inventiveness.

C.D. I feel safe in saying that the place where you spend the most time—where you'd probably like to spend the most time—is the flea market.

D.K. Very true. In Saint-Ouen, north of Paris, where there are a few eagle-eyed dealers I can trust, and in Italy, in Parma. We stumbled across the Parma fair rather by chance, on a visit to my sister-in-law. At the time we were there, almost twenty years ago, I noticed there was this furniture fair, and I discovered that it was in fact the largest Italian fair for furniture from the eighteenth century to today. At that time, there were only four contemporary design stands in the middle of entire aisles of the eighteenth century. I'd just opened the gallery; the discovery was fortuitous. I said to myself, this is going to be easy! I was really lucky, because I got my hands on treasures by Gino Sarfatti and many others. Four years later, there were ten stands, and today there are two whole halls dedicated to design, with many copies and reissues.

I've experienced some genuine moments of joy in secondhand markets, such as when I found a Gino Sarfatti lamp 191 (c. 1951). Although it had featured on the front cover of *Domus* magazine in 1952, no one had seen one since its launch, not even the Sarfatti family. Well, coming across it, tracking it down, going to pick it up in Italy was a pleasure that only highly specialized collecting can offer.

Of course, it's a matter of luck. It's enough for some trader to sell this lamp—without knowing its value exactly—to another, who sells it on to a third, then to a fourth, until someone, realizing what he has on his books, calls me and sells it to me for more than all the previous amounts put together!

I can no longer buy incognito like I used to thirty years ago; all the traders know I collect lamps. The one who is most often "had"—but who is also the happiest—is the collector. He's the only one that attaches a non-monetary value to the lamp.

C.D. Your schedule regularly programs thematic exhibitions: stools, mirrors, jewelry, Italian or French lighting. You've also organized exhibitions dedicated to a period, such as the 1950s, or to a material, such as *Only Wood*, in 2014.

D.K. That's something we really enjoy doing. We work with a curator or critic—for example, Caroline Cros for mirrors, Christian Schlatter for stools—and the pleasure comes from the response of each designer. We send each one a folder with texts and images for reference, and it's exciting to see what they come up with. These exhibitions are really exercises in design. There are also the exhibitions we've designed with Marcel Brient, where we show design, contemporary art, poetry, and art objects all together. It's a direction we've been keen on exploring, notably with Jérôme de Noirmont for the exhibition *Signes des temps* in 2015, and more recently with exhibits around Bertrand Lavier in 2017 and Jean-Michel Sanejouand in 2018. It's a different kind of exhibition that enriches how we, as well as the designers and collectors, see things, in a refreshing and joyful way. That's priceless.

C.D. One characteristic of the gallery is that it maintains the distinction between design and art, with a clear and precise vision of what contemporary design should be, which in turn lets you host contemporary art and other disciplines without the risk of mixing things up.

D.K. I'm constantly reiterating the difference between art and design. An artist knows no constraints. The designer has to face the very important question of use. For me a designer must take into account the history of design and form. In the 2000s they invented something called "design-art." For me that's not design. It's something else. I don't know if it's good or bad, but it's clearly another form of expression.

C.K. There are two things that remain fundamental for us today. The first, in the rather muddled times we live in, is the integrity of the program. You have to be able to resist fashion, trends, the superficial flashiness of things—all those variables we grapple with as we try to keep to our course. The second is the importance of continuing to have fun and being upbeat, of discovering new things, and remaining capable of excitement—and we know that it's thanks to the designers that all this is possible. Didier and I are enthusiasts: every time we take delivery of a new project by one of our designers, it's a delight to start reflecting on it and doing everything possible to bring it to fruition.

D.K. Over the last weeks we've received new projects by Virgil Abloh, Pierre Charpin, Konstantin Grcic, Muller Van Severen, and Marc Newson for their 2020 exhibitions. A new adventure begins.

1. For the history of Galerie Néotù and the activities of Pierre Staudenmeyer, active between 1985 and 2007, see Chloé Braunstein-Kriegel, *Les Années Staudenmeyer: 25 ans de design en France* (Paris: Norma, 2009).

2. For details on Didier and Clémence Krzentowski's lamp collection, see *The Complete Designers' Lights 1950–1990* and *The Complete Designers' Lights II* (Zurich: JRP|Editions, 2011 and 2014 respectively).

Invitation card for Galerie kreo's twentieth anniversary exhibition, September 2019

The vast majority of the pieces produced by Galerie kreo are limited editions
of 8 pieces, plus 2 artist proofs and 2 prototypes. Each edition is signed and numbered.
The captions of the pieces specify their materials (sometimes in a simplified way)
and dimensions. For some of them, only the total height or area is indicated.
When an exhibition view shows a large number of pieces, they are not labeled.
A biographical note is included on the occasion of each designer's first solo exhibition.

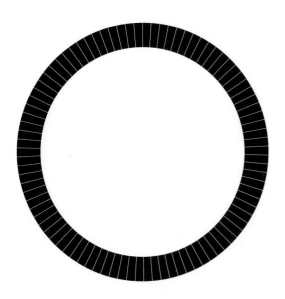

THE
YEARBOOK

EXHIBITIONS 1999–2019, PARIS AND LONDON

Mario Bellini
Achille Castiglioni
Joe Colombo
Garouste & Bonetti
Enzo Mari
Ingo Maurer
Pascal Mourgue
George Nelson
Marc Newson
Verner Panton
Pierre Paulin
Radi Designers
Gino Sarfatti
Ettore Sottsass
Philippe Starck
Martin Szekely

a Invitation card:
   Joe Colombo
   Combi-Center, 1963,
   for Bernini (left)

   Verner Panton
   Wire Lamps, 1969,
   for J. Lüber (right)

a

This June, kreo has opened a gallery to join the six other contemporary art venues on rue Louise Weiss in the 13th *arrondissement*. There Didier Krzentowski, assessor for the French Customs Conciliation and Expertise Commission and member of the French Union of Experts (UFE) and the National Association of Experts (CNE) for contemporary art and design, will show a selection of exceptional furniture pieces and objects from the 1960 to 1970s, as well as from the 1980s to 2000.

Press release, June 1999

The kreo adventure began in the 13th *arrondissement* of Paris in 1999, two years prior to the closure of Staudenmeyer's pioneering Galerie Néotù, the place that gathered a whole generation of design lovers, including Clémence and Didier Krzentowski. Of course, this was no random location, since contemporary art is one of Didier Krzentowski's many passions, and at that time rue Louise Weiss was its French epicenter. It was gallery owners Emmanuel Perrotin and Jennifer Flay who encouraged him to open his own gallery. A number of earlier experiences had already given him a taste for exhibiting, in particular, collaborations with the iconic Galerie Purple, and then with Fondation Cartier for the *Fabulation* exhibition by Radi Designers. And, of course, the activities led by the Agence kreo from 1992 in the field of industrial design. June 1999 witnessed the opening of the first exhibition *Mobilier & Objets (1960–2000)*. Already apparent alongside the contemporary pieces on show was the emphasis on vintage design that has since continued in the patient task of collecting the work of Gino Sarfatti and more recently exhibiting Italian and French lighting.

The invitation to the inaugural exhibition, which was the work of graphic designer Laurent Fétis, featured a trio of lamps, Wire by Verner Panton— the first lamp Didier Krzentowski ever acquired— alongside Joe Colombo's Combi-center, a modular cylindrical wooden storage unit, revolutionary at the time.

Press release for *Une pièce par jour,* Galerie kreo's 100th exhibition, September 2016

Ron Arad
Mario Bellini
Achille Castiglioni
Joe Colombo
Garouste & Bonetti
Enzo Mari
Ingo Maurer
Pascal Mourgue
George Nelson
Marc Newson
Verner Panton
Pierre Paulin
Radi Designers
Gino Sarfatti
Ettore Sottsass
Philippe Starck
Martin Szekely

a Invitation card:
Radi Designers
Sleeping Cat rug, 1999
New Zealand tufted wool,
heating fabric under the
rug, h. 2 ft. × diam. 5 ft. 11 in.
(h. 60 × diam. 180 cm)

Collective founded in
1992 by Claudio Colucci,
Florence Doléac, Laurent
Massaloux, Olivier Sidet,
and Robert Stadler, Radi
Designers was active until
1999. RADI stands for
Recherche Autoproduction
Design Industriel.

b Ron Arad
Little Heavy Chair, 1989,
for One Off; left: patinated
steel; right: polished steel

2

a

Sleeping Cat is an intelligent object, which,
as usual with Radi Designers, works thanks to a
simple but judicious technical solution. Since users
relate to the object sensually, the relationship they
forge with it becomes closer. A manifesto for
a poetics of function and giving free rein to the
imagination, it presents a novel proposal for how
to occupy a space—at once freer, more flexible,
and more emotional, affording us the pleasure of
discovering new ways of experiencing things, just
like reading a book for the second time.

Véronique Baton, in *Radi Designers, Réalité fabriquée*,
exh. cat. (Paris: Fondation Cartier pour l'art contemporain,
1999), p. 52

This rug plays fast and loose with the
clichés of middle-class comfort, whose
archetypes are given a mash-up:
the real fire is reduced to just a show
of flame, warmth comes from heated
underlay under the carpeting, while the
cat is just a motif woven into the rug.

Radi Designers, collection Design & Designer (Paris: Pyramid, 2002), p. 36

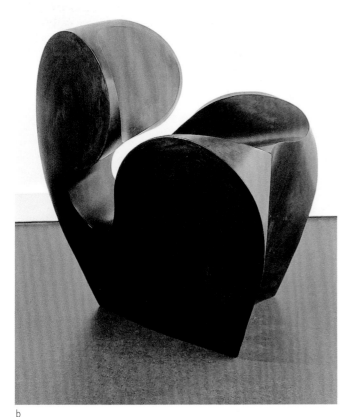

b

Galerie kreo's season opener flies the flag of British design, with the representation of the Israeli-English design giant, Ron Arad, exhibiting a Little Heavy Chair of 1989, issued in an edition of just twenty, for the first time in France. This armchair, presented here in both versions (patinated and polished stainless steel), is the cornerstone of Arad's output, employing materials traditionally associated with heavy industry to make alternative furniture, but heralding his rejection of mass production. Two new kreo editions are also showcased, including the Sleeping Cat rug by the Radi Designers group. Pursuing its eclectic policy, the Galerie kreo exhibits these pieces in the company of works by Martin Szekely and Garouste & Bonetti, not to mention new finds by Didier Krzentowski.

Press release, September 1999

Born in 1970, Laurent Fétis lives in Paris.

———————

a Invitation card: *ZAC 99*, exh. cat. (ARC-Musée d'Art Moderne de la Ville de Paris, Paris, 1999); Graphic designs for Mellow, Atmosphériques, East-West, and Sony, 1997–99

b Didier and Clémence Krzentowski's Renault Espace, parked on rue Louise Weiss and marked with the 1992 Albertville Olympic Games logos

a

This fall, Galerie kreo has chosen the path of innovation, exhibiting graphic work by Laurent Fétis. After a background in architecture and the decorative arts, this young graphic designer founded his studio in 1998. Laurent Fétis embraces the notion of "added value," which "goes beyond the commission," as he works as much in the field of music (Radio FG, Mellow, Grand POPO Football Club) as of art (Henrik Plenge Jakobsen, Fabrice Hyber[t], Arnaud Labelle-Rojoux, catalog *ZAC 99*, bdv [bureau des vidéos]). Not only will he exhibit a fine selection of posters, he will also broaden his outlook by designing a project specific to the exhibition. In his own purpose-built display, the work unveiled in this new space will appear in the company of furniture selected by both Fétis and Didier Krzentowski.

Press release, November 1999

b

When Clémence and Didier suggested I come up with a visual identity for the Galerie kreo, our focus turned to the shape of the invitation cards. I wanted them to have a practical and immediately recognizable format compared to those in use at the time, a kind of "Filofax" format. The invitations also had to be functional as regards content, to present the information they supplied. The idea quickly emerged of simply showing the exhibits, photographed against a background whose color would change each year. For every exhibition, the cards would be numbered and the objects illustrated carefully labeled on the back, a principle that transformed the invitations into filing-cards that can be stored and classified to form a "micro-publication." Later we worked together on "real" publications, such as Ronan & Erwan Bouroullec's first book, *Catalogue de Raison*, published with Laurent Le Bon.

Laurent Fétis, July 2019

PIERRE CHARPIN

Born in 1962, Pierre Charpin lives in Paris.

This exhibition features the first design pieces ever produced by Galerie kreo.

a Invitation card:
Light Module, 1999
Lacquered steel, h. 19 ¾ ×
w. 19 ¾ × d. 5 ⅛ in. (h. 50 ×
w. 50 × d. 13 cm)

b Wall Shelf, 1999
Lacquered laminated
wood, h. 28 ¼ × w. 28 ¼ ×
d. 7 ½ in. (h. 72 × w. 72 ×
d. 19 cm)

c Light table, 1999
Light-diffusing PMMA,
lacquered metal,
fluorescent tubes,
h. 6 ft. 7 in × w. 6 ft. 3 in. ×
d. 2 ft. 7 ½ in. (h. 200 ×
w. 190 × d. 80 cm)

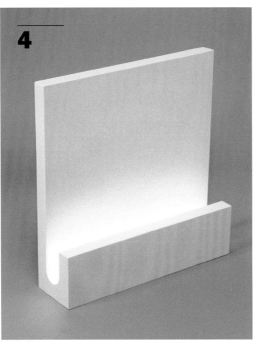

a

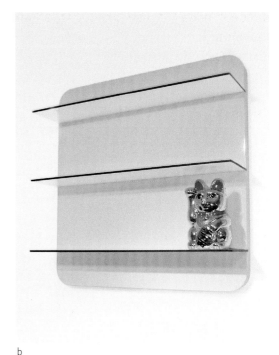

b

Marco Romanelli: You have stated that your objects are "receptors" rather than emitters.

Pierre Charpin: Yes, receptors for meanings. That's something I gradually realized, and which was confirmed in Japan, where I came across objects that "talk about emptiness." Designing objects that talk about emptiness is something I am extremely interested in. Blank objects that everybody can instill with their own meaning, or no meaning at all. I believe that this approach derives from the fact that I envisage objects primarily as forms, and only on a second level as functional, i.e. really as objects. The idea of emptiness and of meaningless objects actually triggers a process of projection and empathy, so others can decide what meaning to give to an object.

Pierre Charpin and Marco Romanelli, "Objects as Receptors," in *Pierre Charpin* (Zurich: JRP|Ringier, 2014), p. 37

Simplifying is undoubtedly one of the striking constants of my practice. Simplifying involves something like offering a suspension of meaning, forms that are not exactly filled, loaded with meaning. It involves offering more breathing space in order to give greater freedom of movement.

Pierre Charpin, 2014

c

Galerie Chez Valentin and Galerie kreo team up to showcase a selection of design pieces by Dominique Mathieu and works by artists represented by Chez Valentin:
Pierre Ardouvin
Véronique Boudier
Franck David
Alain Declercq

Born in 1970, Dominique Mathieu lives in Saint-Ouen.

a Invitation card:
Le Clou side table, 1998

b Exhibition view:

Bleue table, 2000
Epoxy-lacquered steel top and legs, h. 2 ft. 3 in. × w. 3 ft. 5 in. × d. 1 ft. 11 ½ in. (h. 68 × w. 105 × d. 60 cm)

Le Clou side table, 1998
Lacquered aluminum top and legs, lacquered steel base, h. 29 × diam. 19 in. (h. 73 × diam. 48 cm)

Skate lounger, 1999
Structure in lacquered pine struts, seat in plywood h. 1 ft. 3 in. × w. 6 ft. × d. 1 ft. 8 in. (h. 39 × w. 182 × d. 50 cm)

The work on the wall is by Dominique Mathieu.

4²

a

This effect [of adding shading to the drawing of an object in order to make it stand out and situate it in the space] gave me the idea of materializing this shadow, of taking the drawing at its word. Why not try to find the artifice of drawing in reality? This is also a way of literally showing how a designer might develop a project. Once in material form, the shadow of Le Clou became at once plinth and trompe-l'oeil.

Dominique Mathieu, "Une ombre qui devient socle," in *Design(s): de la conception à la diffusion* (Paris: Éditions Bréal, 2004), p. 120

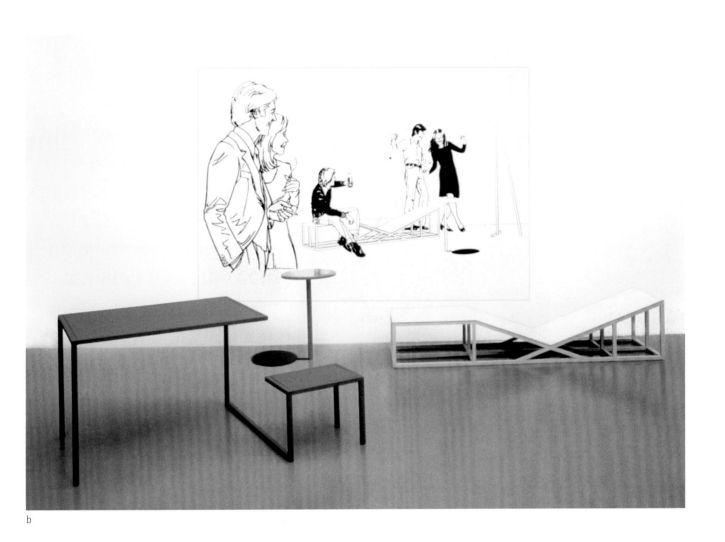

b

An image of the Bleue table might suggest
a relationship between chair and table.
The proportions, however, do not correspond
to the usual dimensions of those two objects
and the height of the main top may lead to
questions as to how a table is defined.

"Portrait de Dominique Mathieu," in *Design(s): de la conception à la diffusion*
(Paris: Éditions Bréal, 2004), p. 113

2000

MOBILIER & OBJETS (1960-2000)

Ron Arad
Mario Bellini
Achille Castiglioni
Joe Colombo
Filière & Dingjian
Garouste & Bonetti
Enzo Mari
Ingo Maurer
Pascal Mourgue
George Nelson
Marc Newson
Verner Panton
Pierre Paulin
Radi Designers
Gino Sarfatti
Ettore Sottsass
Philippe Starck
Martin Szekely

a Invitation card:
Sylvie Filière and
Jean-François Dingjian
Cabane desk, 2000
Structure in lacquered
plywood and "soft" varnish,
h. 2 ft. 1 in. × w. 3 ft. 1 ½ in. ×
d. 2 ft. 2 in. (h. 63 × w. 95 ×
d. 66 cm)

b Sylvie Filière and
Jean-François Dingjian
Reversible Chair, 2000
Lacquered, thermoformed
PVC, h. 24 × w. 16 ½ ×
d. 13 ¾ in. (h. 61 × w. 42 ×
d. 34 cm)

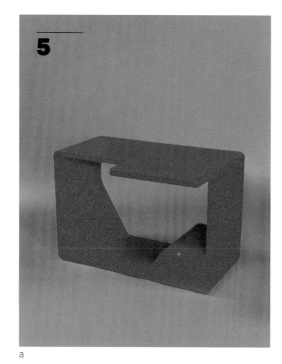

5

a

Though they fulfill specific functions, Filière & Dingjian's pieces appeal to the imagination, without indulging in literal, formal narratives. They form in a kind of in-between, performing both real and fictional uses. Thus, the rocking chair is a toy for the very young, a playground, a relaxation or reading area, deliberately referring to—but without overstating it—the world of skateboarding or rollerblading.

Press release, March 2000

b

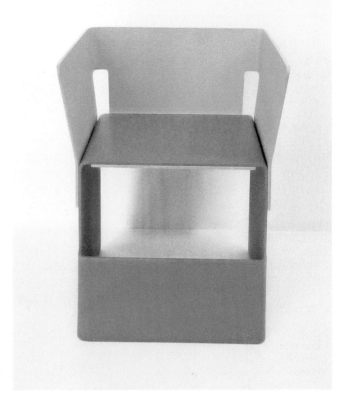

In the realm of design there is a lot of talk nowadays about new uses for new lifestyles, about the inevitable changes the introduction of IT is beginning to bring about in the domestic setting, such as the fusing of work and leisure. We can imagine what the more or less near future might bring and the objects that will constitute its environment. This slew of questions, however, rarely deals with the world of childhood. This is a paradoxical situation, since the universe of the child and its imagery are increasingly to be found in the adult world today. They have crept into homes, by way of little everyday figurative objects, a fashion launched by the firm of Alessi with the Family Follows Fiction collection, but also via gadgets, Japanese in the main (Tamagochi, the Furby soft-toy, Aibo dog), and, more unexpectedly, in computers, with the candy colors of the I-Mac. It seems as if, by dint of appealing to childhood and offering objects verging on the traditional to older consumers, most designers have forgotten their chief and still very real user, the child himself. And it is precisely with children that designers Filière & Dingjian wanted to concern themselves in the field of furniture. As if to exemplify this aforementioned neglect, projects in this area generally veer between small-scale replicas of the adult world and toy furniture that is more or less figurative and more or less educational in nature. How can we get away from these "models"? By diligently striving to consider the child in his or her individuality.... Or the desk-cabin—a space for a child's first bits of homework, but also a place of refuge, a play space, a world that can be transformed at will, as the child's mysteriously wandering mind sees fit. As for the seat, by simultaneously affirming its function as somewhere to just sit and as a chair (for playing "tag"), it generates two quite different apprehensions of space that can encourage a wide variety of scenarios. Finally, the wall storage unit, equipped with retractable clothes hooks and various accessories, teaches adult (dis)order. With the patent desire that this superficial rigor too soon turn into joyous everyday chaos, one part adult fantasies about the child we no longer are, one part recollection of the child we once were, and one part the child we remain: Filière & Dingjian's objects emerge from just this delicate alchemy.

Press release, March 2000

Born in 1951, Ron Arad lives in London.

a Invitation card:
Ron Arad
Narrow Papardelle, 1992, for One Off
Woven and polished mesh steel, welded on a steel chair-frame, w. 3 ft. 6 in. × d. 1 ft. 5 ¾ in. (w. 107 × d. 45 cm); carpet: 9 ft. 10 in. (3 m)

b RTW bookshelf, 1996, for One Off
Patinated steel, ball-bearing system (to keep books horizontal even if the bookshelf rolls), diam. 4 ft. 4 in./5 ft. 11 in. (diam. 1.30/1.80 m)

c Rolling Volume chair, 2000, for One Off
Patinated steel, h. 2 ft. 8 in. × w. 2 ft. 5 ½ in. × d. 3 ft. 4 in. (h. 82 × w. 75 × d. 102 cm)

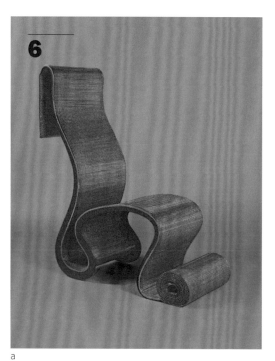

a

He's been called tentative and provocative, risk-taking and problematic, dialectical and destructive, constructive and solar, a punk and a hippy, an Israeli and a Londoner, here but elsewhere, sculptor and mechanic, attentive and light, profound and unfocused, singular, autonomous, free, digressive, and something of a magician. Ron Arad, then, a jack-of-all-trades of genius—a magical director, designer, architect, set designer, whose fun comes from reinventing alphabets and vocabularies, grammars and syntaxes in an endless linguistic game. He has reinvented the wheel, transforming it into a series of moving multi-shelving units, the RTWs, of various sizes and each working differently. Nomadic and poetic, they are as light hearted as they are intelligent. To walk from room to room rolling a 770-lb. (350-kg) bookcase, as if hardly touching it, is nothing short of a miracle. He has reinvented the ellipse, the purest symbol of perfection, famously the path of less resistance for expressing thoughts and whose inferences are so effective. From the New Tel Aviv Opera to the Adidas Stadium and Chalk Farm

Studios, the demonstration is masterful. He has reinvented an old dialectic that confronted, that opposed density and buoyancy, the polished and the rough, the natural and the cultural, the antagonistic and the refined, by crossing it out with a stroke of his pencil, with a click of his fingers, and a sidelong look. The Rolling Volume chair lowers the curtain on this debate. He has reinvented the field of the possible, delighting in making it all bend to his line. The straight line sweeps inward, everything rigid is softened, steel morphs into modeling clay, the solid becomes mesh—on encountering the Industrial Revolution the oriental arabesque morphs into the Narrow Papardelle chair. As Raymond Guidot sees it, Arad has even reinvented the Hebrew alphabet, going beyond the letter/number equivalence, and extending them into form and space, orchestrating the most dialectical, insolent, and imaginative variations imaginable.
Gilles de Bure, press release, April 2000

b

c

Born in 1963, Marc Newson lives in London.

a Invitation card:
Marc Newson
Alufelt Chair, 1993

b Orgone Stretch Lounge, 1993
Polished aluminum, lacquered interior, red version, h. 2 ft. 8 ½ in. × w. 5 ft. 10 ½ in. × d. 2 ft. (h. 83 × w. 179 × d. 62 cm)

c Alufelt Chair, 1993
Polished aluminum, lacquered interior, green version, h. 2 ft. 7 in. × w. 2 ft. 2 ½ in. × d. 3 ft. 4 in. (h. 84 × w. 67 × d. 102 cm)

d Wicker Chair, 1990
Wicker, aluminum, h. 3 ft. 8 ½ in. × w. 2 ft. 5 ¾ in. × d. 2 ft. 9 in. (h. 113 × w. 76 × d. 84 cm)

7

a

Stéphanie Busuttil: How would you define your style?
Marc Newson: That's a difficult question, which I never ask myself. I hope to propose a series of objects, furniture, that is simply effective and aesthetic. It so happens that until now, I've used some colors more easily, but that's only today; tomorrow, those I like now may give way to others. As for the forms, it is true that I tend to like very tense, very tight, organic, biomorphic, slightly futuristic forms, but always adapted to the subject and the service of the subject.

Stéphanie Busuttil: Technically, your parts are often very sophisticated.
Marc Newson : I love to follow through with what I have in mind, explore the materials and always ask for more, whether it's plastics, metal, wood, fabrics; whether I'm working on a bike design for Biomega, a Falcon 900, or a concept car for Ford. There is no difference, and what we discover for one project, once developed or adapted, helps in the realization of another.

Stéphanie Busuttil: You favor the technical side, the technology.
Marc Newson: That's right. I regret that today we no longer have big dreams, as we did in the 1960s and 1970s, that people are no longer optimistic, that we no longer have the fantasy and folly that allowed some people to imagine walking on the Moon. And they succeeded. I am fascinated by space; I could imagine designing a space station, a housing unit, collaborating with NASA or Aerospace.

"Marc Newson: l'Australien qui fait des vagues," *Connaissance des Arts* (no. 574, July–August 2000), p. 67

b

c

d

September 16–November 4, 2000—11, rue Louise Weiss, Paris

GWÉNAËLLE PETIT-PIERRE AND PIERRE LEGUILLON, *CRITIQUE DE LA SÉPARATION*

In September, Galerie kreo starts a new series of exhibitions conceived by guest curators. Its inaugural exhibition is curated by Pierre Leguillon and Gwénaëlle Petit-Pierre.

With
Carl Andre
Pierre Leguillon
Erik Minkkinen
Pierre Paulin

a Invitation card:
   Page from *Famille 2000*, vol. 2, Maison et décoration (Paris: Éditions des connaissances modernes, 1971), p. 98

b Exhibition view with, in the middle, Dos à Dos sofa by Pierre Paulin, 1967 Prototype made by the French Mobilier National for the Louvre Museum Resin structure, polyurethane foam covered with fabric, h. 1 ft. 10 ½ in. × w. 5 ft. 11 in. (h. 57 × w. 180 cm)

a

A prototype of Pierre Paulin's museum piece sofa made by the Mobilier National is surrounded by photographs by Pierre Leguillon (*Flying Carpets after Carl Andre*, c. 2000), and a sound piece by Erik Minkkinen to be listened to through headphones. It all forms a visual environment that can be visited or viewed from the outside. Sitting not permitted!

From a conversation with Pierre Leguillon, 2019

b

49

Born in 1956, Martin Szekely lives in Paris.

a Invitation card: Martin Szekely, Des plats, 2000

b Exhibition view:

Martin Szekely, Des plats, 2000
Sprayed molten glass, various dimensions
Pieces produced in collaboration with the International Center of Glass and Plastic Arts (CIRVA), Marseille

Table 00, Table OO collection, 2000
Varnished birch plywood
Square version: w. 5 ft. 2 ½ in. × d. 5 ft. 2 ½ in. (w. 1.59 × d. 1.59 cm); rectangular version: w. 11 ft. 9 ¾ in. × d. 6 ft. (w. 3.60 × d. 1.83 m); circular version: diam. 6 ft. 5. in. (195 cm); for all three: h. 2 ft. 5 ½ in. (75 cm)

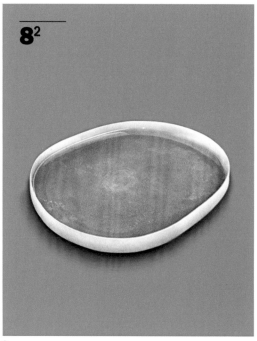

a

A Martin Szekely exhibition has become a rare event—every two or three years he shows his limited edition objects, distinct from his industrial design work: here and there he is searching for "the straight line." A reflection on things, on design, a recurring perspective of specific objects, centered on the definition of the object, on an attention to things—these things we bump into. "Drawing design" is no longer possible: Szekely doesn't "draw design" anymore, apparently since the Perrier glass; he no longer wants to clog up the world with objects, new dishes, tables, chairs; he doesn't ever envisage going back to his wardrobes or his flower pots. He is searching for pieces with a total immediacy. What do these objects have in common? A unique, single material to start with, and with which we get straight to the result, the essential: here everything is visible at first glance. Leaving aside the trappings of seduction, drawing, assembly, the ingenious management of complexity, color, baroque effects and more.... "I do not design these dishes; their shapes are generated by a procedure, a stainless-steel band 3 in. (7 cm) wide and 6 ft. (180 cm) long; I deform it slightly by placing weights on the edge of the band, by doing so the stainless-steel

band takes on a different shape each time—like a spring." The choice of the shape is made on two criteria: the shape must be positive, by which I mean the shape must not be "pinched" but always "more or less round and never a perfect circle"; the second criteria: you must not be able to feel any "will to design these dishes, the distinct pressure exercised by each dish is less of a gesture and more of a simple movement." In this search one would find what is always present: the unity of objects; whether they be wardrobes, flower pots, tables, dishes, the same constitutive unity of the object is there: a piece of metal, a lump of earth, a plank of wood, a chunk of glass. They are never composite, heterogeneous, mechanical objects. Yet again, it is the refusal of the object to be assembled which is the essence of the object.... A design which remains at a critical distance from the gaudiness of the time, following neither the Zen trend nor the ethnic trend. Neither is it a way of giving credence to the idea that no one has done anything, but is instead an attitude to the history of design. Martin Szekely is not revisiting history, he does not come after the heroic actions that make up the history of design; he is trying to remind us of a common history. Here, it is the link between the banquet, the dishes, the tables, and the chairs, a history of primary gestures, of primary behavior, when these objects had to fulfill the function of exchange and giving. An exhibition where the aim is to throw light on—in a photographic sense—the intention of an investigation that must reveal at each stage, with more evidence and sharpness, its outline, its target: the unity, for which "nothing in excess" could be the maxim of its action.

Christian Schlatter, press release, July 2000

These dishes are reduced
to their bare materials.
I made them directly, by
spraying particles of glass.
I want to make things out of
nothing. An object should
just separate man from the
ground, allowing him to sit,
eat.... Nothing else.

From "Entretien avec Anne-Marie Fèvre: Le Moins est un plus,"
Libération, October 18, 2000

b

b

PIERRE CHARPIN, *CÉRAMIQUES, VALLAURIS*
JASPER MORRISON, *CÉRAMIQUES, VALLAURIS*

Born in 1959, Jasper
Morrison lives in London.

a Invitation card:
   Jasper Morrison
   Small square plate, 2000
   Slip, enamel, h. 1 ½ ×
   w. 11 ½ × d. 8 ½ in. (h. 4 ×
   w. 28.5 × d. 22.8 cm)

b Invitation card:
   Pierre Charpin
   Oval plate, 2000
   Chamotte clay, slip, and
   enamel, h. 2 × w. 23 ½ ×
   d. 11 in. (h. 5 × w. 60 ×
   d. 28 cm)

c View of Jasper Morrison's
   ceramic collection

d View of Pierre Charpin's
   ceramic collection

e Pierre Charpin, sketch for
   Oval plate, 2000

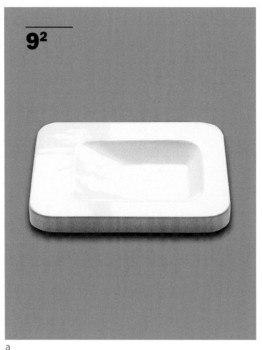

a

b

If we placed less emphasis on form,
we might develop our receptivity
to other qualities of objects. Form
should be the visual and natural
consequence of an idea, a process,
a material, a function, a sensation.
And even then it might be expressed
in a borrowed form or beneath a
surface taken from an object that
already exists.

Jasper Morrison, *Des designers à Vallauris, 1998–2002*
(Paris: Centre National des Arts Plastiques, 2003), p. 70

It's precisely by drawing on simple existing profiles,
borrowed from geometry, that new forms can be
introduced into an apparently closed domain.
That's exactly what I did at Vallauris: super-simple,
archaic forms with just a little interplay between
rough earthenware and smooth enameled surfaces.
But that was enough. Everybody could see that
plenty more could still be said about those forms.
The square still offers so many possibilities!

Pierre Charpin and Marco Romanelli, "Des objets comme
récepteurs," in *Pierre Charpin* (Zurich: JRP|Ringier, 2014),
p. 49

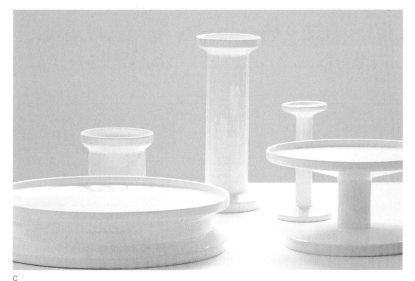

c

In Vallauris, Jasper Morrison has chosen a concept with links to design: the series. Variations on a form. Starting with an elementary form, the column, he fattens it up or pares it down, grows or shrinks it, to create a "family" that includes candlesticks, vases, cups, fruit-dishes, etc. The second series comprises three large dishes that do not function like an ordinary dinner service, but like trays with integrated food plates. They give the illusion of being highly concave, scooped out to the point of resembling "imprints" left by plates—which in fact is the case, since they are molded! They are then multipurpose and ironic. Because, in both the round and rectangular dishes, the bottom is set off-center. The whole Vallauris series is at once funny and moving, elegant and immaculate, its glazed whiteness concealing a pure soul.

Élisabeth Vedrenne, *Jasper Morrison à Vallauris* (Nice: Grégoire Gardette, 2000), p. 13

In Vallauris, Pierre Charpin is working on a collection of tableware. He playfully recreates the magic of a childlike, guileless, larger-than-life world. These cups, trays, and vases are turned on the lathe or "cut to size." He plays fast and loose with glazed, smooth surfaces and with coarse grog clay, as well as on the contrasts between natural, soft colors, such as grays, various greens, warm browns. But for the most part he plays, toys with the size of the rims, widening, expanding them, thereby transforming the perception of the objects entirely. Thus a dish, with its fine, round bowl, resembles, due to its broad, flattened edge, a hat turned upside-down. The tray is a dish without a rim, but upraised to form a charming little table with a red top.... Pierre Charpin's humor and insolence are imbued with the tenderness with which pottery is made.

Élisabeth Vedrenne, press release, September 2000

d

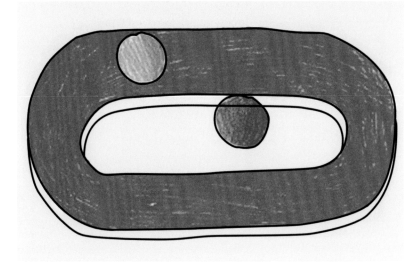

e

Born in 1948, François Bauchet lives in Paris and Bordeaux.

a Invitation card:
Coffee table, 2001
Polyester resin, h. 1 ft. 9 in. × w. 3 ft. 4 in. × d. 2 ft. (h. 53 × w. 102 × d. 60 cm)

b H6L3 bookshelf, 2001
Polyester resin, h. 5 ft. 5 ¾ in. × w. 2 ft. 8 ½ in. × d. 1 ft. 1 ½ in. (h. 167 × w. 82.5 × d. 34.5 cm)

c H5L2 bookshelf, 2001
Polyester resin, h. 4 ft. 5 in. × w. 1 ft. 8 in. × d. 1 ft. 1 ½ in. (h. 135.5 × w. 51.5 × d. 34.5 cm)

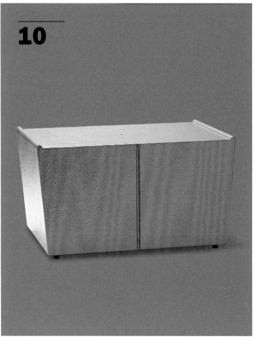

a

What is François Bauchet's position in the French design landscape? Arty-designer, archi-designer, techno-designer. . . ? No matter what the reality is, it must be said that Bauchet has emerged from all these genres, without belonging to any one category.... All his furniture and objects function like a paragraph in one and the same story, a single uninterrupted and much more complex narrative. And the steady determination, deployed with panache over the past twenty years, that it form a single body, a single mass. To make things "physical," to create thickness, presence, density in a world where the virtual seems to want to invade everything, absorb everything. To this, the three pieces he presents today at the Galerie kreo—his most recent productions—bear ample testimony. First of all, a highly structured, very architectural table, with legs with very light indents that, if they proclaim scale, weight, and mass, also make clear its extreme mobility. Then, a monolithic coffee table—just a top possessed of an enclosed, compact body, a smooth, gray block that occupies the space like a truncated stele. Finally, two wonderfully simple elements in the shape of the letters "L" and "T." Employing these two letters, François Bauchet builds, in response to the location or need, the mood or desire, consoles or shelves, tables or benches.... Two letters that speak volumes as to the dialectical and rhetorical scope of François Bauchet's output. Once again, the story expands, the same continuous narrative line that Bauchet unfurls from design to design. This time though with a particular tone and touch: stretched resin in a dull, "leaden" gray. And again, without stint, the palpable sense of density, counterbalanced by the extraordinary simplicity and untrammeled freedom that characterize François Bauchet's work in every last detail. That is, the very antithesis of confinement.

Gilles de Bure, press release, November 2000

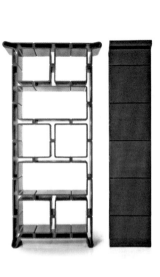

b

c

An exhibition proposal by
Stéphane Corréard

Exhibition of the entire
Metafore series, 1972–
1979

Born in 1917 in Innsbruck,
Ettore Sottsass died in
Milan in 2007.

a Invitation card:
Photo n°23/41, "Design
for the fate of humanity—
Design for humanity's
horrible message to
the other planets, San
Giminiano, 1976," h. 15 ¾ ×
w. 12 in. (h. 40 × w. 30 cm)

b Bookshelf, 1985, for
Galleria Rocca 6
Lacquered wood and
aluminum, h. 7 ft. ×
w. 7 ft. 10 in. × d. 1 ft.
3 ¾ in. (h. 218 × w. 240 ×
d. 40 cm)

a

b

For me, doing design is not about giving form to
a product, a more or less stupid product for a more
or less luxury industry. For me, design is a tool
for discussing life, social relationships, politics,
cooking, and even design itself.

Ettore Sottsass, 1981

Already in 1957, when one of a handful of participants at the First Conference of the Situationist International in Alba, he was thinking along the same lines as he was doing in 1981. Were Sottsass and Debord fighting the same fight? Maybe. Partially unveiled at the Centre Pompidou in Paris in 1994, the first French exhibition of all the photographs in the Metafore series (1972–79) completely transforms our knowledge and understanding of Ettore Sottsass's oeuvre.... The 1970s proved much less productive for Sottsass, at least on the surface. Essentially he was to devote himself to photography, to the five series he later grouped together under the generic title Metafore. Three sets of proposals for utopian designs: for the destiny of humanity, for human rights, for the needs of animals, and two purely Situationist ensembles, Fidanzate and Decorations. Thus, this "objectless" decade was perhaps the richest in design projects. Each photograph in fact records an installation in a natural setting. Each installation is a poetic if ironic attempt to invent new relationships between user and object. The "designs for the destinies of humanity," for example, include proposals for a "design for a door to enter shadows" and a "design

for a staircase to accede to power." In the "designs for human rights" alternative proposals are illustrated, such as "Do you want to sleep or do you want a bed," and "Do you want to sit down or do you want a throne."... For Ettore Sottsass this artistic work, which can only be compared to those of Enzo Mari or Bruno Munari, acted as a transition allowing him to construct a wholly new conception of design. By applying theoretical thought processes to the decorative arts in the service of a "morality" of the object, which, deep down, owes nothing to modernist thinking, he anticipated—the very first to do so, perhaps—the fate of art in the era of its technical reproduction.... Thus, from the early 1980s, the revolutionary proposals contained in the Metafore series became reality: the Memphis furniture and objects designed by Ettore Sottsass were to expunge forever the aura from notions such as functionalism, good taste, and even ease of use in the world of design.

Stéphane Corréard, press release, April 2001

A.R.P.
Osvaldo Borsani
Robin Day
Paul Goldman
Pierre Guariche
Gérard Guermonprez
Louis Kalff
Mathieu Matégot
Joseph-André Motte
Michel Mortier
George Nelson
Pierre Paulin
Gio Ponti
Alain Richard
Gino Sarfatti
Louis Sognot
Claude Vassal

a Invitation card:
   Gino Sarfatti, Floor lamp
   1073/3, 1956, for Arteluce
   George Nelson, Console,
   for Herman Miller
   Pierre Guariche, Armchair,
   1951, for Airborne

b Louis Kalff
   Desk light, c. 1957–59,
   for Philips
   Brass stem, perforated
   lacquered metal
   lampshade, h. 14 × diam.
   13 ¼ in. (h. 36 × diam.
   34 cm)

c Michel Mortier
   Téquel suite, c. 1955, for
   Steiner
   Foam, webbing, and wood
   structure, solid-wood
   pedestal. Sofa: h. 2 ft.
   1 ¼ in. × w. 6 ft. 2 in. ×
   d. 2 ft. 6 ½ in. (h. 64 ×
   w. 188 × d. 77 cm);
   armchairs: h. 2 ft. 1 ¼ in. ×
   w. 2 ft. 3 ½ in. × d. 2 ft.
   6 ½ in. (h. 64 × w. 70 ×
   d. 77 cm)

d Gérard Guermonprez
   Monaco sideboard, c. 1955,
   for Magnani
   Lacquered black-metal
   base, tropical wood veneer,
   h. 2 ft. 7 ¾ in. × w. 7 ft.
   7 in. × d. 1 ft. 5 ¾ in. (h. 81 ×
   w. 220 × d. 45 cm)

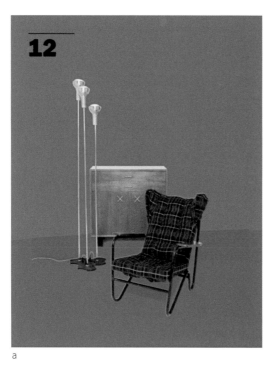

a

b

The 1950s: a somewhat forsaken decade. Galerie kreo continues to play the card of eclecticism…. Committed to showing and defending creation now, its space has also been concerned with the past, dedicated to showcasing rare pieces and little-known artists, alternating solo exhibitions by designers with presentations of historic pieces. At this new exhibition on the 1950s we invite you to discover pieces signed Alain Richard, Joseph-André Motte, Pierre Guariche, George Nelson, A.R.P, Gino Sarfatti, and Gio Ponti—a few of the gallery's "crushes" from a period often unfairly disparaged. Reduced to a handful of myths, the 1950s were in many respects a period of rebirth and of the popularization of new ways of life. Technology and industry invaded the applied arts: on the concrete level, a raft of new materials, from metals to Formica, blazed the trail, also improving flexibility on the artistic level; industrial aesthetics soon had its masters. Ikea's forefathers were on the horizon.

Press release, April 2001

c

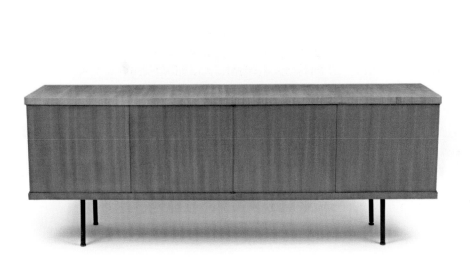

d

Born in 1971 and 1976, Ronan and Erwan Bouroullec live in Paris.

a Invitation card

b Exhibition view:

Cabane, 2001
Plastic and metal structure, woolen cover, h. 8 ft. 2 in. × w. 12 ft. 10 in. × d. 6 ft. 7 in. (h. 2.20 × w. 3.90 × d. 2.00 m)

Module Shelf, 2001
Polystyrene, h. 1 ft. 7 ¾ in. × w. 9 ft. 10 in. × d. 1 ft. 3 ¾ in. (h. 50 × w. 300 × d. 40 cm)

c Exhibition view:

Honda vase, 2001
Lacquered resin with metallic car paint, h. 3 ft. 3 in. × diam. 1 ft. 8 in. (h. 100 × diam. 50 cm)

Parasol lumineux, 2001
Metal stem, variator, h. 6 ft. 1 in. × w. 6 ft. 1 in. × d. 6 ft. 7 in. (h. 1.86 × w. 1.86 × d. 2.00 m)

Grappe carpet, 2001
Wool, surface: 13 sq. in. (84 cm²)

Armchair, 1999
Steel structure, foam, fabric, h. 2 ft. 10 in. × w. 8 ft. × d. 3 ft. 10 in. (h. 85 × w. 245 × d. 114 cm)

Vase lumineux, blue version, 2001
Perforated polyester, h. 20 ½ × w. 26 × d. 6 in. (h. 52 × w. 66 × d. 15 cm)

13

a

The child prodigies of the design world, Ronan and Erwan Bouroullec form a close duo bonded by brotherhood. They are as forthcoming on the subject of their current projects (Vitra, Cappellini, Rosenthal, Magis, etc.) as they are discreet on the subject of themselves. Though nothing filters out of their work methods, the two brothers are ready to hold forth on their approach to their work, which is trying to get away from simple rationalization. "The fact that there is a response to the function does not mean that an object is a success." They are as economic with words as with design, they erase as much as possible so as to avoid closing off avenues to the user. Their design is open to free interpretation to avoid the ritualization of the gesture. "Our objects are tools which make their own solution, they are open questions on ways to live." The seductive power of these creations is such that they cannot leave us indifferent....

Their first exhibition with Galerie kreo is another type of adventure which frees them from the habitual constraints. They have approached the gallery space as a place for experimentation, with a wish to formalize their research. Along the same lines as the Cabane, which was first presented in Hyères at the Villa Noailles (Summer 2000), the Bouroullec brothers are sticking to their idea of micro-constructions, exploring the possible links between design and architecture. Among the new pieces is a flexible structure in foam and wool with slightly rigid plaited strips which forms an object with undefined contours. Half wind-breaker, half shelter, it creates a light, transparent zone of rest. Along the same lines the "indoor parasol" enables the user to define a sub-space within the living area, materialized this time by the neon light which is concentrated under its dome. The exaggerated dimensions give this maxi-lamp which measures 6 ½ × 6 ½ ft. (2 × 2 m) a particular presence which is accentuated by the way in which it acts as a beacon. Ronan & Erwan Bouroullec enjoy upsetting images so as to create the conditions which lead to habits being broken. A twisted mind and a critical eye on the fuss about the coming dematerialization, the brothers occupy their time by making their vases the size of a television or a giant bulb, by lighting them up while covering their outer layer with reflective metallic paint. These highly visible objects say so much more than their mere function would lead us to believe. And this is what makes them so appealing.

Laurence Salmon, press release, May 2001

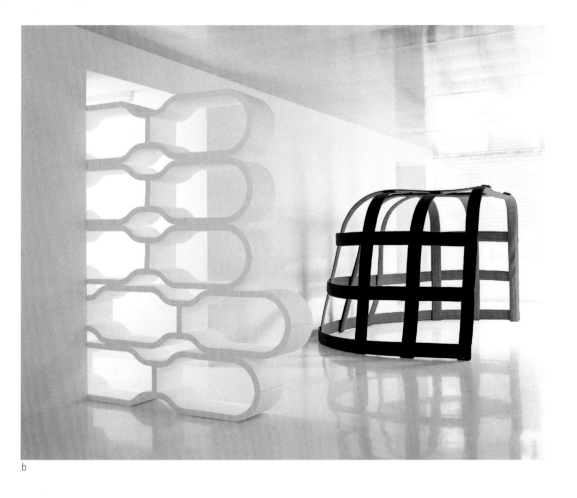

b

Our objects are tools that
make their own solution,
they are open questions
on ways to live.

Ronan & Erwan Bouroullec, 2001

c

ALESSANDRO MENDINI AND DAN FRIEDMAN, *LET'S TALK ABOUT TITANIUM*

Born in 1945 in Cleveland, Ohio, Dan Friedman died in New York in 1995.

Born in 1931 in Milan, Alessandro Mendini died in Milan in 2019.

a Invitation card:
Double Dream wardrobe, 2001
Concave doors and interior shelving in titanium, plated titanium, bronze, and sandblasted glass, interior in polished bronze and onyx, h. 6 ft. 8 in. × w. 3 ft. × d. 1 ft. 3 ¾ in. (h. 203 × w. 90 × d. 40 cm)

b Letter from Mendini to Friedman, 1987

c Exhibition view:

Hip Hop Modernism double cabinet, 2001
Titanium, lacquer, onyx, h. 5 ft. 11 in. × w. 4 ft. 1 in. × d. 3 ft. 6 in. (h. 180 × w. 125 × d. 105 cm)

Tribalism coffee table, 2001
Titanium, h. 1 ft. 5 ¾ in. × w. 4 ft. 1 in. × d. 3 ft. 11 ½ in. (h. 45 × w. 125 × p. 120 cm)

Mutation shelving, 2001
Titanium, h. 4 ft. 1 in. × w. 3 ft. 11 ½ in. × d. 1 ft. 5 ¾ in. (h. 125 × w. 120 × p. 45 cm)

d Memory chest of drawers, 2001
Titanium, lacquered red titanium, onyx, silver, bronze, h. 4 ft. 9 in. × w. 3 ft. 2 in. × d. 1 ft. 8 in. (h. 145 × w. 97 × d. 50 cm)

e Metaphorical Utopia fountain, 2001
Titanium columns with copper basin, h. 4 ft. 9 in. × w. 3 ft. 2 in. × d. 1 ft. 8 in. (h. 145 × w. 97 × d. 50 cm)

14

a

The Double Dream wardrobe is surely the model in which it is easiest to discern the trademark signatures of each of the two designers. Thus, the inward sweep of the red lacquer aluminum-plated titanium doors, the spheres on the surfaces, arranged in an apparently random manner—which reappears on the double cabinet, Hip Hop Modernism—and the sandblasted glass graphics on the side echoing the name of the piece, Double Dream, clearly belong to the American idiom.

On the other hand, when the wardrobe is opened, the geometric structure in bronze and onyx surmounted by a cone—of preeminently Mendinian outline—is redolent of a domestic shrine dedicated to some mysterious divinity and speaks of the work of the Italian.

Claire Fayolle, "Double Dream," *Beaux-Arts* (no. 208, September 2001), p. 102

It's not just to pay tribute to a friend no longer with us, but also because we tried to express things that were new to each of us, things I consider to still be relevant today. We talked about titanium and elementary volumes, about lines in gilt bronze, about polychrome spheres on inclined planes. And about pictograms, water, silence, pantheism, and geometry.

Alessandro Mendini, September 2001

b

c

d

e

This collection of seven original pieces is the upshot of Alessandro Mendini's collaboration with Dan Friedman employing an unusual material for furniture: titanium. Alessandro Mendini, one of the foremost Italian architects and designers of the twentieth century, was awarded a Compasso d'Oro for his lifetime's achievement in 1979. Today, Mendini collaborates with many global brands: Alessi, Cassina, Swatch, and his pieces have entered the collections of the greatest museums around the world. Dan Friedman, one of the most talented graphic designers of his generation, designed logos for Citibank and AIDS research, among others.

Press release, September 2001

2001 MAARTEN VAN SEVEREN

Born in 1956 in Antwerp, Maarten Van Severen died in Ghent in 2005.

a Invitation card:
Bookcase, 2001
Lacquered aluminum, three levels: h. 4 ft. 9 in. × w. 11 ft. 9 in. × d. 1 ft. 4 in. (h. 145 × w. 357.7 × d. 40.8 cm)

b Preparatory sketches, 2001

c Wall Storage Bookcase, 2001
Sanded and lacquered aluminum, h. 1 ft. 2 ¾ in. × w. 11 ft. 9 in. × d. 1 ft. 4 in. (h. 37 × w. 357.7 × d. 40.8 cm)

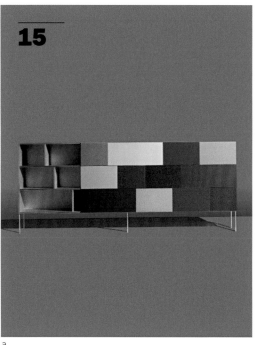

15

a

The piece recalls both Charles and Ray Eames' ESU 421-C storage unit and Donald Judd's "colored boxes." Colorful, movable panels form the front, though without covering it entirely. When they slide apart, they conceal part of the inside and immediately reveal another. This game of hide-and-seek creates an image literally, and even emotionally moving.

Christian Simenc, *Le Journal des Arts*
(no. 203, March 18–31, 2005)

Maarten Van Severen's furniture designs are dwellings. Not only because they settle into the space in a solid and silent way, radiating confidence and clarity, reassuringly certain about their presence, their "being in the world." But because they are in themselves spaces. Humble, calm, soothing spaces. Hasn't Maarten Van Severen described some of his tables, shelves, and bookcases as extensions, projections from the floor or the wall into the void? He likes to quote Hans Holbein's painting of Christ in his tomb, which, in whatever medium it is, literally digs into the sheet of paper it's printed on. Maarten Van Severen's furniture is a home because it originates in tireless attention to the exact volume, surface, line, material, texture, and color required. But also because it derives from an inflection, an expectation, the acceptance that they will receive something other than themselves, a something else that allows them to attain accomplishment, if not existence, thanks to the very presence of this otherness. As if they were ready to "act together." It is, moreover, a real surprise to come across furniture by Maarten Van Severen displayed in an immaculate, deserted store or showroom—or in those idiosyncratic houses built by the Dutch

architect Rem Koolhaas, to which he often contributes—cluttered and piled high with papers, books, artifacts, computers, food, and all those countless things that produce and are secreted by everyday life.... With great simplicity, one of Maarten Van Severen's most recent projects illustrates this point better than any other. For the first time, color has been added to a metal cabinet or storage unit. A color, or colors, borne by as many sliding panels we can assemble, as we like, want, or require. Like shutters before a window, like partitions round an enclosed space. Things on words, words on things. The passage of light, the passage of shade. The passing of time, the passing of life.

Charles-Arthur Boyer, press release, October 2001

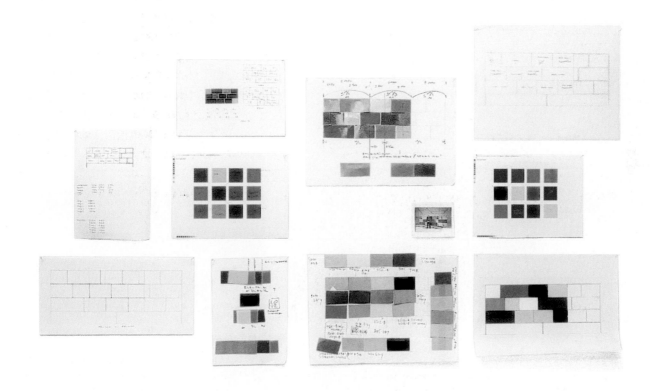

b

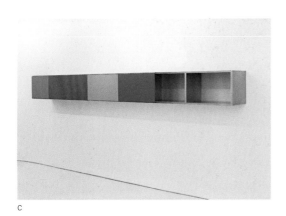
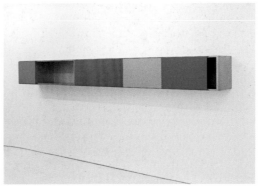

c

2001

SIT DOWN, 1950–2001

François Bauchet
Paul Goldman
William Guhl
Arne Jacobsen
Marc Newson
Pierre Paulin
Verner Panton
Ernest Race
Philippe Starck
Martin Szekely
Maarten Van Severen
Bob Wilson

---

a Invitation card:
   Martin Szekely
   Cork chair, 2000
   Cork and birch plywood,
   h. 32 ¼ × w. 13 ¾ ×
   d. 21 ½ in. (h. 82 × w. 35 ×
   d. 55 cm)

b Paul Goldman
   Cherner chair, 1957
   Walnut-faced molded
   plywood h. 31 ½ × w. 27 ×
   d. 20 ¾ in. (h. 80 × w. 68 ×
   d. 53 cm)

c François Bauchet
   *C'est aussi une chaise
   (Hommage à René
   Magritte)*, 1981
   Lacquered wood, h. 28 ¼ ×
   w. 13 ¾ × d. 15 ¾ in. (h. 72 ×
   w. 35 × d. 40 cm)

d Philippe Starck
   Miss Wirt chair, 1982,
   for Disform, 1983
   Tripod chair with epoxy-
   lacquered steel back, textile
   seating and backing, h. 3 ft.
   8 ½ in. × w. 1 ft. 10 ½ in. ×
   d. 1 ft. 8 in. (h. 113 × w. 57 ×
   d. 50 cm)
   For Disform, 1983

16

a

b

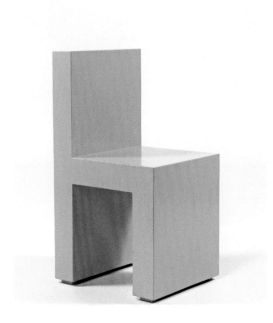

c

I made my first furniture, designed at the time as art pieces, in a reaction against those movements [American minimalism, BMPT, Supports/Surfaces]. The challenge was to propose an approach at once more direct and open to appropriation. In *C'est aussi une chaise* the image is meant to make a statement, in what is a rather simple formal register working on referencing familiar ingredients. The research on narrative also corresponded to what could be seen at that time in Milan, with Memphis and others. That's how I designed my first pieces that became furniture.... The question of the autonomous object, constructed as a complete organism in a single form, by way of a single gesture, has preoccupied me since that very first piece carved out of a solid, entirely homogeneous and coherent.

François Bauchet, interview with Léa Mosconi, paris-art.com, March 2013

d

B.B.P.R.
Osvaldo Borsani
Andrea Branzi
Dan Friedman
and Alessandro Mendini
Alessandro Mendini
Gino Sarfatti
Ettore Sottsass

a   Invitation card:
Andrea Branzi
Piccolo Albero bookshelf,
Amnesia collection, 1991
Anodized aluminum, Italian
beech. h. 6 ft. 8 in. × w. 6 ft.
3 in. × d. 1 ft. (h. 205 ×
w. 190 × d. 30 cm)

17

a

During the fertile period coinciding with the transition from the 1950s to the 1960s, a series of unforeseen social and economic changes took place in Italy. These phenomena led Italian design to adopt a totally autonomous and original stance in relation to European design generally.
In promoting the first authentic interchanges between the generations and the articulation of a new model for collaborating with industry, it had the effect of anticipating the official crisis of modernity by nearly ten years. In the 1960s, Italian design really took off, acquiring an international status that was confirmed at the Museum of Modern Art in New York [with the exhibition *Italy: The New Domestic Landscape*, 1972].

Maddalena D'Alfonso, "La grande époque du design italien," in Andrea Branzi and Marilia Pederbelli (gen. eds.), *Qu'est-ce que le design?* (Paris: Gründ, 2009), p. 188

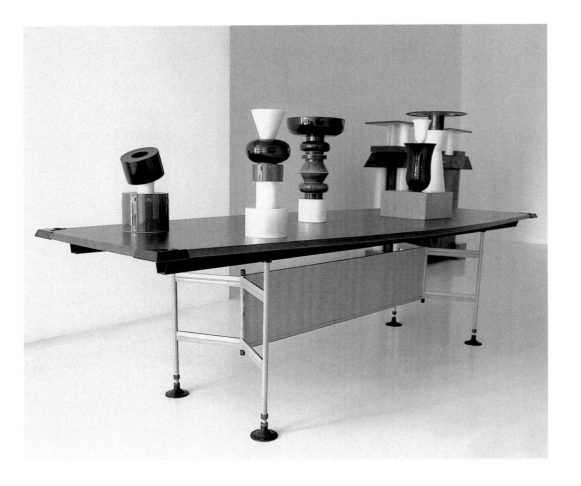

MARTIN SZEKELY, *SIX CONSTRUCTIONS*

a Invitation card:
Martin Szekely
Ladder, 2002
Lacquered steel, aluminum honeycomb, fiberglass,
h. 7 ft. 1 in. × w. 4 ft. 2 in. × d. 1 ft. 3 in. (h. 216 × w. 126 × d. 39 cm)

b Platform, 2002
Lacquered steel, aluminum honeycomb, fiberglass,
h. 2 ft. 5 ½ in.× w. 5 ft. 11 in. × d. 2 ft. 11 ½ in. (h. 75 × w. 180 × d. 90 cm)

c Exhibition view:

Ladder, 2002

Platform, 2002

Box, 2002
Lacquered steel, aluminum honeycomb, fiberglass,
h. 1 ft. 3 in. × w. 4 ft. 1 in. × d. 2 ft. ½ in. (h. 39 × w. 125 × d. 62.5 cm)

Base, 2002
Lacquered steel, aluminum honeycomb, fiberglass,
h. 3 ft. 4 in. × w. 6 ft. 5 in. × d. 2 ft. (h. 102 × w. 195 × d. 60 cm)

Plinth, 2002
Lacquered steel, aluminum honeycomb, fiberglass,
h. 2 ft. 11 ½ in. × w. 2 ft. 11 ½ in. × d. 2 ft. 11 ½ in. (h. 90 × w. 90 × d. 90 cm)

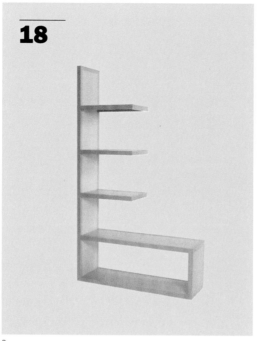

18

a

b

Displace the gaze, displace questions. Design cannibalizes. It feeds on design.

Objects by designers are alienated by their condition of "designer objects": conditioned by their image, by their surroundings, and by fashion. The ambition is to locate oneself as far from the aesthetic canon as possible.

The item of furniture as object is far from self-evident. Why a platter? Why sit? Where to sit? What is a table? A cupboard? What symbolic and exchange values can furniture-as-objects hope to attain? Today, trying to answer questions about the basis of furniture-as-objects means taking account of our current cultural and material environment. Otherwise, the answer will be outdated and passé.

One objective: to break away from the tradition of furniture history. Reconnecting with the most fundamental necessities of our physical and mental humanities. Furniture-as-objects from before the history of design.

These constructions support us, acting as stands for our bodies and our objects. Their real dimensions are dictated by the human body and reflect its measurements.

A body that needs to keep itself off the ground.

Are pieces of furniture plinths? Architecture contains us. Works of art are placed (on display). Furniture props us up and contains us. It is in a humble position.

What would happen if furniture-as-objects lost some of their presence, becoming mere levels, props, bases, and extensions for our bodily needs?

The materials collected for these six constructions are not specific to the domestic sphere. The constructions are not predestined for specific settings. They come from nowhere, and thus from everywhere. Photographed without context, the constructions have no scale; they are monumental.

Signs of furniture?

Martin Szekely, December 2001

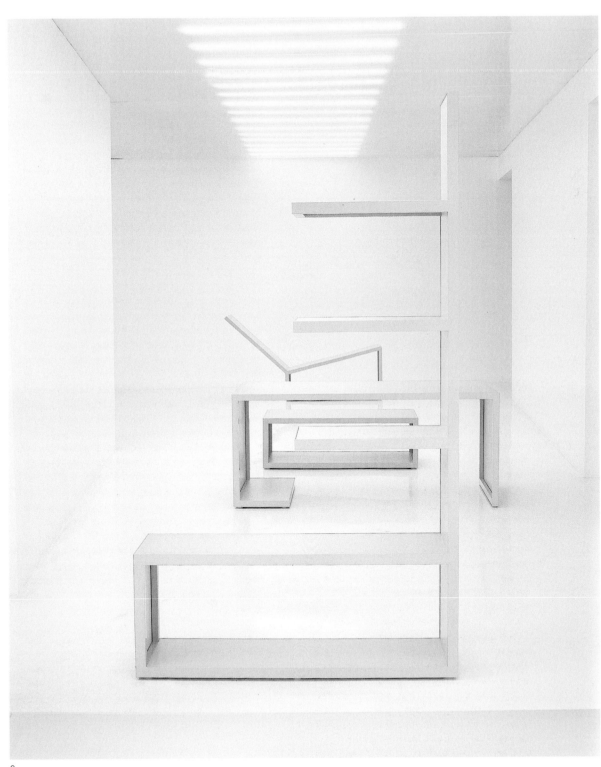

BERTRAND LAVIER AND MARC NEWSON, *EMBRYO*

Born in 1949, Bertrand Lavier lives in Aignay-le-Duc and Paris.

a Invitation card:
Bertrand Lavier
Embryo, 2002
Chair design: Marc Newson; stand design: Halal Rachedi, h. 4 ft. × w. 2 ft. 7 ½ in. × d. 2 ft. 7 ½ in. (h. 122 × w. 80 × d. 80 cm)

b Exhibition view:

Pod of Drawers, 1987
Fiberglass and aluminum sheets, h. 4 ft. 3 in. × w. 2 ft. 4 in. × d. 1 ft. 3 ¾ in. (h. 130 × w. 71 × d. 40 cm)

Alufelt Chair, 1993
Polished aluminum, lacquered interior, red version, h. 2 ft. 9 in. × w. 3 ft. 4 in. × d. 2 ft. 2 ½ in. (h. 84 × w. 102 × d. 67 cm)

Bertrand Lavier
Embryo, 2002

Wicker Chair, 1990
Woven rattan, tubular steel, h. 2 ft. 6 in. × w. 2 ft. 2 ¼ in. × d. 2 ft. 11 ¾ in. (h. 76 × w. 67 × d. 91 cm)

c Exhibition view:

Wicker Chair, 1990

Lockheed Lounge Chair, 1988
Fiberglass and aluminum sheets, h. 2 ft. × w. 5 ft. 11 in. × d. 2 ft. 8 in. (h. 60 × w. 180 × d. 80 cm)

Chop Top Table, 1986
Polished and lacquered aluminum, car-glass table-top, h. 2 ft. 6 in. × w. 5 ft. 11 in. × d. 3 ft. 2 ½ in. (h. 76.5 × w. 180 × d. 97.5 cm)

Embryo Chair, 1988
Neoprene, h. 31 ½ × w. 33 × d. 35 in. (h. 80 × w. 84 × d. 89 cm)

19

a

Here is an object (let's call it that for the moment for the want of a better word) inconspicuously situated at the intersection of several of Bertrand Lavier's "worksites." ... One of his famous "worksites" (but aren't they all, surely?), whose name is usually summarized in "so-called objects," has led him to consign to Mr. Halal Rachedi, a craftsman specializing in the display of primal art objects, objects which, although obviously not primal art, are nevertheless to be treated with equal respect.... The "worksite" with objects on plinths, a vast undertaking in destabilizing the standards of good taste and bourgeois strategies of asserting *distinction*, here overlaps tangentially with other "sites." First there's the "grafts," whose principle rests on adding two objects to make a third: a refrigerator on top of a safe, music by Varèse on a sculpture by Calder, or the subtle *N°5/ Shalimar* (1987), the simultaneous release of the two famous perfumes, a "worksite" for which Lavier often employs elements of contemporary design. A table by Prouvé on a freezer, a Panton Chair (1959) atop a fridge, or, more recently, the same Panton Chair sporting the opening in the Eames Conversation Chair (1948), as well as the seat from a Bertoïa chair on the base of the

Rocking Chair by the same Eames.... *Embryo*, a chair designed by Marc Newson in 1988, was originally intended to be covered with a material whose use for seating subscribes rather to the principle of grafting. The Australian Newson chose to cover this chair with the fabric used in wetsuits—later he was to turn to the actual shape of a surfboard to make a lounger. This act of impertinence probably also stemmed from his unusual professional background: Newson did not study design, but jewelry and sculpture. And does it need recalling that Bertrand Lavier did not study the art of "art," but the art of landscape, at the landscape architecture school in Versailles? Newson familiarized himself with design in the pages of specialized magazines, while every day Lavier would walk past the window of the art gallery next door to where he lived: both honed their skills without the teaching of a master whose practice, it is to be feared, they might otherwise have imitated. When he was born in 1963, Newson had been preceded almost fifteen years earlier by Walt Disney's images of Mickey Mouse in the Museum of Modern Art: a temporal short-circuit that might have gladdened the heart of Bertrand Lavier, who today has handed Mr. Halal Rachedi Marc Newson's cheeky chair, zipped up the back like a diving suit and sitting firmly on its tubular metal legs, asking him to find the most suitable way to display it. In the process, *Embryo* has become an object at once of the present and the past, a memorial and temporal telescoping, endowing it a status that, as with other chairs by Newson, auction houses will be quick to confirm, as occurred with the Lockheed Lounge Chair of 1985, an eye-popping object built like an airplane wing, which recently broke all records in New York. By sanctifying design objects in this way, Lavier coolly mirrors the outlandish process that records productions and registers them in the inventory of "exceptional objects" from what is still just about our time, inviting us, as is his wont, to rethink our value system. He is also urging us to think of an armchair as an art object, since we can be sure that it is not just the fifteen years separating us from its creation that persuades us to do so—though that helps.

Éric Troncy, press release, April 2002

b

c

Tito Agnoli
Ron Arad
Andrea Branzi
Dan Friedman
and Alessandro Mendini
Garouste & Bonetti
Dominique Mathieu
Ingo Maurer
Alessandro Mendini
Angelo Ostuni & Renato Forti
Pucci de Rossi
Claudio Salocchi
Gino Sarfatti
Ettore Sottsass
Martin Szekely
Roger Tallon
Maarten Van Severen
Franz West
Bob Wilson

---

a Invitation card:
   Andrea Branzi
   Piccola gabbia storage
   cupboard, Amnesia
   collection, 1991
   Metal and lacquered
   wood, h. 5 ft. 9 in. × w. 2 ft.
   5 ½ in. × d. 1 ft 10 in.
   (h. 175 × w. 75 × 55 cm)

b Ron Arad
   Well Tempered Chair, 1987,
   for Vitra
   Tempered stainless
   steel, h. 4 ft. 7 in. ×
   w. 3 ft. ½ in. × d. 2 ft. 8 in.
   (h. 140 × w. 93 × d. 80 cm)

20

a

In 1986, Ron Arad decided to tackle an iconic piece of furniture history: the famous club armchair, which he revisited using four curved sheets of stainless steel, bolted together rather than soldered. The resulting Well Tempered Chair is a paradoxical object that combines the comfortable and satisfying forms of a traditional armchair with the coldness of steel, to which is added the instability connoted by this type of assemblage.

Press pack for the Ron Arad exhibition *No Discipline*, Centre Pompidou, Paris, 2008–9

b

75

2002

November 9–December 21, 2002—22, rue Duchefdelaville, Paris

RONAN & ERWAN BOUROULLEC, *LIT CLOS*

a Invitation card:
   Lit clos, 2000
   Lacquered polyester resin,
   wood, metal, h. 7 ft./10 ft.
   7 in. × w. 7 ft. 10 in. ×
   d. 6 ft. 7 in. (h. 2.14/3.24 ×
   w. 2.40 × d. 2.00 m)

21

a

Oversizing, a reaction to the
dematerialization theory.

Totems, human scale, real presence,
absolute lightness, cocoons,
sarcophagi.

Between furniture and architecture,
light techniques, assembled like
an IKEA piece, the importance of
height, evoking childhood, far from
the image of modern comfort.

Ronan & Erwan Bouroullec, in Laurent Le Bon, *Ronan & Erwan Bouroullec:
Catalogue de raison* (Paris: Éditions Images modernes/Éditions kreo, 2002), pp. 22–23

Born in 1968, Jerszy Seymour lives in Berlin.

a Invitation card

b Plan for *Lowlife* exhibition, 2003

c Exhibition view:

Muff Daddy armchair, 2003
Foam covered with black leather, h. 2 ft. 2 ¼ in. × w. 3 ft. 2 in. × d. 3 ft. 7 in. (h. 67 × w. 97 × d. 110 cm)

Bonnie and Clyde sofa, 2001
Polyurethane foam, h. 4 ft. 11 in. × w. 12 ft. 5 in. × d. 6 ft. (h. 150 × w. 380 × d. 182 cm)

Free Wheelin' Franklin table, 2003
Metal, h. 23 ½ in. × diam. 21 ½ in. (h. 60 × diam. 55 cm)

Love and Hate vases, 2003
Murano glass, h. 16 × diam. 10 in. (h. 41 × diam. 25 cm)

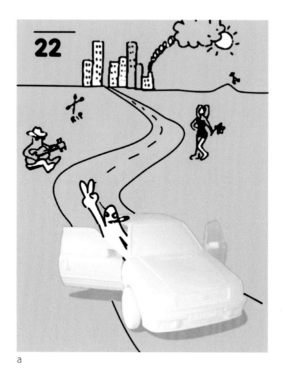

a

The Bonnie and Clyde sofa/bed is molded in expanded polyurethane—normally used for insulation in houses—from a cast taken from a 1984 Ford Escort XR3. Inside is a space which can hold a double bed or seating with a table and light, all molded from polyurethane. It is like a mini-architecture or maxi-furniture; you could even live in it. The idea was to sample a shape that was already ideal in terms of its dimensions, as it is an object already made to fit the human body, but steel is too heavy, so it was converted to expanded polyurethane making it a light object. It is also a reaction to the ubiquitous white sofa, where quality of life is represented by how big a widescreen TV you have. Down with disco, here's Bonnie and Clyde robbing banks, in love, popular heroes, chased and killed by the police—all in a car. If they were alive in the 1980s they might have even driven an XR3.

Press release, January 2003

More peace and love to your material consumption.

Jerszy Seymour, 2002

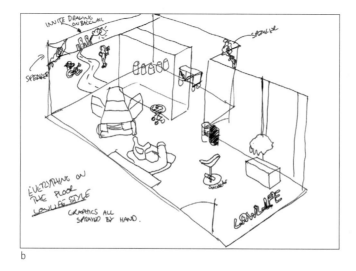

b

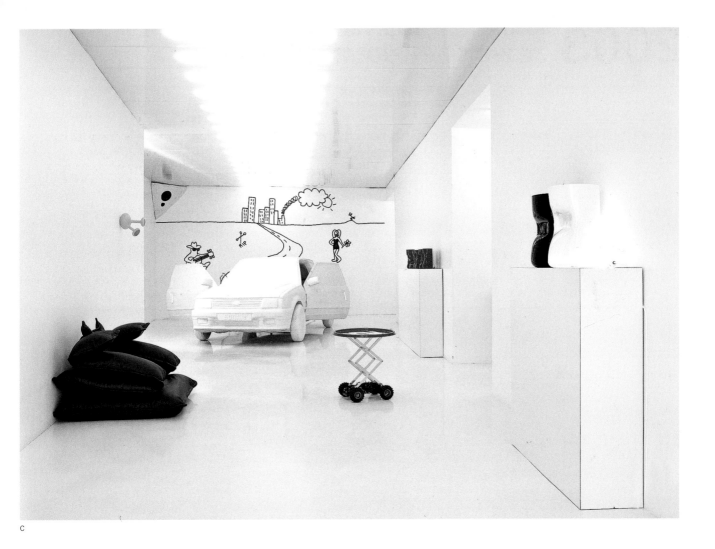

c

Not all of his narrative, masquerading pieces indulge in humor for humor's sake. They remain functional and explore new technologies and materials without seeming to do so. Above all, they are more committed than they might look. For this great, soft-hearted punk one might think that Bonnie and Clyde is just the sacralization of the myth of lovers on the run, molded in white polyurethane. Or the revenge of a young man who was "knocked down by a Ford Capri GTX in 1981" and wanted to petrify it like a salt statue. But the Ford Escort XR3, metamorphosed into snow-white evanescent "maxi furniture," the interior fitted out like a complete mini living room, is also a perversion of white—a critical rebuttal to the dominant white sofa of the 1990s. Thus he blows up the elegant showroom.

Anne-Marie Fèvre, "Politiquement incorrect," *Beaux-Arts Magazine* (special issue, 2003), p. 76

Ronan & Erwan Bouroullec
Kwok Hoi Chan
Marc Newson
Claudio Salocchi
Jerszy Seymour
Ettore Sottsass
Martin Szekely
Maarten Van Severen

a Invitation card:
  Marc Newson
  Zenith Chair, 1998/2002
  Polished aluminum, h. 31 ×
  w. 23 ½ × d. 30 ½ in.
  (h. 79 × w. 60 × d. 77 cm)

b Entry about Claudio
  Salocchi's Aloa floor lamp
  in *Repertorio 1950–1980*,
  p. 355

c Exhibition view:

  Marc Newson
  Embryo Chair, 1988
  Neoprene, h. 31 ½ × w. 33 ×
  d. 35 in. (h. 80 × w. 84 ×
  d. 89 cm)

  Claudio Salocchi,
  Aloa floor lamp, 1971,
  for Sormani
  Metal, black lacquer,
  halogen lamp, h. 5 ft. 8 ½ in.
  (h. 174 cm)

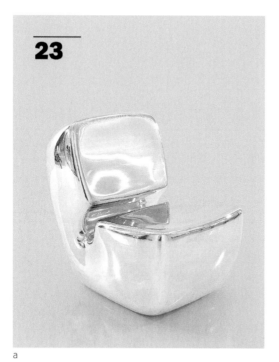

23

a

The piece was made by British coachbuilders specializing in the restoration of Aston Martins, with whom Marc had worked to make his earlier aluminum pieces. Whereas the previous aluminum pieces had played with the relationship between the interior and the exterior, the Zenith Chair presented him with an interesting challenge to try a completely enclosed form.

Marc-Newson.com, 2019

b

Claudio Salocchi
Aloa
*Lampada da terra
orientabile sul basamento.
La sorgente puntiforme
è realizzata utilizzando
una lampada alogena,
il basamento sferico
è zavorrato con sabbia
e contiene
il trasformatore.*
Sormani

c

a Invitation card:
Sliding Arch, 2003
Oregon pine, aluminum,
epoxy finish, h. 5 ft. 5 in. ×
w. 6 ft. × d. 1 ft. 4 ½ in.
(h. 166 × w. 184 × d. 42 cm)

b Exhibition view:

Closed Sideboard, 2003
Oregon pine, aluminum,
epoxy finish, h. 26 × w. 34 ×
d. 24 in. (h. 66.5 × w. 86 ×
d. 60.5 cm)

Upright Storage, 2003
Oregon pine, aluminum,
epoxy finish, h. 5 ft.
3 ¾ in. × w. 1 ft. 1 ¾ in. ×
d. 1 ft. 1 ¾ in. (h. 162 ×
w. 35 × d. 35 cm)

c Vertical Partitioned
Storage, 2003
Oregon pine, aluminum,
epoxy finish, h. 4 ft. 7 in. ×
w. 5 ft. 9 ½ in. × d. 1 ft.
1 ¾ in. (h. 139.5 × w. 176.5 ×
d. 35 cm)

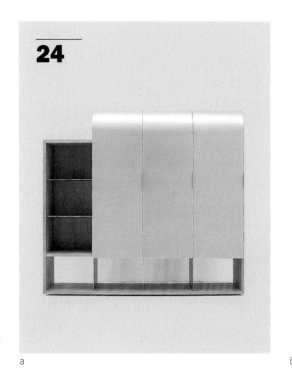

24

a

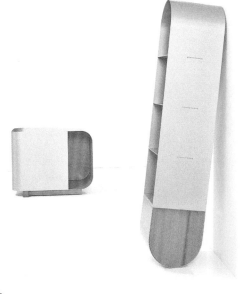

b

The main role of the pieces in the Hadar collection is to give structure to the space they occupy. Their very deliberate physical presence punctuates the space like so many enigmatic markers. They try to go against type through their shape and their system of construction so as to open up their use. One must invent ways to use them.

François Bauchet, April 2003

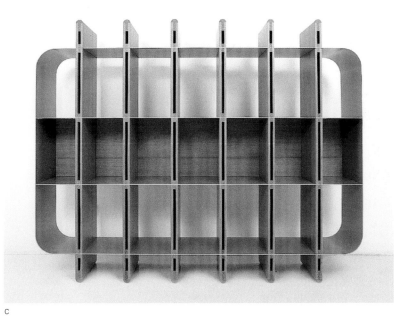

c

Born in 1952, Mattia
Bonetti lives in Paris.

———

a   Invitation card:
Smarties round coffee
table, 2003
Polyester resin, metallic
paint, h. 31 ½ × diam. 9 ¾ in
(h. 42 × diam. 142 cm)

b   H2O floor lamp, 2003
Metallic structure,
Plexiglas, h. 6 ft. 6 in. ×
diam. 1 ft. 4 in. (h. 197.5 ×
diam. 42 cm)

c   Smarties armchair, 2003
Chromium-plated steel
frame, lambskin covers,
h. 3 ft. 2 in. × w. 2 ft. 2 in. ×
d. 2 ft. (h. 97 × w. 66 ×
d. 61 cm)

d   Exhibition view:

H2O floor lamp, 2003

Smarties round coffee
table, 2003

Tartan closet, 2003
Trellis of black-and-white
nickeled-brass wire strips,
h. 4 ft. 11 in. × w. 3 ft.
4 in. × d. 1 ft. 4 in. (h. 150 ×
w. 101 × d. 41 cm)

Smarties sofa, 2003
Chromium-plated steel
frame, lambskin covers,
h. 3 ft. 1 ½ in. × w. 4 ft.
6 in. × d. 2 ft. 1 in. (h. 95 ×
w. 137 × d. 63 cm)

25

a

b

c

d

With enchanting tree-like forms or decorative pastiches, Garouste & Bonetti have been giving French design a disorienting, extroverted twist for twenty years. Their separation was ratified in 2001 with a magnificent retrospective at the Musée du Grand-Hornu in Belgium. Mattia Bonetti today unveils his first solo exhibition. Of course, the temptation is to search for traces of the now defunct barbarian duo in his work. Is it the Galerie kreo's minimal white frame that gives the impression of forms purified, simplified? For a now deco-pop sofa, the scrolls have disappeared, replaced by Smarties. Exit the glass with the H2O floor lamp; enter an elegant shower of Plexiglas. An improbable round pink table looks like candy. The totem of the whole ensemble, the Tartan closet stands tall. Built in black and white nickel-plated brass, all space and solid, it is a trompe-l'oeil piece, a broken mirror within a (broken) mirror—a small, abstract architecture reflecting Bonetti's new "geometries" and his own personal path to date.

Anne-Marie Fèvre, "Mattia Bonetti en solo," *Libération Next*, June 24, 2003

B.B.P.R.
Ronan & Erwan Bouroullec
Pierre Guariche
Jacques Hitier
Alessandro Mendini
Pierre Paulin
Martin Szekely

a Invitation card:

Ronan & Erwan Bouroullec,
Cabane, 2001
Plastic and metal structure,
woolen cover, h. 8 ft. 2 in. ×
w. 12 ft. 10 in. × d. 6 ft. 7 in.
(h. 2.20 × w. 3.90 ×
d. 2.00 m)

Martin Szekely,
S. L. Table, 2003
Honeycomb aluminum,
Corian, glossy polished
inox legs, h. 2 ft. 5 ½ in. ×
w. 6 ft. 3 in. × d. 2 ft. 5 ½ in.
(h. 75 × w. 190 × d. 75 cm)

26

a

Brigitte Fitoussi: Collector, gallerist, design producer: How do you define yourself?

Didier Krzentowski: Design producer or gallerist is fine for me. In reality, I'm not at all an intellectual in this area, but, without wishing to sound pretentious, I know I have a good eye. I often buy things I don't understand. When I don't understand, I start by looking.... The choice of a work must always be a way of asking a question.

Brigitte Fitoussi and Didier Krzentowski, "Fusion," *Numéro* (no. 47, October 2003), p. 122

a Invitation card:
Alessandro Mendini
Autoritratto mirror, 2013
Mirrored glass, black
laminated wood panel,
h. 31 ½ × w. 27 × d. ½ in.
(h. 80 × w. 69 × d. 1.5 cm)

b Olivier Gagnère
Cyclops mirror, 2003
Lacquered polyester resin,
h. 31 ½ × w. 31 ½ × d. 4 ¼ in.
(h. 80 × w. 80 × d. 11 cm)

c Jerzy Seymour
Make Up mirror, 2003
Resin stereolithography,
h. 20 ½ × w. 6 ¾ × d. 10 in.
(h. 52 × w. 17 × d. 36 cm)

d Martin Szekely
A.A. mirror, 2003
Rotating mirror in polished
stainless steel, diam.
24 ¾ × d. 3 ½ in. (diam.
63 × d. 8.7 cm)

e François Bauchet
Be mirror, 2003
Dark silvered Pyrex bowl,
diam. 9 ½ × d. 4 in. (diam.
24 × d. 10 cm)

f James Irvine
Four View mirror, 2003
White-lacquered aluminum,
mirrored glass, panel
with four pivoting mirrors,
h. 11 ¾ × w. 3 ft. 6 ½ in. ×
d. 2 ½ in. (h. 30 × w. 108 ×
d. 6.5 cm)

g Harri Koskinen
Peili mirror, 2003
Mirrored glass, h. 9 ¼ ×
w. 11 ¾ × d. 6 in. (h. 23.5 ×
w. 30 × d. 15 cm)

h Mattia Bonetti
Triangle mirror, 2003
Laminated wood, mirrored
glass, h. 31 ½ × w. 9 ¾ in.
(h. 80 × w. 25 cm)

i Jasper Morrison
Mirror, 2003
Mirrored glass, h. 1 ft.
3 in. × w. 3 ft. 11 in. ×
d. 1 in. (h. 38 × w. 119.8 ×
d. 2.5 cm)

27

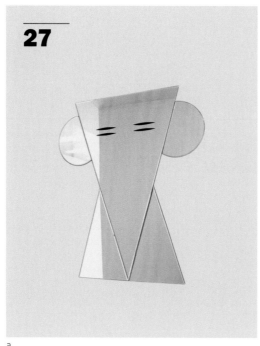

a

To begin with, we must insist on the difficulty in defining the mirror, this surface which is saturated with innumerable paradoxes (front/back, light/dark, illusion/truth, feminine/masculine, domestic/public, intimate/social, friend/enemy, virtue/vice, static/nomad, opaque/transparent, solid/fluid, concave/convex, discreet/decorative, religious/profane) which in themselves explain the interest it continues to provoke.

Among these confrontations, let's deal with the feminine and the masculine first. The mirror is present at every stage of the life of a woman, companion to her feminine desires, pleasures, and secrets. In ancient times it was part of the funerary rite, bearing witness to the refinement, elegance, and beauty of the dead woman. In the Middle Ages, the mirrors were referred to as "demoiselle" or "valet," or hidden in sculpted ivory mirror cases. An extension of the body, the mirror is a silent and positive figure of trust, a refuge, but also a wonderful trap (for example Alice's trip to the other side) which can enslave those who get caught. The design of the portable i-Mac in the shape of a giant compact, a sort of "electronic" mirror for twenty-first-century woman is proof of its irresistible power of seduction. But there is another mirror, alive and imperceptible, facing the woman—the perception of others. Full of erotic and Freudian symbols, the mirror transmits the projection of the other onto oneself and vice versa. It carries the stamp and the mark of this enchanting face to face. If the use of mirrors was forbidden for men in ancient times, they appropriated it through symbols. Man is in search of inner beauty, of truth, "Know yourself" said Socrates. Mirrors are tools of conscience which symbolize this test of self or of others. In Plato's *Symposium*, the cup that contains the wine, the dappled liquid, this drinkable mirror reveals the truth of the soul, one's own and, above all, that of others; wine is the mirror of the soul, according to Aeschylus and Alcaeus.

A tool of thought, speculation, the mirror is also a metaphor for philosophical subjects like time, knowledge, language, and space: "The mirror pushes us forward, into the future of reflections to come and at the same time, it sends us back in the direction from whence the image comes, the past. This spatial game is a transformation of our situation in time," said artist Michelangelo Pistoletto.

b

c

d

e

f

g

h

i

j

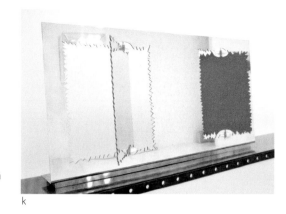
k

l

m

m

j Konstantin Grcic
   Me-Myself-And-I mirror,
   2003–4
   Silver mirror in wine
   glass, h. 5 ½ × d. 3 ⅛ in.
   (h. 14 × d. 8 cm)

k Tsé & Tsé
   Sept Ans de Bonheur
   mirror, 2003
   Polished and lacquered
   steel, variable
   dimensions

l Hella Jongerius
   Jubilee Plates mirrors,
   2003
   Transparent sanded
   glass, pink opaque glass
   with silvery sheen. Small
   model: diam. 16 ½ ×
   d. 3 in. (diam. 42 ×
   d. 8 cm); large model:
   diam. 17 × d. 4 ¾ in.
   (diam. 43 × d. 12 cm)
   Produced by CIRVA,
   Marseille

m Andrea Branzi
   Giardino mirror, 2003
   Formica external
   structure (bottom
   image), internal
   structure covered with
   mirror plates (top image),
   solid oak base, h. 4 ft.
   8 ¾ in. × w. 2 ft. ½ in. ×
   d. 2 ft. ½ in. (h. 149.5 ×
   w. 62 × d. 62 cm)

n Marc Newson
   Black Hole mirror, 2003
   Polished stainless steel,
   diam. 31 ½ × d. 4 in.
   (diam. 80 × d. 10 cm)

o Christophe Pillet
   Mirror, 2003
   Solid silver, h. 10 ¾ ×
   w. 3 ¼ × d. 1 in. (h. 27.7 ×
   w. 8.5 × d. 2.3 cm)

p François Azambourg
   Outline mirrors, 2003
   Pine frame, polyester.
   Small model: h. 13 ×
   w. 7 ½ × d. ¾ in. (h. 33 ×
   w. 19 × d. 1.8 cm); large
   model: h. 29 × w. 19 ¾ ×
   d. ⅞ in. (h. 73 × w. 50 ×
   d. 2.2 cm)

q Ronan & Erwan
   Bouroullec
   Black Mirror, 2003
   Anodized aluminum,
   mirrored glass, h. 17 ¾ ×
   w. 28 ¼ × d. 2 ¾ in.
   (h. 45 × w. 72 × d. 7 cm)

Self-knowledge is replaced by a knowledge of the world and the mirror is a common symbol as it reflects the world. It is thus the perfect symbol of creation itself: "God was born from an unseen mirror: the world is a mirror that gets murkier." Divine mirrors: "The Bible is an unstained mirror." An object of prudence and wisdom with medieval speculum literature, mirror books, mirror encyclopedias, which gather together all the knowledge of the world, the vanity of man who thinks he sees "the shape of the world as if in a mirror." The mirror can be spiritual and moral, with mirrors for princes, treaties of behavior and policy which list the codes and customs to which an "ideal" man should adhere. "Look at the world in which you live (mirror). Observe the role you play (painting). Meditate on what you are really (skull)."

The mirror is an eye, a machine which transmits and receives images and symbols. Optical recreation has arisen from the mirror—hence the success of catoptric or paraboloidal mirrors, a form of entertainment which appeared with the century of the Lumière brothers, a visionary science which would give rise to the cinema.

Final mirrors, these fleeting, moving surfaces constitute an inevitable passage.

In the time of the Pharaohs, the other life was perceived as a universe where faces are inverted. Even though the representation of the mirror is quite rare in Egyptian civilization, it can be found in the dance with mirrors found in the tomb of Mereruka in Saqqara. This dance scene shows the protective role of the mirror and its affinities with the sun, the golden mirror, symbol of energy. In the West, the relationship between mirror and death is darker. Assimilated with the image of the devil in the Middle Ages, its reflections are dangerous and fatal (the myth of Narcissus), like deafening echoes.

Taking into consideration this reminder of the multiple facets of the mirror, what other finalities or symbolism would you like to add? In short, given total freedom in terms of materials, uses, of the concept and creation of a mirror "object" (the format of which would be limited to 80 cm) what do you propose?

Caroline Cros, proposal text sent to the designers
for the *Miroirs* exhibition, May 2002

m

m

n

o

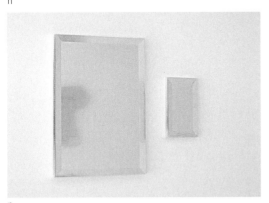

p

q

r

s

t

r Ettore Sottsass
Dioniso mirror, 2003
Internal structure in
mirror-covered
laminated wood, visible
structure in anodized
aluminum and mirror,
h. 31 ½ × w. 31 ½ ×
d. 15 ¾ in. (h. 80 ×
w. 80 × d. 40 cm)

s Andrée Putman
Your Turn to Play, 2003
Lacquered wood,
stainless steel, mirror,
h. 3 ft. × w. 3 ft. × d. 1 in.
(h. 90 × w. 90 × d. 3 cm)

t Michael Young
Kreo mirror, 2003
Lacquered wood, mirror,
h. 13 ¾ × w. 8 ¾ in.
(h. 35 × w. 22 cm);
base: w. 24 ¾ × d. 3 ½ in.
(w. 63 × d. 8.5 cm)

a Invitation card:
 Orgone coffee table,
 1989/2003
 Lacquered and polished
 aluminum, lacquered
 fiberglass top, h. 13 ¼ in. ×
 w. 5 ft. 3 in. × d. 2 ft. 6 in.
 (h. 34 × w. 160 × d. 71 cm)

b Diode lamps, 2003
 Base and head in Corian,
 tubular legs in anodized
 aluminum. Large model:
 h. 5 ft. 11 in. × w. 2 ft. ×
 d. 9 in. (h. 180 × w. 60 ×
 d. 22.5 cm); small model:
 h. 3 ft. 11 in. × w. 2 ft. ×
 d. 9 in. (h. 120 × w. 60 ×
 d. 22.5 cm)

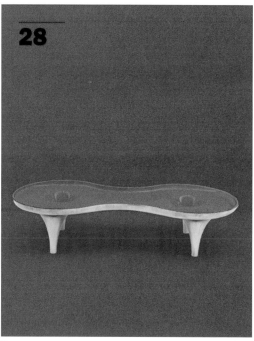

a

"More than any other design gallery in the world, Galerie kreo has helped my wife Jackie and I to build our contemporary design collection. The relationship that the gallery has to the designers as well as its ability to engage in the process of production has continually led to extraordinary results. One great example is the Chop Top Table by Marc Newson, which I acquired almost fifteen years ago. It took almost two years for the Aston Martin coachbuilders to produce the work. We have had it in our home ever since."

Craig Robins, collector and entrepreneur, cofounder of Design Miami and developer of the Miami Design District, Miami, 2019

Invited by Dupont, the manufacturer of Corian, to design a piece demonstrating the kinds of creative possibilities of the material, Marc decided to design a sculptural lamp that was made from thermoformed Corian. This was made possible by a factory in Germany that had capabilities in thermoforming technology. By heating up the material, it could be placed in a mold; this way, it could also be made thin enough to shine light through. This was a completely novel application of the material.

marc-newson.com, 2019

b

2004

COHABITATION

François Bauchet
Mattia Bonetti
Ernesto Gismondi
Pierre Guariche
Hella Jongerius
Kwok Hoi Chan
Joseph-André Motte
Jasper Morrison
Martin Szekely

a   Invitation card:
Mattia Bonetti, Tube sofa,
2004
Wood structure, pony-skin
upholstery, h. 4 ft. × w. 7 ft.
2 in. × d. 3 ft. 9 in. (h. 1.21 ×
w. 2.20 × d. 1.15 m)

b   Marcel Brient in front of
Hella Jongerius's
White Blizzard Bulb lamp
(2002), 2004

a

I needed furniture that would go with modern and contemporary art—something that, over time, was done with fervor. I was going to discover, love, and possess: Donald Judd, Jorge Pardo, Marc Newson, Konstantin Grcic, Franz West, Hella Jongerius, Ron Arad, Mattia Bonetti, Andrea Branzi, Naoto Fukasawa, and many others besides. Thank you to the artists; thank you, Didier.

Marcel Brient, collector, 2019

b

April 24–May 29, 2004—22, rue Duchefdelaville, Paris

RONAN & ERWAN BOUROULLEC,
ASSEMBLAGES 250, 150, 60

a Invitation card

b Assemblage #1, 2004
Metal, leather, Corian,
paint; structure h. 4 ft.
2 ½ in. × w. 4 ft. 11 in. ×
d. 6 ft. 11 in. (h. 1.28 ×
w. 1.50 × d. 2.10 m)

c Assemblage #2, 2004
Metal, Corian, paint;
structure h. 5 ft. 4 in. ×
w. 8 ft. 10 in. × d. 3 ft.
2 ½ in. (h. 162 × w. 270 ×
d. 98 cm)

d Assemblage #3, 2004
Metal, leather, paint;
structure h. 6 ft. 10 in. ×
w. 4 ft. × d. 3 ft. 1 in.
(h. 208 × w. 120 ×
d. 95 cm)

e Assemblage #4, 2004
Aluminum, metal, leather,
Corian; structure h. 5 ft.
11 in. × w. 8 ft. 5 in. × d. 6 ft.
6 ¾ in. (h. 1.80 × w. 2.56 ×
d. 2.00 m)

f Assemblage #5, 2004
Metal, Corian; structure
h. 5 ft. 11 in. × w. 8 ft. 4 in. ×
d. 3 ft. 3 in. (h. 1.80 ×
w. 2.55 × d. 1.00 m)

a

To pose, to place, to center, to align.... This collection is built around different levels which begin horizontally then become vertical to form "assemblages." Light, paint, materials outline the particularity of each level. An indecisive particularity in terms of use but very precise in terms of the balance of each ensemble. "Assemblages": with heights, depths, and points of view.

Ronan & Erwan Bouroullec, April 2004

b

c

d

e

f

Tito Agnoli
B.B.P.R.
Achille Castiglioni
Joe Colombo
Alberto Fraser
Dan Friedman
and Alessandro Mendini
Alberto Lago
Alessandro Mendini
Gaetano Pesce
Denis Santachiara
Gino Sarfatti
Superstudio
Massimo Vignelli

a Invitation card:
   Alessandro Mendini,
   Proust Chair, 1990
   Hand-painted plastic,
   h. 3 ft. × w. 2 ft. × d. 2 ft.
   (h. 90 × w. 60 × d. 60 cm)

b Andrea Branzi
   Cucus chair, Animali
   Domestici collection, 1985,
   for Zabro
   Wood and lacquer, h. 3 ft.
   6 ½ in. (h. 108.5 cm)

c Exhibition view:

   Alessandro Mendini
   1990 coffee table, 1990, for
   Divisione Nuova Alchimia
   Lacquered wood, glass,
   h. 2 ft. × diam. 3 ft. 3 in.
   (h. 61 × diam. 100 cm)

   Gino Sarfatti
   Floor/wall light
   1045/VT/A, 1940-48,
   for Arteluce
   Metal, aluminum, h. 3 ft.
   3 in. to 5 ft. 3 in. × diam. 2 ft.
   4 in. (h. 100–160 × diam.
   28 cm)

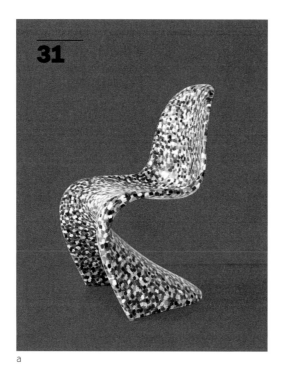

a

b

c

In 1985, Andrea Branzi presents his first solo exhibition, *Animali Domestici*. In a somber atmosphere, dramatized by powerful plays of light, radically-, essentially-shaped seats coexist. One is struck immediately by the strength of these hybrid components, artificial geometric seating, in neutral gray colors, into which are grafted natural tree trunks serving as seatbacks and armrests.... Pieces which escape the everyday world to appeal to a very powerfully evocative memory.

"Animali Domestici, un tournant décisif," in *Branzi* (Paris: Éditions Gallimard, 2014), p. 31

January 8–February 26, 2005—22, rue Duchefdelaville, Paris

RONAN & ERWAN BOUROULLEC, *BELLS*

a Invitation card

b Exhibition view:

Bells lamp, 2004
Lacquered copper,
metallic paint, metal table
covered in leather.
Large model: h. 6 ft. ×
w. 2 ft. 2 ¼ in. × d. 2 ft. 1 ½ in.
(h. 185 × w. 67 × d. 65 cm);
small model: h. 5 ft. 4 ½ in. ×
w. 2 ft. 2 ¼ in. × d. 2 ft. 1 ½ in
(h. 164 × w. 67 × d. 65 cm)

Suspension Bells, 2004
Lacquered resin, metallic
paint, h. 17 × diam. 23 ½ in.
(h. 43.8 × diam. 60 cm)

Bells coffee table, 2004
Lacquered copper,
metallic paint, metal table
covered in leather, h. 15 ×
diam. 23 ½ in. (h. 38 × diam.
60 cm)

32

a

Bells is a series of lamps and side tables taken from the
Assemblages collection, for which we had developed these
bell-shaped lamps. They are made out of hand-embossed
copper, which is then lacquered. These high-level,
handmade techniques enable us to produce objects with
an incredible finish. It seemed obvious to us to extract
these elements and to release them as single lamps and
side tables, which would be simpler and easier to handle
than the Assemblages. The "bell" as a shape is simple
and at the same time complex: it refers to some kind of
archetype, conveying a certain softness and familiarity.
On the flip side, when turned upside down, it gives a visual
instability to the tables.

Ronan & Erwan Bouroullec, 2005

a Invitation card:
T3 Shelves, 2004

b T3 Shelves, 2004
4G aluminum, Nextel paint,
h. 5 ft. 7 in. × w. 6 ft. 9 in. ×
d. 1 ft. 3 ¼ in. (h. 170 ×
w. 206 × d. 39 cm)

c T5 Shelves, 2004
4G aluminum, Nextel paint,
5 ft.7 in. × w. 6 ft. 9 ½ in. ×
d. 1 ft. 3 in. (h. 259 ×
w. 344× d. 46 cm)

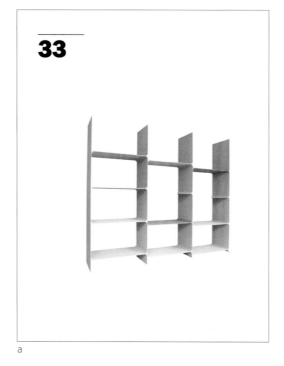

33

a

Measurements? Yes.

The height of the shelf is essential, it is the measure of man and his gestures, plus any potential extensions, reaching out his arms, his hands; beyond such dimensions, we need protheses, stepladder, ladder, or it's unusable. The depth of the shelf is dictated by usage: two books are stored on it, edge to edge, or an object; a shelf, not placed against a wall, but accessible from both sides.

A very peculiar shelf, a separation wall would be straighter, an architectural element sharing "a space that's always rowdy" (Georges Bataille), where a shelf fulfilling its functions would tend to dissolve, a posture similarly recurrent in Martin Szekely's oeuvre. This vertical object called "shelf" clutters up the visual field as little as possible, until it disappears at the precise moment when it satisfactorily performs its functions of placing, tidying away, and classifying books and objects.

The unity of the shelf stems from this sum of forces distributed and multiplied by triangles, ledges, or shutters that have also become almost invisible on the shelf. A narrowing of focus that articulates and unifies Martin Szekely's position and each of his projects.

This narrowing is measured here by the limits of the material employed, those of its bearing capacity, as well as those of its stability and equilibrium, a question of the construction or structure of the object, by which it can still fulfill its function and use.

An infinitesimal too many, an infinitesimal too few, and the outcome is collapse or explosion. It might be observed that the most successful objects of recent years are surely those that fully perform their functions and yet which disappear when these same functions are raised to their highest intensity, saturation, culmination.

Another type of disappearance, this time deriving from the materials used, especially in storage units arranged at the place where the zenithal light inside the— decidedly "rowdy"— space that makes a mess of the furniture, that literally vaporizes by temporarily disappearing, an intermittency that photography alone can reveal or conceal.

A shelf self-constructs, self-generates, self-reflects, always starting out from itself, a freestanding element, it unfolds, ascends; it occupies a position of self-sufficiency (the principle of construction and command) and autonomy (with its own law), against those who thought fit to claim the illusory right to design it. It can only be that and nothing else, and that, to the nearest infinitesimal.

Christian Schlatter, *Des étagères* (Paris: Bernard Chauveau, 2005), pp. 4–5

b, c

2005

May 28–July 23, 2005—22, rue Duchefdelaville, Paris

COLORS

Mattia Bonetti
Fernando and Humberto
Campana
Hella Jongerius
Dominique Mathieu
Alessandro Mendini
Radi Designers
Tejo Remy
Jerszy Seymour
Ettore Sottsass
Martin Szekely

a Invitation card:
Fernando and Humberto
Campana, Vitoria Regia
Medium stool, 2002
Metallic tubes, fabric,
h. 15 ¾ × diam. 31 ½ in.
(h. 40 × diam. 80 cm)

b Tejo Remy
Rag Chair, no. 74, no. 83,
and no. 87, 1991
Steel structure covered in
rags connected by plastic
bands, h. 31 ½ × w. 24 ×
d. 23 ½ in. (h. 80 × w. 61 ×
d. 60 cm)

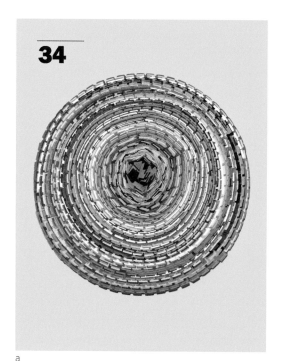

34

a

b

This chair is layered from the contents of fifteen bags of rags. It arrives ready-made but the user has the option to recycle his own discarded clothes to be included in the design. Each piece is unique—a treasure chest of memories.

Droog Design website, 2019

b

b

Born in 1963, Hella Jongerius lives in Berlin.

a Invitation card:
Cupboard #1, 2005
White-lacquered ash wood, silk-screened Plexiglas, wood piece from an old cupboard: one front door, h. 3 ft. 3 in. × w. 1 ft. 10 ½ in. × d. 1 ft. 10 ½ in. (h. 99 × w. 57 × d. 57 cm)

b Cupboard #3, 2005
White-lacquered ash wood, silk-screened Plexiglas, wood pieces from an old cupboard: three shelves and one drawer on the front, h. 34 ½ × w. 22 ¼ × d. 18 ¾ in. (h. 87.5 × w. 56.5 × d. 47.5 cm)

c Cupboard #5, 2005
White-lacquered ash wood, silk-screened Plexiglas, wood pieces from an old cupboard: three shelves on the front, h. 3 ft. 4 ½ in. × w. 1 ft. 8 in. × d. 2 ft. ¾ in. (h. 103 × w. 51 × d. 63 cm)

d Cupboard #10, 2005
White-lacquered ash wood, silk-screened Plexiglas, wood pieces from an old cupboard: two front doors with opening on one shelf and two drawers, h. 3 ft. 1 ½ in. × w. 1 ft. 7 ¼ in. × d. 1 ft. 10 ½ in. (h. 95.5 × w. 49 × d. 57 cm)

The exhibition also featured a selection of screens made of felt and mixed textiles, with embroidery and silkscreen printing by JongeriusLab

35

a

The Cupboards are sketches, 3D-sketching with old and new materials. Trying to find the right balance for a new product, what is authentic and would work with that in new materials. One antique cupboard became, after cutting and gluing, several new cupboards, like a collage of models. When does the new product visual flip over from the old, towards a new style? How strong is this old cupboard in our memory? What if the new parts have decoration integrated in artificial materials? This project is a study in form and material, with a trial-and-error method, just a step along the search in a new language. Rupture and the past is the theme I'm working on at the moment.

Hella Jongerius, July 2005

b

c

As a designer I have a lot to learn from what has already been done, just as industry can learn from craftsmanship.

Hella Jongerius, 2005

d

2005

November 5–December 23, 2005—22, rue Duchefdelaville, Paris

ECAL–ÉCOLE CANTONALE D'ART DE LAUSANNE, *INDUSTRIAL DESIGN*

Nicolas Aebischer
Laetitia de Allegri
Stéphane Barbier Bouvet
Fabio Biancaniello
Olivier Burgisser
Christine Buclin
Julie Cosendai
Sophie Depéry
Sophie Depéry and
Erik Pierrat
Luciano Dell'Orefice
Aude Genton
Gaëlle Girault
Emanuelle Jaques
Moulouhi Hadji
Andrea Knecht
Édouard Larmaraud
Letissia Perrin
La Chanh Nguyen
Roberto Prato
Damien Regamey
Damien Regamey and
Sergio Streun
Adrien Rovero
Augustin Scott de
Martinville and
Adrien Rovero
Augustin Scott de
Martinville and
Antoine Vauthey
Sibylle Stoeckli
Klara Zavadilova
Raphaële Zenger

a Invitation card:
ECAL/Augustin Scott de
Martinville and Antoine
Vauthey, Birdfeeder, 2004
Wood, porcelain, h. 8 ¼ ×
w. 9 ¾ × d. 7 ½ in. (h. 21 ×
w. 25 × d. 19 cm)

36

a

The result presents an overview of student production over recent years. Whether they are classics brought out by major companies—the Ramo ladder for Serralunga, the DrinkTray for Ligne Roset—or were produced in workshops run by renowned designers (Crystal Clear for Swarovski with the Campana brothers, the jewel redefined with Florence Doléac, a workshop about birdfeeders), or even just diploma projects, ECAL demonstrates how its teaching integrates every field of contemporary design.

Press release, November 2005

I do not like schools. However, the singularity of the ECAL suits me: its pedagogy is unconventional and porous, it tackles all fronts, handles media wonderfully, and doesn't care about the narrow confines to which schools restrict themselves. Its policy of infiltration makes ECAL visible everywhere, from New York's Museum of Modern Art to the Shanghai Museum of Contemporary Art, from the London Design Museum to the numerous galleries and international design fairs. In a few years, under the leadership of its director Pierre Keller and Alexis Georgacopoulos, Head of Industrial Design, this small Swiss school showed that it made fun of prejudice, that it became much more than a simple outsider.

Ronan Bouroullec, September 2005

These are not student pieces. Some are ready to be produced. It's design for pleasure and I like it.

Didier Krzentowski, in Anne-Marie Fèvre, "L'école calée et décalée," *Libération*, November 18, 2005

Konstantin Grcic
Julia Lohmann
Angelo Ostuni & Renato Forti
Gino Sarfatti
Martin Szekely

a Invitation card:
   Julia Lohmann
   Belinda Cowbench, 2005
   Wood, leather, foam,
   h. 2 ft. 3 ½ in. × w. 4 ft.
   11 in. × d. 1 ft. 7 ¾ in.
   (h. 70 × w. 150 × d. 50 cm)

a

A leather bench or bovine *memento mori*. We don't want our food to remind us of the animal it is made of but, at the same time, we are able to create living materials through advances in biotechnology. The Cow Bench explores the threshold between animal and material.

Julia Lohmann

a Invitation card:
   Large DB coffee table,
   2005
   Brushed and lacquered
   aluminum structure, h. 1 ft.
   1 ¾ in. × w. 3 ft. × d. 4 ft.
   1 ½ in. (h. 35 × w. 90 ×
   d. 126 cm)

b Exhibition view:

   Y mirror, 2006
   Lacquered and polished
   stainless steel, h. 3 ft. ×
   w. 4 ft. 10 ½ in. (h. 90 ×
   w. 146.4 cm)

   Medium T coffee table,
   2005
   Brushed and lacquered
   aluminum structure, h. 1 ft.
   1 ¾ in. × w. 4 ft. 6 in. ×
   d. 2 ft. 6 ¾ in. (h. 35 ×
   w. 137 × d. 78 cm)

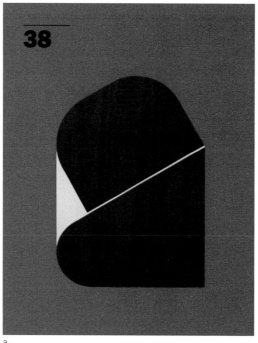

a

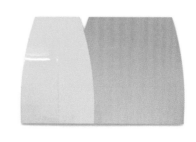

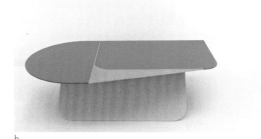

b

One of the characteristics of my work is the series.
This is more obvious in the very specific context of
a project for the gallery, where I am more
interested in designing a series of objects than an
object in a series. This does not involve the search
for the ideal design (the only one possible), but is,
on the contrary, an exploration, a search for
possible content in an intuition, an idea, a principle,
a drawing.... What makes a series is the
materialization of this collection of possibilities, to
draw a pathway between the different possibilities,
and in so doing, to highlight the principle of
research, before the object itself.

The *Platform* exhibition proposes a series of six
coffee tables of different dimensions, designed
for the Galerie kreo in the autumn of 2005.
By definition, a platform is a flat, horizontal shape,
either high or low, a surface on which other objects
are to be placed. The coffee tables are made of
three parts that are cut out and then assembled;
two are colored and one anodized, and they rest
on a base of folded metal. In addition to this series
there is a series of three mirrors in stainless steel,
made with the juxtaposition of two almost identical
shapes, one shiny and the other colored.

Pierre Charpin, January 2006

BIG-GAME
Ronan & Erwan Bouroullec
Adrien Rovero

a Invitation card:
Adrien Rovero
Dés-ordre carpet, 2004

b Adrien Rovero
Dés-ordre carpet, 2004
Hand-tufted wool, l. 11 ft.
6 in. × w. 8 ft. 2 in. ×
d. ½ in. (l. 350 × w. 250 ×
d. 1.5 cm)
Edition Galerie kreo/ECAL

c Ronan & Erwan Bouroullec
Grappe carpet, 2001
Wool, surface: 13 sq. in.
(84 cm²)

d BIG-GAME
Flatpack carpet, 2006
Hand-tufted wool,
l. 8 ft. 2 in. × w. 5 ft. 11 in. ×
d. ½ in. (l. 250 × w. 180 ×
d. 1.3 cm)

a

Working in the furniture and exhibition design sectors, Adrien Rovero has developed an uncluttered and effective—often offbeat—style that draws inspiration from his close scrutiny of everyday life. He enjoys assembling and repurposing shapes, materials, references and uses. He questions the interplay of scales: fiddling with reduced or blown-up sizes of his objects, he invites us to enter a disconcerting world of Gulliver and Lilliput.

Press pack for the exhibition *Adrien Rovero: Landscale*, MUDAC–Museum of Contemporary Design and Applied Arts, Lausanne, 2012

b

c

d

JASPER MORRISON, *CARRARA TABLES*

a Invitation card

b Variation #5 Carrara
   Tables, 2005
   Aluminum honeycomb,
   Carrara marble.
   Small unit: h. 11 × w. 29 ½ ×
   d. 15 in. (h. 28 × w. 75 ×
   d. 38.5 cm); large unit:
   h. 11 in. × w. 5 ft. 5 ¾ in. ×
   d. 15 in. (h. 28 × w. 167 ×
   d. 38.5 cm)

c Variation #13 Carrara
   Tables, 2005
   Aluminum honeycomb,
   Carrara marble.
   Small unit: h. 11 × w. 29 ½ ×
   d. 15 in. (h. 28 × w. 75 ×
   d. 38.5 cm); medium unit:
   h. 11 in. × w. 4 ft. × d. 1 ft.
   3 in. (h. 28 × w. 121 ×
   d. 38.5 cm); large unit:
   h. 11 in. × w. 5 ft. 5 ¾ in. ×
   d. 15 in. (h. 28 × w. 167 ×
   d. 38.5 cm)

d Sketch for the seventeen
   variations of the Carrara
   Tables, 2006

40

a

The Carrara Tables by British designer Jasper Morrison demonstrate how the specificity of a form can spawn a new typology of objects, which, as a result, naturally takes its place in the history of design. The story starts with an old wooden coffee table, of Korean origin, an object the designer lives with. An archetypal form, familiar from the interiors of Asian homes, it recalls the custom of sitting on the floor.... To develop this new collection Jasper Morrison chose the vocabulary of modularity, a system once celebrated by modernists, to whom the designer here pays modest tribute. Instead of using it as it is, however, he reconfigures it, reinterprets it, playfully appropriating its potential for adaptability.... Depending how they are placed within a space, a Carrara Table can serve as a bench-table or, on the other hand, as a table-bench, or even act as a table-bench-shelf.... In order to ensure the feasibility of this fusion between module and marble, i.e. to reduce weight and improve stability, honeycomb aluminum plating is inserted into the top. Circular indentations milled into the surface indicate where the legs of other marble tables can stand, if required. Aside from their function, these hollows possess an ornamental character reminiscent of traces left by some extinct civilization or of industrial markings. The shape of the legs recalls the calculations made for columns in ancient Greek temples. Virtually imperceptible, once made aware of it, it is a detail that increases one's aesthetic pleasure.

Laurence Mauderli, *Jasper Morrison: Répertoire pour une forme* (Paris: Bernard Chauveau, 2006), p. 3

b

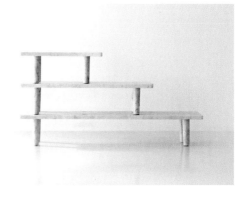

c

c

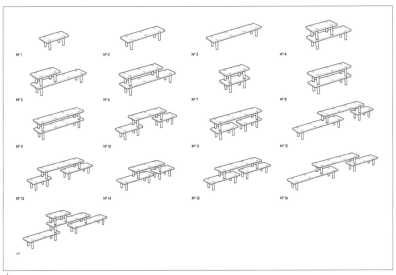

d

I found a low wooden table in a crafts shop in Tokyo: it came from Korea, they told me, and is apparently a typology made in a wide variety of versions on the same theme. I have been living with the original for a number of years now and have come to appreciate it more and more. When Didier Krzentowski asked me to do a show at Galerie kreo, the first idea I had was to do a series of tables in Carrara marble. Somehow I got side-tracked and decided to use this table as a stacking, modular system. I remember sometime in the 1970s a new piece of furniture was invented: it was a long, low shelf, usually fixed to the wall of the living room, and used very simply to put books and objects on, or to sit on. The modular version of this can be composed by stacking various combinations of the three members of the system. The marble tops have been hollowed out and a sheet of honeycomb aluminum inserted to lower the weight and increase the strength, so adjusting the combination is not so implausible.

Jasper Morrison, *A Book of Things* (Zurich: Lars Müller Publishers, 2015), p. 236

JASPER MORRISON, *MUSEUM PIECES*

a Invitation card:
   Museum Pieces–Cabinet
   A, 2006

b Museum Pieces–Cabinet
   A, 2006
   Cabinet in Securit glass
   and natural varnished oak,
   collection of fifteen objects
   made in black or white
   resin, h. 6 ft. 2 in. × w. 2 ft.
   1 ½ in. × d. 2 ft. 1 ½ in.
   (h.186 × w. 65 × d. 65 cm)

c Museum Pieces–Cabinet
   B, 2006
   Cabinet in Securit glass
   and natural varnished
   oak, collection of fifteen
   objects made in black or
   white resin, h. 6 ft. 1 in. ×
   w. 3 ft. 3 in. × d. 1 ft. 3 ¾ in.
   (h. 186 × w. 100 × d. 40 cm)

a

For some time now I have been visiting archeology museums whenever I find myself in a new town and photographing some of the beautiful examples of everyday life from long ago. Looking through the images recently I started to form the idea of making a synthetic collection of antiquities. It has become very difficult for people to buy these things recently, with plenty of debate about the illegal trade in them and an abundance of fakes on the market. The function these pieces serve is purely symbolic, and yet as reminders of the beauty of past cultures and displayed in special cabinets, they are an instant collection. Of course you don't get the beautiful patina of the originals, as these ones are cast in resin from 3D computer data, but once you have bought the collection at least you can be sure it's yours.
Jasper Morrison, *A Book of Things* (Zurich: Lars Müller Publishers, 2015), p. 238

b

c

This show? Fifteen black resin pieces, fifteen white resin pieces, thirty pieces in all, that when displayed become the "museum pieces" of the title.

Where is Jasper Morrison going with this gesture of enclosure? Is he shifting the territory of his pieces, here, "museum pieces"? Does it mean that his pieces are leaving expected territory and that he has suspended their use through this movement of enclosure, put function on hold to make them pieces to be looked at exclusively?

The second gesture, their making, abolishes all possible use; some pieces are solid or single blocks, others give the impression that here, too, something is awry, when others seem to retain the promise of use. We could start by describing the first ones by calling them vases with blocked necks, but we must go further—these vases are solid, their function is not merely suspended due to the display case, they can have no function. A bowl? We can just about use the term receptacle, even though we would be hard pressed to find an element that could be contained in it; the impression of a suspended use, of a distant functionality returns. A jewelry box, a receptacle for medicine? We could perhaps associate them with archeological pieces, cosmetic accessories for Ugaritic women, but the container and its lid are one.

What will these thirty pieces, enclosed in display cases, become exactly? Pieces to show, to look at, of course. These museum pieces resemble Morandi's work in places, perhaps they are objects from Chirico's metaphysical period, perhaps also, they remind us that the painter used to say he could only capture certain objects when "surprised by certain arrangements of objects" and that the whole mystery of the question was, for him, contained in that word: "surprise." So with these pieces, a new understanding of objects, seen up close, from afar, but always enclosed in a display case, what have they become? Can we possibly envisage a return to Jasper Morrison's archetypal figures, objects finally rid of all formality?

Christian Schlatter, July 2006

2006

MAARTEN VAN SEVEREN

a Invitation card:
   Bakelite desk, 2001

b Bakelite desk, 2001
   Bakelite, h. 2 ft. 4 ½ in. ×
   w. 8 ft. 10 in. × d. 3 ft. 3 in.
   (h. 72.5 × w. 270 ×
   d. 100 cm)

42

a

There is nothing deceptive or extraneous in Maarten's work.

Rolf Fehlbaum, 2001

A piece of furniture in space is simultaneously confronted with the dividing lines of the wall and floor, but also a window, which adds the possibility of a horizon line.

Sophie Tasma Anargyros, "Maarten Van Severen," *Intramuros* (no. 69, February/March 1997), pp. 30–34

b

In the courtyard of his workshop in Ghent, Maarten Van Severen installed a work by the sculptor Philippe Van Isacker: a gray, perfect parallelepiped, almost levitating above the ground, held by four steel jacks: *For the Right to Doubt*. Indeed, Maarten Van Severen, the Belgian designer, was prone to doubt himself. It happens even to the most brilliant. Never to his pieces. They are, on the contrary, sure, precise, precious. He worked on the essential, both in terms of shape and material. Evidence of which are the two posthumous pieces shown here: a wall-mounted bookshelf and a desk. The first piece, an oblong bookshelf, is made from aluminum with a facade made up of moveable panels covered in a phosphorescent lacquer. When they slide, they hide a fragment of the interior while revealing another. The piece rarely looks the same. It is, above all, unusually long. Not 3.58 meters. Nor is it even 3.60 meters: "rounding off" was not part of Van Severen's philosophy, especially when it was a question of "angles." The bookshelf measures exactly 3.577 meters. Or, more to the point, 3.577 millimeters, the only tolerable unit of measure according to Van Severen. The man himself made his pieces with his own hands, using a die. The evidence can be seen

to the nearest millimeter. The second of the two pieces presented, a black Bakelite desk, was thought through in the same manner. Ultimate starkness: four legs, a plateau, the same thickness of material throughout, the same color. It is almost an archetype, an idea. The object is both initial and definitive. Its proportions are equally breath-taking, in particular the size that eulogizes the horizontal. 2.700 millimeters, exactly. The desk has no "style" as such. It says nothing, about its feasibility, its genesis. It is merely itself, with proof. An incontestable presence. It is simply there. And simply everything. The last paragon of a precise, ascetic, and silent body of work. We were aware of Maarten Van Severen's desire for perfection. With time we discover that he explored existence in its most infinitesimal dimensions.

Press release, October 2006

Andrea Branzi
Pierre Charpin
Hella Jongerius
Michele de Lucchi
Angelo Mangiarotti
Alessandro Mendini
Ettore Sottsass

---

a Invitation card:
Andrea Branzi
Antheia vase, 2006
"Bucchero" ceramic
and gold-colored metal,
h. 17 ¼ × d. 13 ½ in. (h. 44 ×
d. 34 cm)

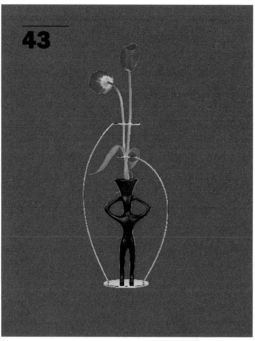

a

A vase is a simple support, and designers have always been rather lazy about its function: they have never sought to make it perfect. It's a marvelous support because there are very few rules about its use, which allows for a certain freedom. But vase production is cyclical. All designers—ourselves included—produced many of them in the 1980s and 1990s. And then we stopped designing them. Now they're coming back. There's a sort of love-hate relationship with this object.... Historically, vases have always been rather special objects, which have clearly absorbed successive styles. This has been going on since Antiquity. Nevertheless, the vases of Ettore Sottsass or Angelo Mangiarotti, who worked a lot with ceramics... are still exceptional due to their formal balance.

Ronan Bouroullec, in Nicolas Trembley, *Sgrafo vs. Fat Lava* (Zurich: JRP|Ringier, 2012)

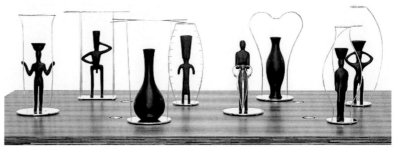

Andrea Branzi
Fernando and Humberto
Campana
Pierre Charpin
Ettore Sottsass
Martin Szekely

a Invitation card:
Martin Szekely, V.R.G.D.
coffee table, 2006
Steel mesh, tatami mat,
Corian, three inseparable
elements, h. 17 ×
w. 16/23 ½ × d. 13/19 ¼ in.
(h. 43 × w. 41/60 ×
d. 33/49 cm)

b Alessandro Mendini
Cleome Elegans cabinet,
Museum Market collection,
1993, for Design Milano
Lacquered wood,
fiberglass, bronze, glass,
h. 5 ft. 3 ½ in. × w. 5 ft.
3 ½ in. × d. 1 ft. 6 in.
(h. 161 × w. 106 × d. 45 cm)

c Ettore Sottsass
Armadio per la stanza de
un nomade, 2005, for Clio
Calvi Gallery
Storage unit made of
two panels of cork, one
mirror, one blackboard,
and a drawer. Drawings on
the blackboard made by
Miquel Barcelo and Ettore
Sottsass, h. 6 ft. 1 in. ×
w. 2 ft. × d. 2 ft. (h. 185.5 ×
w. 60 × d. 60 cm)

44

a

b

Alessandro Mendini likes to say, "My objects are like characters in a theater." The Cleome Elegans cabinet is a rare vintage piece, which illustrates the freedom, the vitality, and the construction of the designers' pieces. It is a combination, or rather a set of colors and shapes placed one upon the other: a box topped with a fish head, on top of a cone-shaped pleated base. A kind of personage, who brings in the viewer.

Press release, March 2007

c

The Closet [*Armadio*] is conceived like a "box," with different panels: wood and cork panels, where pictures, invitations, and drawings are pinned, chosen by the designer, or black slate on which appears in chalk, like on a school blackboard, texts and a signature of Miquel Barcelo and Ettore Sottsass. In this piece, we can find the base of Sottsass's work: geometrical shapes, the use of primary colors and different mixed materials, which define an unusual language, and challenge industrial and uniform production.

Press release, March 2007

Pierre Charpin
Roberto Gabetti, Aimaro
Isola, Guido Drocco,
and Luciano Re
Vittorio Gregotti, Lodovico
Meneghetti, and Giotto
Stoppino
James Irvine
Hella Jongerius
Dominique Mathieu
Alessandro Mendini
Jasper Morrison
Marc Newson
Claudio Salocchi
Gino Sarfatti
Wieki Somers
Martin Szekely
Raphaële Zenger

a Invitation card:
   Wieki Somers, Bathboat
   Tub, 2005

b Wieki Somers, Bathboat
   Tub, 2005
   Oak, red cedar, h. 2 ft. ×
   w. 6 ft. 5 in. × d. 2 ft. 8 ½ in.
   (h. 62 × w. 195 × d. 83 cm)

a

A bathtub. It provides a new experience through a simple intervention. It started with watching a fisherman's boat floating on a lake one morning. Peaceful, timeless, somehow mysterious and deeply banal at the same time. Boating and bathing in the water evoke similar feelings. Here they are combined in one object.... Bathboat is not a joke, but a dream.

Wieki Somers, 2005

b

François Bauchet
Ronan & Erwan Bouroullec
Pierre Charpin
Demakersvan
Hella Jongerius
Jasper Morrison
Marc Newson
Radi Designers
Ettore Sottsass
Martin Szekely
Maarten Van Severen

a Invitation card:
Hella Jongerius,
Rhinoceros mirror, 2007
Mirror, black walnut, h. 2 ft.
6 ¾ in. × w. 3 ft. 9 in. ×
d. 2 in. (h. 78.5 × w. 115 ×
d. 3 cm)

b Hella Jongerius,
Vulture mirror, 2007
Mirror, black walnut, h. 23 ×
w. 34 × d. 1 ⅝ in. (h. 58 ×
w. 87 × d. 4 cm)

c Hella Jongerius,
Fennec mirror, 2007
Mirror, black walnut,
h. 9 ½ × w. 17 ¼ × d. 1 ⅝ in.
(h. 24 × w. 44 × d. 4 cm)

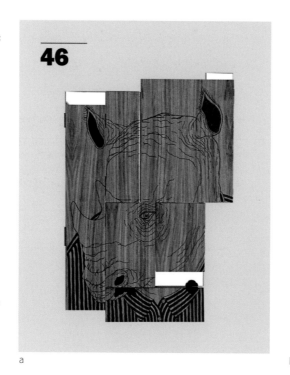

46

a

b

a

c

Playing with the mirrored image of oneself and
the fragments of an animal's "face," the Fennec,
Vulture, and Rhinoceros mirrors are conceived
as interactive pieces for the viewer. Each of
the elements is specially designed, including the
hinges, which, paired with the warm walnut wood,
recall a variety of natural elements.
Press release, April 2007

François Bauchet
Ronan & Erwan Bouroullec
Andrea Branzi
Kwok Hoi Chan
Pierre Charpin
Michele de Lucchi
Vittorio Gregotti, Lodovico
Meneghetti, Giotto
Stoppino
Jasper Morrison
Marc Newson
Pierre Paulin
Gino Sarfatti
Martin Szekely
Franz West

a Invitation card:
   Martin Szekely
   Black 103 console, 2006
   Inox steel, glossy black
   finish, h. 3 ft. 4 ½ in ×
   d. 1 ft. 2 in. (h. 103 ×
   d. 36 cm)

47

a

A few months after *A White Show*, here's
A Black Show, for which dark is the rule,
except inside the Giardino mirror (2003)
by Andrea Branzi, enthroned in the middle
of this black-clad space: reflecting out to
infinity, as if on a quest for the black hole.

Press release, June 2007

2007

TABOURETS

François Azambourg
François Bauchet
Ronan & Erwan Bouroullec
Andrea Branzi
Fernando Brizio
Fernando and Humberto
Campana
Pierre Charpin
David Dubois
Rena Dumas
Olivier Gagnère
Elisabeth Garouste
Konstantin Grcic
James Irvine
Hella Jongerius
Julia Lohmann
Alessandro Mendini
Philippe Million
Jasper Morrison
Andrée Putman
Adrien Rovero
Jerszy Seymour
Wieki Somers
Martin Szekely
Michael Young

a Invitation card

b Andrée Putman seated in
her Baldaquin stool, 2007
White-lacquered metal
structure, transparent glass
bead curtain, white leather
upholstery, h. 6 ft. ½ in.
(h. 1.84 m)

48

François Azambourg
François Bauchet
Ronan & Erwan Bouroullec
Andrea Branzi
Fernando Brizio
Humberto & Fernando Campana
Pierre Charpin
David Dubois
Rena Dumas
Olivier Gagnère
Elizabeth Garouste
Konstantin Grcic
James Irvine
Hella Jongerius
Julia Lohmann
Alessandro Mendini
Philippe Million
Jasper Morrison
Andrée Putman
Adrien Rovero
Jerszy Seymour
Wieki Somers
Martin Szekely
Michael Young

a

**Andrée Putman often told a
story—a tale, almost—to describe
her design pieces. For Baldaquin,
it would start like this: A young
woman is sitting on a stool.
A handsome young man opens
the curtain, and the story begins.**
Didier Krzentowski, 2019

b

a   Studio Wieki Somers
    Frozen Stool, 2007
    Ash wood, UV topcoat,
    polyester resin, h. 13 ½ in.
    (h. 34 cm)

b   Martin Szekely
    Z.Z. stool, 2007
    No. 1, French walnut,
    h. 17 × w. 16 × d. 14 ¼ in.
    (h. 43 × w. 41 × d. 36.5 cm)

c   Konstantin Grcic
    Vol. II stool, 2007
    Foam, wood, natural-
    colored leather upholstery,
    h. 23 ½ in. (h. 60 cm)

d   Fernando and Humberto
    Campana
    Terrastool, 2007
    Clay structure, "sushi"
    cushion, h. 18 in. (h. 46 cm)

e   Pierre Charpin
    Occasional stool, 2007
    White beech, h. 16 ½ in.
    (h. 42 cm)

f   Fernando Brizio
    Alice stool, 2007
    Wood, stainless steel,
    h. 17 in. (h. 43.5 cm)

g   Rena Dumas
    Stool, 2007
    Gabon ebony, or black
    anodized aluminum, or
    leather, h. 14 in. (h. 35 cm)

h   Philippe Million
    Stool, 2007
    Lacquered aluminum,
    h. 20 ¾ in. (h. 53 cm)

i   Michael Young
    Barstool, 2007
    Lacquered, satin-finish
    M.D.F., leather, steel,
    h. 29 ½ in. (h. 75 cm)

j   François Bauchet
    Stool, 2007
    Samba (clear), Wenge
    plywood, h. 20 ¾ in.
    (h. 53 cm)

k   David Dubois
    Stoolbox, 2007
    Cardboard, black leather,
    h. 12 ¼ in. (h. 31 cm)

l   Ronan & Erwan Bouroullec
    Stool, 2007
    Tinted and varnished
    sculpted oak, h. 10 ½, 11,
    and 12 in. (h. 26.5, 28, and
    30 cm)

m   Julia Lohmann
    Lasting Void stool, 2007
    Black lacquered resin,
    h. 15 ¾ in. (h. 40 cm)

n   François Azambourg
    Silver stool, 2007
    Layered 0.3 mm silver
    leaf, stool made of
    folded pieces assembled
    by brazing, h. 16 in.
    (h. 41 cm)

o   Jasper Morrison
    Three-legged stool,
    2007
    Polished aluminum,
    h. 13 in. (h. 33 cm)

p   Andrea Branzi
    Stool, 2007
    Vitra legs designed by
    George Nelson and
    birch wood seat, h. 31 in.
    (h. 79 cm)

q   Hella Jongerius
    Backpack stool, 2007
    Walnut, handmade
    upholstery, polyester
    resin boxes, h. 24 ½ in.
    (h. 62 cm)

r   Adrien Rovero
    Pimp stool, 2007
    Anodized aluminum,
    h. 17 in. (h. 43 cm)

s   Olivier Gagnère
    Stool, 2007
    Metal, wood, leather,
    h. 17 ¾ in. (h. 45 cm)

t   James Irvine
    Blow stool, 2007
    Murano glass, h. 15 ¾ in.
    (h. 40 cm)

u   Alessandro Mendini
    Enigma stool, 2007
    Lacquered resin, h. 18 in.
    (h. 46 cm)

v   Élisabeth Garouste
    Fantasia stool, 2007
    Lacquered resin, wood,
    h. 19 ½ in. (h. 50 cm)

There is a piece of furniture that inexplicably constitutes a sort of rite of passage for any designer worth his or her salt, the ultimate quest, without which there can be no recognition: the chair. The stool cannot claim such a status. Probably because what the dictionary describes as "a seat usually without back or arms supported by three or four legs" does not support the whole human body, only its least noble part: the posterior. That is as it may be. The short history of design is replete with notorious specimens: the Ulm stool designed by Max Bill and Hans Gugelot, the Butterfly by Sori Yanagi, the Mezzadro by the Castiglioni brothers, the Rocking by Isamu Noguchi, the Eames Time-Life…. The stool is an ultra-functional object. Compared to the naturally sedentary chair, the stool is more of a nomad. Sitting astride a stool, one sees things differently. Isn't one's point of view different when closer to the ground? This project was inspired by a memory, that of the old rustic seat used by farmers in Alpine valleys: the "milking stool," known in Swiss as the "*botte-cul*." The same one that Charlotte Perriand adapted so perfectly as a three-legged version for houses in the skiing resort of Alpine Meribel-les-Allues.

The present exercise consists of questioning today's designers on this archetype of yesterday. Each one answered differently. Each object possesses its own particularities: a material, a shape, a logic. The stool is not an ordinary object. In Africa, this seat is "one of the articulations of a complex system of thought built on the ties that bind together the earth, the Gods, the ancestors, society, the individual; the myths, rites, everyday gestures; matter, the object, the word" (Jean-François Pirson, *Le Corps et la chaise* [Taviers: Metaphores, 1990]). In the chief's palace, the "Stool House" is a room without windows. Only certain people have the right to enter and the guardian comes regularly to offer gifts. The twenty-three stools on show here are all in a line. A mystical procession or joyful parade? Silence is essential. In 1965, in a performance entitled *Teaching Painting to a Dead Hare*, Joseph Beuys sat on a stool to explain the meaning of art to a stuffed animal he held in his arms.

Christian Schlatter, Fall 2007

a

b

c

d

e

f

g

h

i

j

k

l

m

n

o

p

q

r

s

t

u

v

Award created by
Jean-Baptiste Danet
Artistic Direction:
Martin Szekely

BIG-GAME
David Dubois
Adrien Rovero

a Invitation card

b BIG-GAME
Wood Work reading light,
2007
Balsa, epoxy resin,
aluminum, fluorescent
tube, h. 4 ft. 7 in. × w. 4 ft. ×
d. 4 ft. 3 in. (h. 1.40 ×
w. 1.20 × d. 1.30 m)

c David Dubois
MD Light, 2007
Folded white-lacquered
steel plate, h. 9 × w. 5 ¾ ×
d. 4 ¾ in (h. 23 × w. 14.5 ×
d. 12 cm)

d Adrien Rovero
Portico lamp, 2007
Inox structure, aluminum,
Plexiglas box, h. 6 ft. 7 in. ×
w. 7 ft. × d. 2 ft. 4 in.
(h. 200 × w. 210 × d. 71 cm)

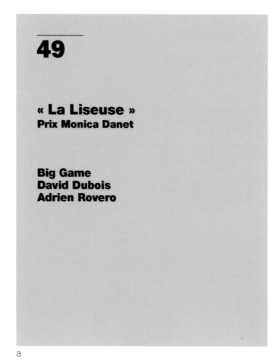

———
49

« La Liseuse »
Prix Monica Danet

Big Game
David Dubois
Adrien Rovero

a

Monica Danet was the art director of Christofle for almost ten years. "Monica was cultivated and a fine observer," remembers Jean-Baptiste Danet. "Fascinated by the beauty and purity of objects that have a meaning, not necessarily useful. It was in contact with designers that she lived life to the full." "She appreciated objects and their authors," adds the designer Martin Szekely, who worked with her at the beginning of the 2000s to design objects for Christofle. Monica left us at the age of forty-four, after a long illness.

Created this year on Jean-Baptiste Danet's initiative, the Monica Danet Prize wishes to pay tribute to Monica's passion and determination.... For its first edition, the prize was awarded to three young designers, or design groups: the Swiss designer Adrien Rovero (b. 1981), the French designer David Dubois (b. 1971), and the BIG-GAME trio. All have realized a prototype of their own light. In a painting by Vermeer entitled *The Reader by the Window*, a young woman is lost in the reading of a letter. On the window there is a reflection of a face.

Press release, September 2007

b

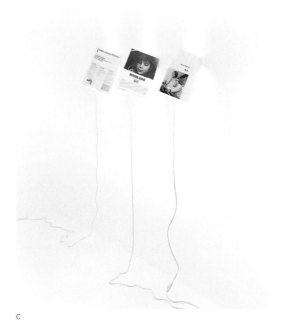

c

d

b, c, d

The Monica Danet Prize aims
to encourage three young designers,
offering them financial support
to create, develop, and produce
an original piece. Monica was
passionate about books, which is
the reason for the chosen theme:
la liseuse, or reading light.

Press release, September 2007

a Invitation card

b Exhibition view:

Sofa, 2008
Tinted and varnished oak,
foam, wool, fabric, h. 6 ft.
7 in. × w. 9 ft. 2 in. × d. 3 ft.
4 in. (h. 2.00 × w. 2.80 ×
d. 1.02 m)

Icefield coffee table, 2008
Gel coat, fiberglass,
h. 7 in. × w. 9 ft. 3 in. ×
d. 3 ft. 4 ½ in. (h. 18 ×
w. 282 × d. 103 cm)

Double Black Light, 2008
Aluminum, fiberglass, car
paint, Plexiglas, steel cable,
fluorescent light, h. 3 ft.
9 in. × w. 7 ft. 11 ½ in. ×
d. 3 ft. 9 in. (h. 115 ×
w. 243.5 × d. 115 cm); bell:
diam. 19 ¾ in. (50 cm)

Triple Black Light, 2008
Aluminum, fiberglass, car
paint, Plexiglas, steel cable,
fluorescent light, h. 3 ft.
9 in. × w. 7 ft. 11 ½ in. ×
d. 4 ft. 3 in. (h. 115 ×
w. 243.5 × d. 130 cm); bell:
diam. 19 ¾ in. (50 cm)

c Exhibition view:

Rice Field coffee table,
2008
Gel coat, fiberglass,
h. 9 ¾ in. × w. 6 ft. 9 in. ×
d. 3 ft. 11 ½ in. (h. 25 ×
w. 206 × d. 120 cm)

Blue Screen, 2008
Painted steel, painted
aluminum, wool, steel cable,
h. 6 ft. 7 in. × w. 8 ft. 6 in. ×
d. 1 ft 5 ¼ in. (h. 200 ×
w. 260 × d. 44 cm)

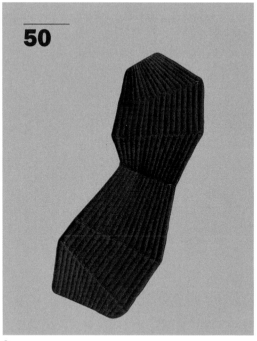

50

a

For Ronan & Erwan Bouroullec, working with galleries is a chance to breathe outside the usual constraints that characterize their enthusiastic contribution to industrial design. Their need to go "over the top" shows their almost childlike joy in escaping the ties that bind them when working on a brief. The unique proportions of these new pieces are free from existing typologies and domestic conventions. They free themselves from defined and definitive shapes. The Bouroullec brothers travel between the known and the unknown, moving in an "in-between" space that still leaves plenty of room for practical use. The disturbing, long black lamp invents a pivoting principle that leans on the ceiling. It moves like a living organism, like a three-headed hydra. The exaggerated diameter evokes the imposing size of Venetian chandeliers.

The molded polyester tables, with their synthetic appearance, are huge monolithic shapes that are barely off the ground. Their white and unreal aspect makes them seem like floating ice floes. The sofa—can we still refer to it as such?—is a black box, one of the elementary shapes that Ronan & Erwan Bouroullec love so much. The intriguing shape (9 ft. 10 in. × 6 ft. 7 in. [3 × 2 m])

makes us wonder about the true nature of the object. Is it a piece of furniture or an alcove? The pile of covers clears any doubts about its function: it is a place of comfort, a shelter for rest and retreat, a sort of spatial parenthesis. Just as impressive in terms of dimension (7 ft. 2 in. × 13 ft. [2.20 × 4 m]), the screen is more of a "fabric wall" than a mobile separation. One is seduced by these patches of wool in abstract, geometric, stitched shapes in clashing colors. The design of the aluminum chassis on which these huge wool covers are "placed" reminds us of a saddlemaker's workshop with skins hanging on metal trestles. These four objects do not constitute a collection by any means, as they were all designed at different times. However, they do represent the constant research of the Bouroullec brothers into the notion of the "quality of the atmosphere." The use of fabric is one answer. In this case, it is a vehicle for color, and the huge, flat, monochrome surfaces bring to mind abstract paintings. After having explored a more pointillist and vibrant touch with the fabric tile Kvadrat, the two designers are today experimenting with the strict and lyrical rhythm of collections and fitted shapes, associated with layers of color. Ettore Sottsass said, "Color is life." Ronan Bouroullec ironically says that "color is as complicated as life." In any case, the two brothers refuse to invent any kind of theory on the subject. They tame color with method, letting themselves be guided by their intuition. This is a delight and an open door every time as their aesthetic visibly gathers strength.

Laurence Salmon, January 2008

b

c

"Erwan and Ronan Bouroullec are rooted in the Bigouden country, in this Breton land that has given so much to the creation of modern times. This would be reason enough for me to take an interest in their work, especially since they now enjoy impressive international recognition. What attracts me to their work, however, is the conviction that it is major, some of the best in the history of design. They both know how to reconcile the delicacy of formal research with the intelligence of materials, the scrupulous respect for use and the ambition to make their productions accessible to all, in this complex relationship between the creations and the two people who make them. Here, we are in the very definition of design and its own genius. This is why I wanted them to be associated with a project that is particularly dear to me, that of the development of the Paris Bourse de Commerce and its surroundings."

François Pinault, Paris, 2019

a Invitation card:
   Concrete desk, 2007

b Concrete coffee table,
   2007
   Lafarge Ductal fiber
   concrete and aluminum
   honeycomb, h. 1 ft. 3 ¾ in. ×
   w. 4 ft. 3 in. × d. 3 ft. 3 in.
   (h. 40 × w. 130 × d. 99 cm)

c Concrete desk, 2007
   Lafarge Ductal fiber
   concrete and aluminum
   honeycomb, h. 2 ft. 5 ½ in. ×
   w. 6 ft. 7 in. × d. 4 ft. 3 in.
   (h. 75 × w. 200 × d. 129 cm)

d Concrete round table with
   central leg, 2007
   Lafarge Ductal fiber
   concrete and aluminum
   honeycomb, h. 2 ft. 5 ½ in. ×
   w. 6 ft. 8 in. × d. 6 ft. 4 ¼ in.
   (h. 75 × w. 203 ×
   d. 194 cm)

e Concrete table, 2007
   Lafarge Ductal fiber
   concrete and aluminum
   honeycomb, h. 2 ft. 5 ½ in. ×
   w. 9 ft. 6 in. × d. 4 ft. 8 in.
   (h. 75 × w. 290 ×
   d. 143 cm)

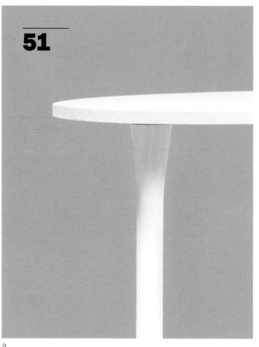

51

a

b, c

The Ductal concrete produced by Lafarge initially comes as a powder of fine particles and additives. Organic fibers are put into the concrete to structure it. Water is added to form a paste that takes the shape of its mold.

The project was to create a large tabletop using mineral materials that would be an appropriate weight for household use. This represents a shift away from the culture of the building trade and the intended destination of concrete on building sites.

My ideas were shared by Sylvain Quidant, the engineer and codirector on a project that had never been tried before: working concrete not as a heavy mass, but in light, poured, pressed sheets, stratifying a composite sandwich of concrete/aluminum honeycomb/concrete. At this stage, we realized that each component of the composite was fragile in itself. A composite material is more solid and resistant than each component on its own. The cohesion produced a new material that guaranteed the table would be rigid, flat, and present no acoustic problems, making the most of the material's qualities and characteristics without conforming to convention.

The indefinite outline of the tabletop results from the mass of soft concrete being flattened by a roller rather than from a drawing. Furthermore, the appearance of the surface is a reminder that the material was almost liquid at one point. The top dries out to a smooth, matte, pale gray that is silky to the touch. The top is raised to the desired height by cylindrical legs that flare out gently at the top, or, in some models, by a single broad cylindrical base. The entire set of data, shapes, dimensions, and positions of the legs are the result of a calculation to determine the table's resistance to the impact of users over time. The shape is welcoming, with no head of the table and no set number of places—from a single person to a group sitting all round it.

The tables owe their apparent simplicity to the maximization of the intrinsic qualities of the concrete and the principle of economy that underpins the project as a whole. Just enough, and everything in its place, to let use make its own way. Complexity is contained.

Martin Szekely, November 2007

d

e

a Invitation card:
  Pierre Charpin and
  Alessandro Mendini
  All'Aperto bench, 2007

b Exhibition view:

  Pierre Charpin
  All'Aperto table, 2008
  Bisazza mosaic, fiberglass
  structure, h. 2 ft. 5 ½ in. ×
  w. 4 ft. 10 ½ in. (h. 75 ×
  w. 149 cm)

  Pierre Charpin
  Flower pot, 2007
  Bisazza mosaic,
  polyurethane structure,
  h. 4 ft. ½ in. × diam. 2 ft.
  6 ½ in. (h. 123 × diam.
  75 cm)

  Pierre Charpin and
  Alessandro Mendini
  All'Aperto bench, 2007
  Bisazza mosaic,
  polyurethane structure,
  h. 1 ft. 3 ¾ in. × w. 6 ft.
  3 in. × d. 1 ft. 8 in. (h. 40 ×
  w. 190 × d. 50 cm)

  Pierre Charpin
  All'Aperto coffee table,
  2007
  Bisazza mosaic, fiberglass
  structure, h. 1 ft. 2 ½ in. ×
  w. 4 ft. 3 in. × d. 3 ft.
  4 ½ in. (h. 37 × w. 129.5 ×
  d. 103.5 cm)

52

a

"I had just moved back to Paris and moved in with my future wife. We had assembled the few pieces of furniture we had. The All'Aperto table was our first purchase from Galerie kreo and quite definitely the nicest thing we had. We were drawn to its freehand lines and organic shape and by the pleasure we got running our fingers across it. It became the cornerstone of our collection, which grew with other works from Pierre Charpin and other designers. It was the start of a friendship and of a wonderful journey."

Léopold Meyer, collector and Chairman of the Friends of Centre Pompidou, Paris, 2019

This odd couple here unveils what is a magnificent piece. A sarcophagus-shaped bench of great formal purity, rhythmically suffused by color, at once rigorous and playful. The game is on and discussions take place between the two designers. Communicating by email, they test the water before allotting their roles: Pierre Charpin will provide the form and Alessandro Mendini the motif. Created in tandem and bearing the title All'aperto, this perfectly harmonious work makes its point with aplomb—a path linking one generation to the next, a bridge between inside and out.

Anne Bony, paris-art.com, June 2008

The All'aperto project unites the designers Alessandro Mendini and Pierre Charpin on the common theme of the Bisazza mosaic technique applied to furniture objects, intended to be outside. We could also say: a game of mosaics, like a game of words. Isn't design always a thing of variations around those equivocals? However, All'aperto indicates without ambiguity the adopted direction, the one of the outside, of the opened (*aperto*), echoing like a "Down" with the smell of chalk dust—a cry that's always a badge of pride for the undisciplined one of design. Mosaic is also an exterior: the material hides the structure on which it is laid. It prevents it being identified and makes it insignificant. The appearance remains a mystery: the material is here an enigma that contains the object and the subject, it carries the inside and the outside world. A drawing and a pattern remain, thus, a silhouette and the nuances of its dress,

worn by some elementary functions: an armchair, a flower stand, a bench, and two tables compose the gallery's proposal. All is in front, in the decor, in the convention and the game. If mosaic talks about detour, of the game and its rules, it convenes also the distance, of physical nature as well as cultural. With time, the age and the resistance of the material and the one of space, the apprehension, will change according to whether one is closed or not. Included in the All'aperto proposition is the hypothesis of the Powers of Two: it could refer to the collaboration of two designers, Mendini and Charpin, to the change of perception that takes place because of the image's enlargement of the Eames' exercise, Powers Of Ten. In mosaic, it is a question of reproduction, not in the sense of technique, but of love.

Pierre Doze, press release, May 2008

b

2008

September 13–October 19, 2008—31, rue Dauphine, Paris

16 NEW PIECES

François Bauchet
Ronan & Erwan Bouroullec
Fernando Brizio
Pierre Charpin
David Dubois
Front Design
Naoto Fukasawa
Konstantin Grcic
James Irvine
Hella Jongerius
Alessandro Mendini
Jasper Morrison
Marc Newson
Jerszy Seymour
Wieki Somers
Martin Szekely

---

a Invitation card

b Exhibition view:

Marc Newson
Carbon Ladder, 2008
Carbon fiber, h. 6 ft. 7 in. ×
w. 1 ft. 5 in./1 ft. 8 ¾ in. ×
d. 2 ½ in. (h. 201.5 ×
w. 43/52.5 × d. 6 cm)

Ronan & Erwan Bouroullec
Geta coffee table, 2008
Lacquered oak, h. 9 ½ in. ×
w. 6 ft. 3 ¾ in. × d. 3 ft.
1 ¼ in. (h. 24 × w. 157 ×
d. 95 cm)

Pierre Charpin
Moon mirror, 2008
Polished stainless steel,
diam. 4 ft. (diam. 122 cm)

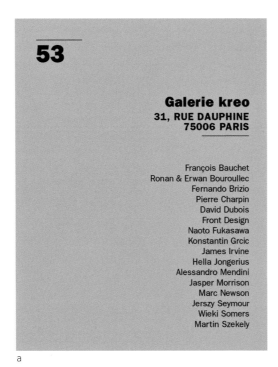

53

Galerie kreo
31, RUE DAUPHINE
75006 PARIS

François Bauchet
Ronan & Erwan Bouroullec
Fernando Brizio
Pierre Charpin
David Dubois
Front Design
Naoto Fukasawa
Konstantin Grcic
James Irvine
Hella Jongerius
Alessandro Mendini
Jasper Morrison
Marc Newson
Jerszy Seymour
Wieki Somers
Martin Szekely

a

Roxana Azimi: You're leaving the 13th *arrondissement* for the 6th. What are the benefits of the space and the new neighborhood?

Didier Krzentowski: I had this picture of the 6th as a district for antique dealers, but the fact that contemporary art galleries such as Fabienne and Kamel Mennour are here too suits me fine, because my activity is not unlike theirs. That there are dealers in Art Deco and the 1950s nearby will surely prove a plus, too. Customers may like to mix and match. Foreign visitors also come to the 6th more readily, either to walk around, or to stay. I couldn't have held my opening show in the 13th *arrondissement*. I'm unveiling sixteen new pieces by sixteen different designers, from Marc Newson to Hella Jongerius. There will be two designers who've just joined the gallery, Wieki Somers with a floor-lamp made of braided electric cable, and David Dubois, with a bench enclosing a fountain. Sitting down, you can hear the sound of the water.

"Le mot design ne veut plus rien dire," *Le Journal des Arts*, no. 286, September, 2008, p. 22

b

A ladder. What could be simpler?
A structure made from two sides and
eight bars in black carbon fiber
(mastering materials). A flight that
rises to 6 ½ ft. (2 m) and that weighs
less than 5 lb. (2.1 kg) (mastering
weights and measures). An airy
ensemble where every bar can take
up to 220 lb. (100 kg) (mastering
loads). A thin line that is 19 in.
(48 cm) at the foot and 15 in.
(38 cm) at the head (mastering
balance). A controlled, stated
mastery of all parameters.

A ladder. What could be simpler?
A simple ladder, simply a ladder,
then. But one that involves attributes
that are clearly and always affirmed,
singular, unique. A symphony of
moving shapes, an assembly of
unexpected and changing figures,
like an elusive wave. And always
this virtuosity of design, this feeling
of an ellipse and of movement that
incessantly brings us back to the
immensity of the ocean.
Gilles de Bure about Marc Newson

This is a shape that was sculpted in
our workshop using digital modeling
on the one hand, and trials in
cardboard and sponge on the other.
First of all we refined it, looking for
the outer lines. Then we sculpted the
thickness of the contour, slightly
broader on one end like a drop,
leaning toward the center. The part
of the contour that tends toward the
inside was harder to approach, it had
to be hollowed out to become a type
of receptacle that went to the center
of the piece, but it also had to
maintain a certain flatness for use.
Finally, it all ends with the light that
reveals a surface that the hand
would find hard to decode. It is a
solid wood table, carved in one piece,
but here the cutter is a digital chisel
we control with a computer.
Ronan & Erwan Bouroullec

I tried something insane: to hold the
moon over the couch.
Pierre Charpin

c Wieki Somers
Bellflower lamp, 2008
Carbon, fiberglass, epoxy,
LEDs, h. 6 ft. 1 in. × w. 4 ft.
5 in. × d. 19 ¾ in. (h. 185 ×
w. 135 × d. 50 cm)

d Jerszy Seymour
Metal Scum light, 2008
Galvanized metal, h. 3 ft.
10 ½ in. × diam. 15 ½ in.
(h. 118 × diam. 39.5 cm)

e Martin Szekely
Concrete console, 2008
Lafarge Ductal fiber
concrete, h. 33 ¾ in. × diam.
20 ½ in. (h. 86 × diam.
52 cm)

f Naoto Fukasawa
Hanger, 2008
Oak, aluminum, h. 3 ½ ×
w. 25 ¼ × d. 2 ¾ in. (h. 9 ×
w. 64 × d. 7 cm)

g Fernando Brizio
HB Drawing shelf, 2004
Lacquered wood, HB
pencils, h. 5 ¾ in. × w. 4 ft.
3 in. × d. 1 ft. 4 in. (h. 14.5 ×
w. 130 × d. 41 cm)

h Jasper Morrison
Object Frames, 2008
Oak
Model A: h. 1 ft. 1 in. ×
w. 3 ft. 7 ¼ in. × d. 9 ½ in.
(h. 33 × w. 110 × d. 24 cm);
model B: h. 1 ft. 5 ¾ in. ×
w. 2 ft. 7 ½ in. × d. 9 ½ in.
(h. 45 × w. 80 × d. 24 cm);
model C: h. 23 ½ ×
w. 23 ½× d. 9 ½ in. (h. 60 ×
w. 60 × d. 24 cm)

i Konstantin Grcic
Karbon lounge chair, 2008
Carbon fiber, h. 2 ft.
1 in. × w. 6 ft. 6 in. × d. 1 ft.
7 ½ in. (h. 63.5 × w. 180 ×
d. 50 cm)

c

Bellflower is the intriguing fusion of form, content, and high-tech means of production. The lamp is produced with the so-called "overbraider," a digital weaving machine for high-tech fabric in three dimensions. The shade, base, connecting arch, and the carbon fibers that work as the conductors of electricity are woven in one production line, which is a remarkable innovation in production. So far the technique of "overbraiding" was used only within aerospace engineering, but as this lamp design has proven, it might be employed for interior design as well. Technique plays a powerful role, not only in the production of the lamp and in the way it functions, but also on an aesthetic level. Apart from the visible high-tech appeal of the lamp, the shape and color have a crafted appeal. The shade refers both to a flower and a traditional lampshade. However, this lampshade creates a galaxy feeling when seated underneath it, due to the scattered LEDs in the shade.
Louise Schouwenberg about Studio Wieki Somers

d

His lamp looks heavy and difficult to move, but no. It is not feather-light but it can be moved at wish. It is made of polyurethane that was subsequently galvanized with platinum. This lamp is not a sculpture, insists Seymour, it evokes the notion of solidity in our real, fluctuating world.
Christian Simenc about Jerszy Seymour

e

Designed in the fibered concrete Ductal, which contains synthetic fibers inside the concrete—these fibers play a traditional reinforcing role, but make the material much more effective—the Concrete console is made up of two identical elements that can be put together or separated from one another or the walls. No ostentatious details—on the contrary. A simple, practically invisible joint, that merely tells of the object's construction principle.
Christian Simenc about Martin Szekely

f

Human beings have always had an instinct that enables us to pick up and transform values from the surrounding environments into our life, prior to the birth of the word "design" our history. Take nails on walls as an example: one of our collected values allows us to sense an ability to hang things on them, such as our coats. What really interests me is that, the more natural the behavior from which we try to pick up such values, the less we recognize them in ourselves. In another words, the more we spontaneously harmonize with our environment, the less we recognize our behaviors.

Naoto Fukasawa

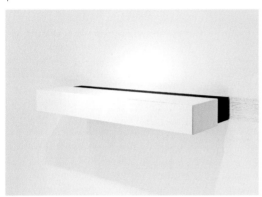

g

Show a gesture, materialize an action. That could be the starting premise for this piece by Fernando Brizio. A unique shelf with a multitude of pencils. What is its rightful place on the wall? Usual question. Uncertainty and hesitation. Show the movement of whoever hangs it, placing it in one place, and then changing the position. The lines will be straight or crooked, whatever. The pencils will sketch the doubt, inevitably.... This piece is part of a vaster project in which a collection of pieces of furniture with the same crayons draw the same parallel lines. The lines connect the pieces, or evoke possible links. This is a metaphor: write down in black and white how everyday objects mold our lives.

Christian Simencs about Fernando Brizio

h

Four planks, nothing more. Three possible dimensions, nothing more. An extremely sophisticated, practically invisible wall-hanging system, nothing less. Smooth oak. Neutral surface. Not easy to read. Emptiness, hollow so much more than full. Free to choose. Free to use. A misleading economy of means. A total absence of gesticulation, complication, simplism. On the contrary, restraint, complexity and simplicity reign. Nothing remarkable here. Everything is normal, "super-normal" even.... Do we need to convoke minimal art in order to evoke conceptual art? Of course not! Without hesitation, we prefer the words "idea" and "evidence" to the words "concept" and "minimalism": simpler, righter, rarer. It brings to mind what Matisse said: "It took me years of work so that people would say, 'that's all Matisse does.'"

Gilles de Bure about Jasper Morrison

i

The Karbon chaise longue is tempestuous, perhaps even offensive. Here, we will find no calming orthogonality, and the succession of straight lines is too curved to rest our eyes. The softness of the lines of the seat is endlessly troubling in its (supposed) submission to the laws of gravity. In its opposition to straight lines and to the deviant axis of the seat back, the chaise longue becomes an equivocal object. The rigidity that retains the memory of a certain suppleness expresses a strange strength, an authority: it presents a type of threat, straight and precise. The aggressiveness is latent, it comes from the material, from carbon fiber's long list of physical qualities.

Pierre Doze about Konstantin Grcic

j James Irvine
   Casino shelf, 2008
   Anodized aluminum,
   h. 5 ft. 3 ¾ in. × w. 2 ft.
   9 in. × d. 2 ft. 9 in.
   (h. 162 × w. 84 ×
   d. 84 cm)

k Front Design
   Levitating lamp, 2007
   Chromed brass, white
   fabric, h. 6 ft. 7 in.
   (h. 2 m)

l François Bauchet
   Claustra bookshelf,
   2008
   Oregon pine, h. 6 ft.
   3 in. × w. 4 ft. 7 in. ×
   d. 2 ft. 2 ¾ in. (h. 190 ×
   w. 140 × d. 68 cm)

m Hella Jongerius
   Swatch coffee table,
   2008
   Walnut, multicolored
   resin, matte and
   glossy finish, h. 13 ¾ ×
   w. 25 ¼ × d. 33 ½ in.
   (h. 35 × w. 162 ×
   d. 85 cm)

n David Dubois
   Water Bench, 2008
   Cedar, zinc
   compartments, water
   pumps, h. 1 ft. 8 ½ in. ×
   w. 6 ft. 7 in. × d. 1 ft.
   5 ¾ in. (h. 52 × w. 200 ×
   d. 45 cm)

o Alessandro Mendini
   Tavolino coffee table/
   bench, 2008
   Fiberglass, Bisazza
   mosaic, h. 1 ft. 1 ¾ in. ×
   w. 5 ft. 3 in. × d. 2 ft.
   9 in. (h. 40 × w. 160 ×
   d. 84 cm)

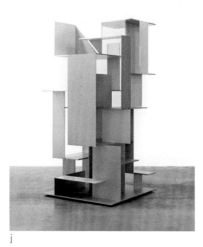

j

What is great about working with kreo is that you can really experiment. By this I mean create objects or furniture which would never be made by normal industry. Outside of normal logic. This does not mean that what one creates is not useful. On the contrary, the object can be "extra" useful because one can design out of the system and usually systems mean things have to be standardized. So the distance between shelves for books is a nice logical distance and more or less always the same. But our lives are full of many different objects with many different forms. Tall, wide, short, and fat. "Casino" means mess in Italian. So for our messy lives with messy things we need an object which in itself is rather disordered. Disorder to create order for disorder.

James Irvine

k

Our new collection is magical. We have created design with impossible characteristics that seem to defy the laws of nature. We collaborated with magicians and learned their secrets. In the collection you find design pieces that make other objects disappear, a chair that balances on one leg and a chest of drawers that separates and floats away and a lamp with an invisible light source and a levitating lampshade.

Front Design

l

Claustra is an adaptable bookshelf that can redefine space.

Constance Rubini about François Bauchet

m

n

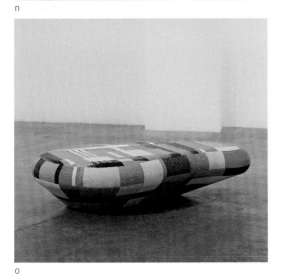

o

Hella Jongerius created a table in which the idea of having options is visualized on many levels. First of all, the tabletop consists of a field of many colors, not one. The same notion of many colors and not one is even included in each individual color. Not one of them is merely what it is. All colors contain a sense of deviation from a primary color and the awareness of the mutual existence of other colors. And last but not least, the reference to many more possibilities is visible in the outline of the tabletop; as all elements vary in shape, many different end results are imaginable. The tables have been handcrafted, using both old and new techniques, a theme that surfaces in many other works of Jongerius.

Louise Schouwenberg about Hella Jongerius

It is a long parallelepiped made of cedar, a strict box that appears to be closed. A flat surface outlines a seat and naturally invites one to sit down. So, it's a bench. But is that the noise of lapping water? A sonic hallucination? This bench is hiding something—it's a water bench. Inside the box runs a little invisible fountain, like a domestic water table. "I like to recover lost spaces, to federate and graft objects," he explains. The bench seems inert, even though the cedar is fragrant. However, it must be fed, it must be filled with water, otherwise it is cut off from its vital and mysterious source. The bench's discreet charm comes from this dissimulation, its basic requirement.

Anne-Marie Fèvre about David Dubois

An oblong, asymmetrical seat: Tavolino is a block with amiable angles that presents itself as a pebble in a harlequin's outfit. It gives off a sweet, immediate familiarity: an idea of a founding pebble, as the irregular layout of the geometrical and brightly colored motifs appeals to an elementary sensibility that we could be tempted into thinking is devoid of a trace of culture and calls for a naturally more instinctive reaction. It reveals a neo-plastic language, a primitive creative expression. The shape of the palm of the hand seems to be made to caress the curves, as the object itself seems to have been hand-crafted. The archaic nature of the mosaic also adds to this quick intimacy. Mosaic speaks of time and decor, convention and a palpable sliding movement. Framework or target, it is a précis of decomposition. The porous meets the vaporous, the watertight is happily evanescent. An exercise in dissipated design, a gaseous passion in a fossil state.

Pierre Doze about Alessandro Mendini

François Azambourg
Andrea Branzi
Pierre Charpin
Front Design
Olivier Gagnère
James Irvine
Hella Jongerius
Julia Lohmann
Alessandro Mendini
Marc Newson
Andrée Putman
Radi Designers
Adrien Rovero
Martin Szekely

a Invitation card

b Exhibition view:
Marc Newson
Super Guppy Lamp, 1987
Chromed aluminum, glass,
h. 6 ft. 9 in. × w. 2 ft 8 ½ in. ×
d. 2 ft. 5 ½ in. (h. 205 ×
w. 83 × d. 75 cm)

James Irvine
Four View mirror, 2003
Lacquered aluminum,
mirrored glass, panel
with four pivoting mirrors,
h. 11 ¾ in. × w. 3 ft. 6 ½ in. ×
d. 2 ½ in. (h. 30 × w. 108 ×
d. 6.5 cm)

Radi Designers
Whippet Bench, 2000
Lacquered resin,
h. 1 ft. 11 in. × w. 4 ft. 11 in. ×
d. 2 ft. 5 in. (h. 58.5 ×
w. 150 × d. 74 cm)

c Exhibition view:
François Azambourg
Outline mirrors, 2003
Pine frame and polyester
Small model: h. 13 × w. 7 ½ ×
d. ¾ in. (h. 33 × w. 19 ×
d. 1.8 cm); large model:
h. 28 ¾ × w. 19 ¾ × d. ¾ in.
(h. 73 × w. 50 × d. 2.2 cm)

Hella Jongerius
Backpack Sofa, 2007
Wood, wool, cotton, linen.
Bench: h. 3 ft. 9 in. ×
w. 6 ft. 5 in. × d. 3 ft.
3 ½ in. (h. 115 × w. 195 ×
d. 100 cm); stool: h. 28 ¼ ×
w. 17 ¾ × d. 10 ½ in. (h. 72 ×
w. 45 × d. 27 cm)

54

a

b

c

The Backpack Sofa refers to the
demands of backpack travelers, who
need options and flexibility while
traveling. The representation of having
options is an important theme that
surfaces in many of my works.

Hella Jongerius, 2007

a Invitation card:
Monolith, 2008

b Exhibition view:

Cargo coffee table, 2008
Matte varnished aluminum,
h. 1 ft. × w. 6 ft. 3 in. × d. 2 ft.
3 ½ in. (h. 30 × w. 190 ×
d. 70 cm)

Monolith, 2008
Polished black resin,
h. 5 ft. 10 in. × diam. 4 ½ in.
(h. 178 × diam. 11 cm)

Séquence bookshelf, 2008
Metallic varnished
aluminum, h. 3 ft. × w. 7 ft.
2 in. × d. 3 ft. 8 ½ in.
(h. 93 × w. 219 × d. 113 cm)

Wave bookshelf, 2008
Metallic varnished
aluminum, h. 5 ft.
7 ½ in. × w. 2 ft. 3 ½ in. ×
d. 2 ft. (h. 172 × w. 70 ×
d. 60.2 cm)

Parabola floor light, 2008
Metallic tube, resin,
h. 6 ft. × w. 1 ft. 10 in. ×
d. 2 ft. 1 in. (h. 185 ×
w. 55,5 × d. 63 cm);
lampshade: diam. 4 ft.
3 in. × d. 1 ft. 3 in. (diam.
130 × d. 37.8 cm)

c Faro storage, 2008
Varnished aluminum box,
painted steel base, h. 6 ft.
3 ½ in. × w. 2 ft. 7 ½ in. ×
d. 1 ft. 8 in. (h. 192.4 ×
w. 80 × d. 50 cm)

d UFO pendant, 2008
Brilliant white resin,
metallic string, h. 17 ½ ×
diam. 15 in. (h. 45 × diam.
38 cm)

e Eclipse floor lamp, 2008
Glossy lacquered resin,
metal, h. 7 ft. 4 in. × diam.
15 ¾ in. (h. 224 × diam.
40 cm)

55

a

While it is true that I often like to work in series, I also take care to avoid being trapped in a system, a formula, becoming repetitive—doubtless to stave off boredom for my own sake and spare those who follow the progress of my work from boredom also. So for this new exhibition, I have deliberately aimed for a collection of eight pieces that are all different from one another. In fact, I have the impression that I have designed a collection of things rather than a collection of objects.

I am not necessarily trying to outline the distinction between what defines an object and what defines a thing, but I tend to think that objects fulfill functions, while things propose uses; that functions are to be used but uses can be imagined; that objects have a precise definition, while the definition of things remains more or less vague, out of focus, and always depends on the appreciation of the person involved.

We could consider the things I have designed for this exhibition to be the materialization of thoughts, objects for meditation, like suggestions, objects open to interpretation. We could consider these things as literal objects, concise expressions of three-dimensional shapes, like presences that are austere and sensual, intense and stimulating.

Or we could take these things to be beautiful objects, objects of a glittering, transcending beauty.

It is the extremely shiny surface and the luster of the material of one thing that absorbs our attention, stimulates our perception, and encourages us to touch it. The repetition of the material, lacquered plaques of aluminum, creates the kinetic vibration that attracts us to another. The emptiness created by the design of the base of another, the empty space for no particular purpose, enables the compact, colorful volume to levitate. The way a wall-mounted satellite dish ("*parabole*" in French) is dimensioned creates a contour, a shape, a shadow and gives the light depth in another. With another, we are intrigued by the shape of the suspension in terms of its stability, materiality, and use. Another gives the impression of being perhaps unfinished, through the visible assembly instructions, the soldering lines that enable the volume to be built, the memory of an action past. Another, through the action of an articulated and off-kilter arm creates a play on light and shade with a gesture of extreme simplicity, without the use of abstract or sophisticated technology.

More than ever, I feel I am taken up in a movement that is to be found and proven in moving forward, a movement where the design of a thing is dependent on the design of the following thing, where it is more and more difficult for me to express why, only how, where it is more and more difficult to understand how these things can happen, find their place in the complexity and panorama of our contemporary landscape.

Pierre Charpin, November 2008

b

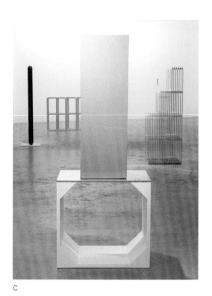

c

d

e

HELLA JONGERIUS,
NATURA DESIGN MAGISTRA

a Invitation card:
   Frog Table, 2009

b Artificial Vases series,
   2009
   Colored and frosted glass
   flowers, leather, paper,
   wood and/or ceramic (all
   handmade), in ceramic
   vases, various dimensions

c Exhibition view:

   Turtle Coffee Table, 2009
   Resins of different colors,
   wood, h. 2 ft. ¾ in. × w. 3 ft.
   9 in. × d. 3 ft. (h. 63 ×
   w. 115 × d. 93 cm)

   Frog Table, 2009
   French walnut, lacquer,
   transparent resin, h. 4 ft. ×
   7 ft. × 3 ft. 6 in. (h. 120 ×
   w. 215 × d. 107 cm)

d Sketch for the Frog Table,
   2009

e Model for the Snail Coffee
   Table, Hella Jongerius
   studio, Rotterdam, 2009

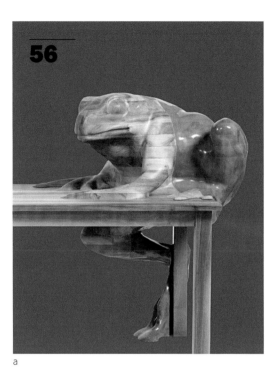

56

a

Now internationally recognized, Hella Jongerius
made her name with a singular body of work that
tirelessly explores the limits as well as the
possibilities of craftwork and industrial techniques.
In many of her pieces she manages to ensure
uniqueness in mass-production processes by
exploiting to the utmost happenstance and even
error. In addition to a fascination with the technical
aspect, the storytelling quality of her productions
has always played an important role. Her manner
of reinterpreting the history of decorative motifs,
combined with an imaginative use of floral and
animal imagery, gives the impression that, hidden
behind her works, scarcely emerging at the
surface, lie stories. Exploring the narrative and
technical potential of design, Hella Jongerius
never transgresses the "natural" boundaries of
her chosen field of action. In understated,
structural links, the object alludes to material
traces of craftsmanship—and this is how a flower
morphs into design, a table into a frog.

Louise Schouwenberg, 2008

b

c

"We live with a magical frog prince. He is often the fourth at lunch, overhearing conversations with colleagues, artists, writers, and fellow dealers. Before sitting, we stroke him. Trevor is smooth to the touch. He brings us luck."

Jeanne Greenberg Rohatyn, collector and Salon 94 gallery founder, New York, 2019

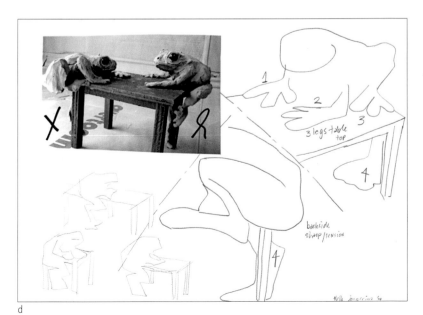

d

e

François Bauchet
BIG-GAME
Ronan & Erwan Bouroullec
Andrea Branzi
Fernando Brizio
Pierre Charpin
Demakersvan
Hella Jongerius
Michele de Lucchi
Ingo Maurer
Alessandro Mendini
Jasper Morrison
Radi Designers
Adrien Rovero
Gino Sarfatti
Jerszy Seymour
Ettore Sottsass
Martin Szekely

a Invitation card

a

Each group exhibition is the chance to create connections between the pieces by the gallery's designers, to combine materials, surfaces, forms, and approaches, thereby enriching our understanding of the approach of each designer.

Clémence Krzentowski, 2019

François Bauchet
Andrea Branzi
Ronan & Erwan Bouroullec
Pierre Charpin
Fernando and Humberto Campana
David Dubois
Front Design
Naoto Fukasawa
Konstantin Grcic
James Irvine
Hella Jongerius
Bertrand Lavier
Julia Lohmann
Alessandro Mendini
Jasper Morrison
Marc Newson
Radi Designers
Adrien Rovero
Jerszy Seymour
Wieki Somers
Martin Szekely
Maarten Van Severen

---

a Invitation card:
  Naoto Fukasawa
  Drilling Table, 2009

b Naoto Fukasawa
  Drilling Table, 2009
  Concrete legs (drilled into
  the floor of the Galerie
  kreo), wood tabletop, h. 2 ft.
  4 in. × w 7 ft. 10 in. × d. 3 ft.
  3 in. (h. 72 × w. 240 ×
  d. 100 cm)

a

b

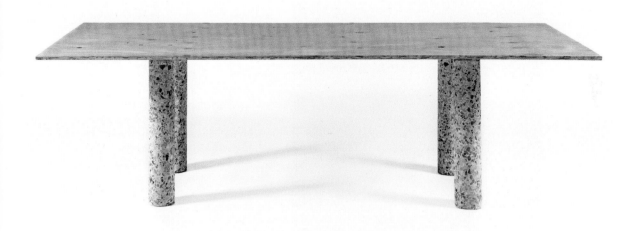

b

Ten years already. Ten years of exhibitions (nearly sixty), ten years of research and experimentation (nearly five hundred models produced). Is it a gallery? Certainly! But even more it's a kind of laboratory dedicated to research work by designers, with a strong commitment to production and to bringing out new pieces. And always with the best these designers and creatives can offer in their research, the best that is by those whose style exalts autonomy, identity, difference, those whose practice rejects the facile and all compromise. In short, those who have a taste for risk, innovation, exclusivity. So, at this precise moment, on the tenth anniversary, how can we look back from 2009 to 1999, year on year, take stock and point out what left its mark on the era, what was a milestone? By presenting the best of the best! Some already produced and exhibited by kreo, others with whom a new adventure is beginning. Interlinked, cross-fading from one into another, next to Naoto Fukasawa's Drilling Table, which plays with memory and foresight, with rootedness and surging, with the recent past and the near future, in a piece whose legs are in fact a core of stone blocks, some from the gallery floor.

Gilles de Bure, press release, September 2009

November 7–December 19–31, rue Dauphine, Paris

MARTIN SZEKELY, *HEROIC SHELVES & SIMPLE BOXES*

a Invitation card:
   Cork 3 storage, 2009
   Natural waxed cork, Corian,
   h. 4 ft. × w. 3 ft. 3 in. × d. 1 ft.
   7 ¼ in. (h. 120.5 × w. 99.5 ×
   d. 49 cm)

b Exhibition view:

   Cork box, 2009
   Natural waxed cork, Corian,
   h. 26 ¼ × w. 21 ½ × d. 26 in.
   (h. 66.8 × w. 54 × d. 66 cm)

   Cork desk, 2009
   Natural waxed cork, legs
   in metal copper finish,
   h. 2 ft. 5 ½ in. × w. 7 ft.
   4 in. × d. 2 ft 5 ½ in. (h. 75 ×
   w. 225 × d. 75 cm)

   Cork coffee table, 2009
   Natural waxed cork, h. 1 ft.
   4 ½ in. × w. 4 ft. 4 in. ×
   d. 1 ft. 3 in. (h. 42 × w. 132 ×
   d. 39 cm)

c 365 shelf, Heroic Shelves
   series, 2009
   Panels in honeycomb
   aluminum and anodized
   aluminum, h. 7 ft. 7 in. ×
   w. 2 ft 8 ½ in. × d. 1 ft. 2 in.
   (h. 232.6 × w. 83.6 ×
   d. 36.5 cm)

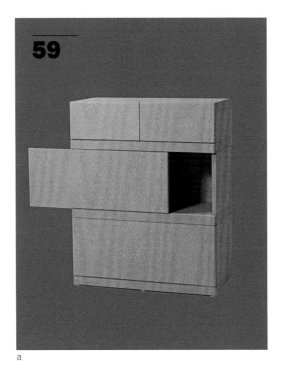

a

Simple Boxes reminds us once again that all furniture is, to some extent, made up of boxes. For example, a table or a stool are boxes that have had parts replaced, a wardrobe is a perfect box, and so on. Simple Boxes are made up of calibrated waxed cork panels made of compressed cork particles. The project was built around these panels: two cupboards with sliding doors and drawers, a chest of drawers, a coffee table, and a table-top on metal legs. Each panel is in the right place and the thickness is determined according to its function and structural limitations. The visible indentations on the surfaces correspond to the dimensional edges of each panel. Cork absorbs physical shocks and sound. It is an insulating material. It is light, soft to the touch, and waterproof. The cork provides a protective covering for the boxes: it protects the contents from the elements. Portuguese fishermen used to make little pieces of furniture and objects from cork to take on their boats as they were safe from falls and water. Simple boxes of an economic nature.

Martin Szekely, November 2009

b

Heroic Shelves follows on from the *Des étagères* show in Galerie kreo in 2005. The structure of the *Des étagères* was built to avoid catching the eye. Once filled, the shelves disappeared in favor of the content, books or other objects. The Heroic Shelves use even fewer elements. The gap between the horizontal tables that was essential to the structure of the *des étagères* no longer exists. What remains is a structure made of flat surfaces that cross at 90-degree angles. The horizontal *Des étagères* and the vertical sides are made from aluminum honeycomb four millimeters thick and of two layers of anodized aluminum "skin" one millimeter thick, which makes a composite material in sandwich form that totals six millimeters. The horizontal and vertical elements are held together with a cross-shaped aluminum profile that is industrially extruded and anodized. Once assembled and glued at each intersection, this cross-shaped profile maintains the Heroic Shelves straight and strong. The triangular profile and uneven shelving gave a charming, attractive image to the earlier *Des étagères*, almost a musicality. That has all disappeared with the Heroic Shelves. Vertical lines cross over horizontal lines. The design is radical but it is also the realization of a builder's dream.

Martin Szekely, November 2009

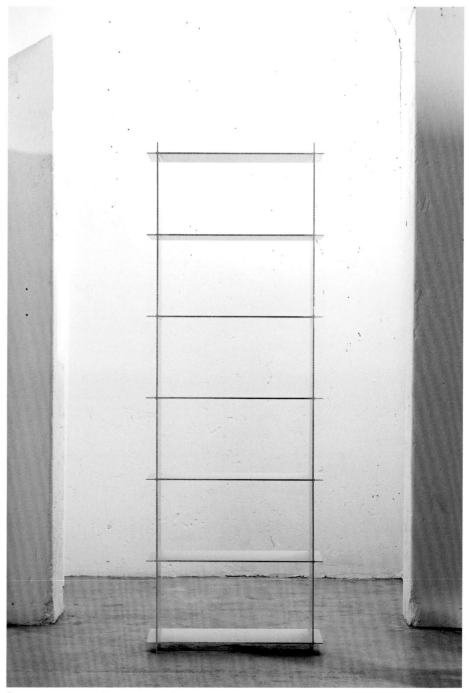

c

2010

STUDIO WIEKI SOMERS, *FROZEN IN TIME*

Studio Wieki Somers
was founded in 2003
by Wieki Somers and
Dylan van den Berg.

_____

a Invitation card

b Image from *IJzekboek*
(Uitgeverij Profiel, 1997)

c Frozen Spring Lamp, 2010
Resin, silk flowers, UV
topcoat, h. 16 × w. 12 ¼ ×
d. 3 ¼ in. (h. 41 × w. 31 ×
d. 8 cm)

d Frozen Leaf Vase, 2010
Silk flowers, UV topcoat,
h. 15 ¾ × w. 8 × d. 5 in.
(h. 40 × w. 20 × d. 13 cm)

e Frozen Carafe, 2010
Resin, silk flowers, UV
topcoat, h. 10 ¼ × w. 7 ¾ ×
d. 4 in. (h. 26 × w. 20 ×
d. 10 cm)

f Frozen Hogweed Vase,
2010
Silk flowers, UV top coat,
h. 21 ¾ × w. 7 ¾ × d. 5 in.
(h. 55 × w. 20 × d. 13 cm)

g Frozen Lantern, 2010
Fabric net, resin, metal,
fishing-rod wood, UV
topcoat, h. 5 ft. 8 ¾ in. ×
diam. 2 ft. 4 ¾ in. (h. 175 ×
diam. 73 cm)

a

b

"In her pale eyes, as Wieki Somers spoke
of that day when the landscape had frozen
in a single night, I saw sparks, and all the
poetry of the Frozen Cabinet unfolded like
a perfect line of verse, a seer's illumination.
Before the two doors, the magic of the dream
turned the objects within into magnificent,
imaginary forms. It is then possible to create
a useful form and that is also a poetic dream.
How extraordinary life is!"
Jacques Seguin, amateur, Paris, 2019

Flowering springs seem to merge with a lamp, the
construction of stools hides within a transparent
skin and branches bow under the weight of icy
layers, seemingly for a few moments only.
The objects look like frozen moments in time....

The inspiration for the project was taken
from the photographs of a natural phenomenon
that struck the northeast of the Netherlands
on March 2, 1987, when several inches of icy
rain poured down from the sky. The glazed frost
brought public life to a complete standstill and
produced a layer of ice on everything it landed
on: branches of trees, lampposts, clothes lines
from which drops of ice were drooping. The half-
transparent ice connected things in a matter-of-
fact and extremely poetic way. For one day the
sidewalk, bicycles, and trees merged into one,
while cars seemed to stick to the streets for ever.
Only one day. When the ice started to melt, trees
could continue to grow their blossoms and cars
could pursue their tours. What struck Studio Wieki
Somers at first was the formal, visual beauty. Well-
known forms, hiding beneath a transparent skin,
had gained a melancholy glow. But there was more.
On a deeper level the items seemed to have turned
into tales from another, yet still familiar world.
Through the metamorphosis, caused by nature, the
strangely familiar items seemed to communicate
something which had always been there and was
only waiting to be unveiled. Paradoxically the cover
of ice caused a dis-covering.
Press release, January 2010

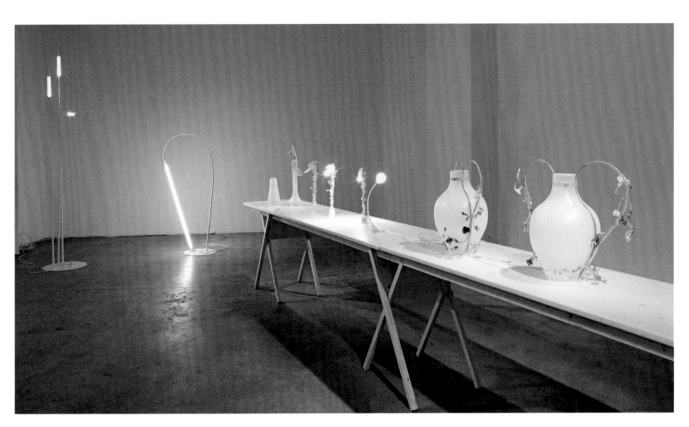

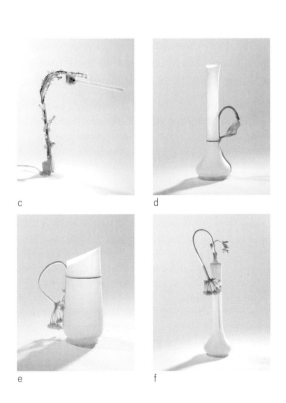

c

d

e

f

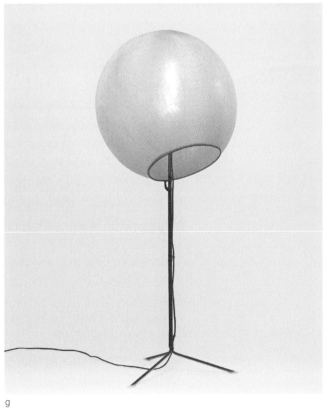

g

a Invitation card:
   Roches 5, 2010
   Lacquered fiberglass,
   various dimensions

b Conque 5 wall light, 2010
   Glossy lacquered
   fiberglass. Each: h. 13 ¾ ×
   w. 6 ¾ × d. 6 in. (h. 35 ×
   w. 17.5 × d. 15.5 cm)

c Liane 15+ ceiling lights,
   2010
   Resin and leather, various
   dimensions

a

Our interest in industrial design is linked to the unlimited reproduction of objects. Nevertheless, for the past ten years we have been producing work in the unique framework provided by the Galerie kreo. This helps us to breathe in between other projects. This unique context has often led us to compare our work for the gallery to the use of a sketch pad, a more instinctive form of research free from the constraints imposed by industry, the norms, weight, size, or other issues more or less justified by mass production. Here, we give ourselves the time to explore different media and extraordinary techniques that are rejected by industry, to approach unique skills. Our work for the Galerie kreo has always produced exceptional events. Our research here is about magic as much as use. This new exhibition has a certain delicacy: we use leather to cover electric wires, we cover a set of shelves with a strangely matte mineral-looking paint, and we make mirrored conch lamps. In search of mystery.

Ronan & Erwan Bouroullec, April 2010

"Delphine and I have admired and collected the work of Ronan & Erwan Bouroullec for many years. We feel so fortunate to be able to live with the beauty that they have created. It's difficult to choose a favorite piece, but the vast, sinuous, and illuminated Liane that hangs in our New York City library is particularly special because it occupies a space we use every day."
Delphine and Reed Krakoff, collectors, New York, 2019

b

c

2010

SIMON LEE À PARIS & LA GALERIE KREO À LONDRES

Simon Lee Gallery artists
exhibited in Paris:
John M Armleder
Angela Bulloch
Larry Clark
George Condo
Matias Faldbakken
Hans-Peter Feldmann
Bernard Frize
Donald Judd
Sherrie Levine
Claudio Parmiggiani
Michelangelo Pistoletto
Jim Shaw
Christopher Wool
Toby Ziegler
Heimo Zobernig

Galerie kreo designers
exhibited in London:
Ronan & Erwan Bouroullec
Pierre Charpin
Konstantin Grcic
James Irvine
Hella Jongerius
Alessandro Mendini
Jasper Morrison
Marc Newson
Andrée Putman
Studio Wieki Somers
Martin Szekely

a Invitation card

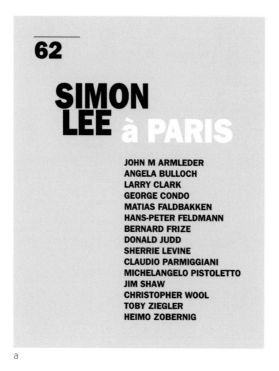

a

Simon and Carine, and Clémence and I have all
been great friends for more than fifteen years,
and we have always bought work from one another.
We knew Simon before he had the gallery.
To organize this swap seemed to work because we
are both working with collectors on either side of
the Channel and we wanted to do something to be
close to them. And some of our designers are
English, too, which is another nice touch.
Didier Krzentowski in Nancy Alsop, "Galerie kreo and Simon
Lee Gallery swap spaces," *Wallpaper* (September 20, 2010)

Pierre Charpin
Naoto Fukasawa
Ettore Sottsass
Martin Szekely
Maarten Van Severen

a Invitation card:
  Martin Szekely
  Heroic Carbon desk, 2010
  Detail

b Ettore Sottsass
  Foresta desk, 2002, for
  Clio Calvi Rudy Volpi
  Mirror, wood, metal, h. 5 ft.
  5 ¾ in. × w. 6 ft. 5 in. ×
  d. 3 ft. 9 in. (h. 167 ×
  w. 196 × d. 115 cm)

63

a

A selection of pieces 29 ½ inches (75 centimeters) high, the standard height for desks and tables.

b

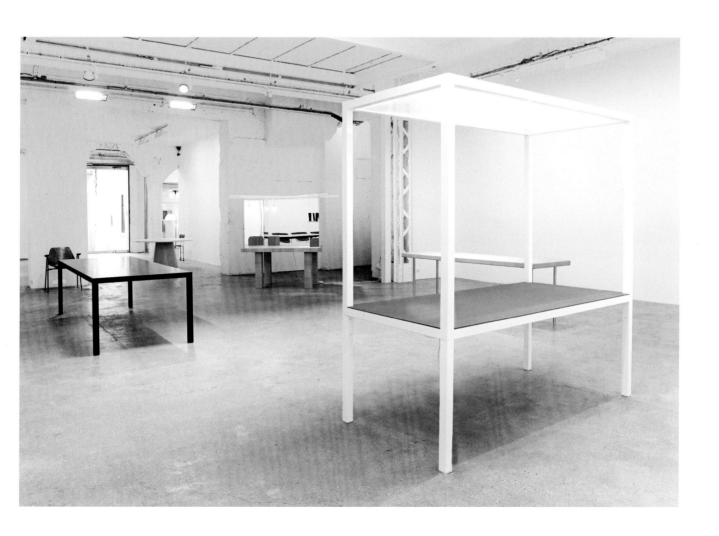

Before leaving us in 2007, Ettore Sottsass
was producing with the same energy as in 1947,
the year he opened his workshop in Milan.
The Foresta desk is a testimony to this. It raises
the issue of confinement linked to the intensive
use of computers and the Internet. The solitude
imposed by these new technologies is subverted
by a fiction-producing apparatus. The desk-box is
lined with mirrors that reflect the image of the user
or others, random suspension lamps are set in
motion due to the movement of life. Ettore
Sottsass thus recreates a domestic landscape,
a box in a box, a place for life and amazement.
Centre d'innovation et de design du Grand-Hornu website,
2019

2011

A NEW GENERATION OF LIGHTS—L'ECAL À PARIS

BIG-GAME
Camille Blin
Fabien Cappello
Michel Charlot
Béatrice Durandard
Delphine Frey
Alexis Georgacopoulos
Tomas Kral
Nicolas Le Moigne
Florian Pittet
Julien Renault
Adrien Rovero
Guillaume Schweizer

a Invitation card:
   Delphine Frey
   Slim & Strong desk light,
   2008

b Camille Blin
   Marble Light, 2010
   Marble and electronic
   components: h. 11 ¾ ×
   w. 19 ¾ × d. 3 in. (h. 30 ×
   w. 50 × d. 8 cm); light: h. 7 ×
   w. 6. ¾ × d. 2 ¼ in. (h. 18 ×
   w. 17 × d. 6.5 cm)

c Delphine Frey
   Slim & Strong desk light,
   2008
   Carbon, copper cable,
   LEDs, h. 11 × w. 36 ½ ×
   d. 4 ¾ in. (h. 28 × w. 93 ×
   d. 12 cm)

64

In 2011, Galerie kreo is hosting *A New Generation of Lights*: an exhibition of lighting designed by students and staff from the industrial design department of the ECAL over the past five years. These young, offbeat, innovative designers, who already enjoy an international career, have mastered Swiss knowhow and the constraints of both classic production and new technologies.

Press release, January 2011

a

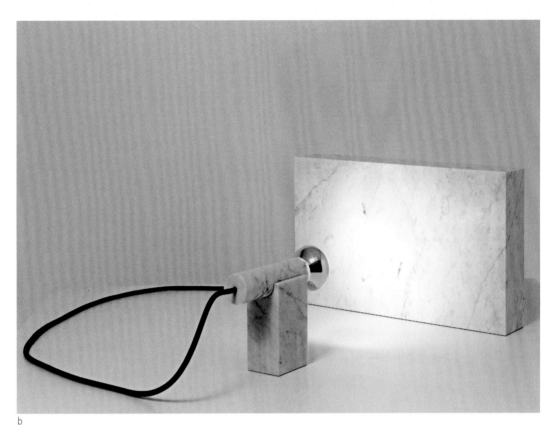

b

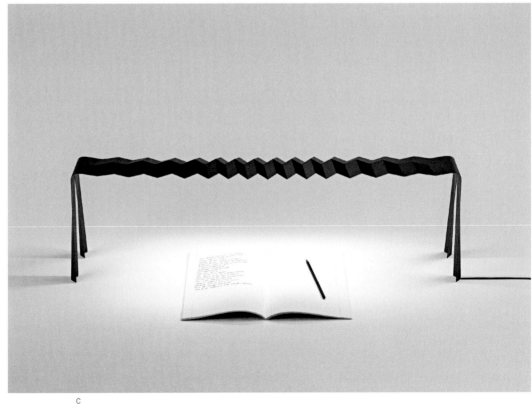

c

171

February 10–May 15, 2011–31, rue Dauphine, Paris

MATIÈRES À RÉFLEXION

Ronan & Erwan Bouroullec
Fernando and Humberto Campana
Pierre Charpin
Front Design
Olivier Gagnère
Konstantin Grcic
Hella Jongerius
Marc Newson
Studio Wieki Somers
Martin Szekely
Maarten Van Severen

---

a Invitation card:
Hella Jongerius
Snail Coffee Table, Natura Design Magistra collection, 2010
Bleached, brushed oak, enameled and unglazed porcelain realized by Manufacture Bernardaud, h. 3 ft. 1 ½ in. × w. 4 ft. 9 ½ in. × d. 3 ft. 5 in. (h. 95 × w. 146 × d. 105 cm)

b Floor plan of the exhibition, January 2011

From May 20 to July 23, 2011, Galerie kreo also put on the exhibition *Sgrafo vs. Fat Lava*, organized by Nicolas Trembley and devoted to his collection of ceramic vases produced in postwar Germany

65

a

Matières à réflexion is an exhibition which gathers together the very latest pieces by Fernando and Humberto Campana, Pierre Charpin, Olivier Gagnère, Hella Jongerius, and Martin Szekely at the Galerie kreo. These new pieces are all "off-the-tracks": they have been produced outside of any collection or exhibition, in unusual materials such as carbon fiber, porcelain, feathers, lacquer, etc.

Press release, February 2011

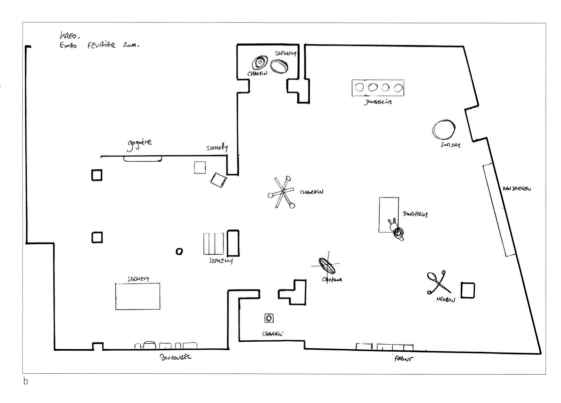

b

173

2011

KONSTANTIN GRCIC, *CHAMPIONS*

Born in 1966, Konstantin Grcic lives in Munich.

a Invitation card:
APACHE table, 2011
Lacquered aluminum, glass, h. 2 ft. 5 ½ in. × w. 8 ft. 10 in. × d. 3 ft. 3 in. (h. 75 × w. 270 × d. 100 cm)

b Exhibition view:

JAXONE table, 2011
Lacquered aluminum, glass, h. 2 ft. 5 ½ in. × d. 4 ft. 3 in. (h. 75 × d. 130 cm)

BANZAI table, 2011
Lacquered aluminum, glass, h. 2 ft. 5 ½ in. × w. 8 ft. 10 in. × d. 3 ft. 3 in. (h. 75 × w. 270 × d. 100 cm)

JETDOG table, 2011
Lacquered aluminum, glass, h. 2 ft. 5 ½ in. × w. 8 ft. 10 in. × d. 3 ft. 3 in. (h. 75 × w. 270 × d. 100 cm)

PODIFY table, 2011
Lacquered aluminum, glass, h. 2 ft. 5 ½ in. × w. 8 ft. 10 in. × d. 3 ft. 3 in. (h. 75 × w. 270 × d. 100 cm)

NADA table, 2011
Lacquered aluminum, glass, h. 2 ft. 5 ½ in. × diam. 4 ft. 3 in. (h. 75 × diam. 130 cm)

66

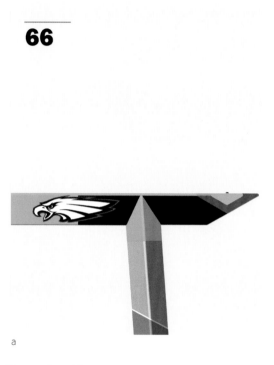

a

"I want the tables to appear like they are Formula 1 cars lined up on the starting grid of a racetrack," Konstantin Grcic says, standing in his studio space in Munich on a spring morning in 2011. We are flicking through a thick dossier of print-outs of computer renderings of the new table bases: aluminum trestle-like constructions with either circular or rectangular glass surfaces. The dossier details the various stages of the rigorous research and design process: the structural designs, the graphic logos, the colors, and the numerous fonts that have all been tried out. As we continue our conversation, Grcic's eyes move to a sleek black ski pole propped up against a bookshelf; he reaches out for it. Lettering runs up and down the stick: the larger lettering reads "Salomon," while the smaller insists this is "High Performance" equipment. "After all, it's not such a leap between these two things. What I particularly like is how the graphics on sports equipment refers to performance. They create the illusion that the object with them is faster or more powerful than the one without. The graphics on the six tables are fake—totally made up." . . .

Grcic's designs for the new tables are loosely derived from the juxtaposition of these two

disparate sources: the world of Formula 1 racing cars and sports equipment on the one side and that of Prouvé on the other. By staging the disjunction that exists between the anonymous designs of the sports world and a signature design by Prouvé, Grcic reshuffles the otherwise static relationship between the high and low in the product design world.

One of the early problems encountered during the research and design process for the new tables was how to ensure the graphics didn't feel extraneous to their design—i.e., to ensure that the three-dimensional and the two-dimensional vocabularies productively interrelated. This objective was achieved by rejecting the transfer foils that are routinely used in sports equipment and instead opting to collaborate with the highly revered lacquerer, Walter Maurer, who worked directly with Andy Warhol and Frank Stella in Germany on their art cars for BMW in the mid-1970s. The way Maurer painstakingly builds up a graphic language by using many layers of paint is crucial. The graphic vocabulary seems as if it's embedded into the aluminum tables, like a series of inlays.

Received wisdom has it that Grcic inherits the legacy of the product designers Marcel Breuer and Dieter Rams from the pre- and postwar periods respectively. But this smooth lineage is too simplistic to really hold since it fails to take into account Grcic's flexible way of responding to even the tightest briefs within the context of industrial product design. In fact, with these new tables, it's as if Grcic sets out to deliberately refute the lineage pinned on him, introducing a playful graphic vocabulary thoroughly alien to the functionalist designs of Breuer and Rams. By transferring the precision that derives from the research and design process from his industrial product designs to these new gallery-bound tables, Grcic has been able to question these two genealogies central to the history of product design: of Prouvé, Breuer, and Rams with their strict principles and geometries on the one hand, and Studio Alchimia and Memphis, with their panoply of ersatz decorative signs and playfully Pop shapes on the other. Instead of just being a tautological game, this is nothing less than a speculative design process aimed at generating a vocabulary of product design for the future.

Alex Coles, press release, June 2011

b

The CHAMPIONS tables are such clearly constructed and very legible pieces. In terms of reading, you may think and feel many different things at the same time: it is solid and liquid; it is chronos and Kairos; it is about mobility and immobility, about racing and yet having to make a pit stop; it is a mask and a totemic or ceremonial table. I could even imagine a potlatch or the Eucharist, and yet it could also be an homage to another great inventor of "good" tables, like the late Flemish designer Maarten van Severen.

Chris Dercon, 2011

a Invitation card:
Ignotus Nomen box, 2011
White Krion, satiny black
resin, h. 5 ft. 2 in. × w. 3 ft.
3 in. × d. 1 ft. 6 in. (h. 158 ×
w. 100 × d. 46 cm)

b General view of the Ignotus
Nomen collection, 2011

c Exhibition view:

Ignotus Nomen desk, 2011
White Krion, satiny black
resin, h. 4 ft. 2 in. × w. 6 ft.
10 in. × d. 2 ft. 7 ½ in.
(h. 127 × w. 210 × d. 80 cm)

Ignotus Nomen shelf, 2011
Oak, glossy white resin,
h. 7 ft. 1 in. × w. 5 ft. 5 in. ×
d. 1 ft. 4 ½ in. (h. 216.5 ×
w. 161 × d. 42 cm)

d Exhibition view:

Ignotus Nomen lamp, 2011
Frosted glass, satiny black
resin, h. 16 ½ × diam. 12 in.
(h. 42 × diam. 30 cm)

Ignotus Nomen coffee table,
2011
White Krion, glossy white
resin, h. 2 ft. 2 ¾ in. × w. 3 ft.
9 in.× d. 3 ft. 9 in. (h. 68 ×
w. 115 × d. 115 cm)

Ignotus Nomen vase, 2011
Frosted glass, glossy white
resin, h. 27 ½ × d. 7 in.
(h. 70 × d. 18 cm)

d Exhibition view:

Ignotus Nomen shelf, 2011

Ignotus Nomen bench,
2011
White Krion, satiny black
resin, h. 6 ft. 7 in. × w. 7 ft. ×
d. 1 ft. 6 in. (h. 120 ×
w. 213 × d. 48 cm)

67

a

When I think about the meaning and the reasons that drove me to draw this new collection, I have the feeling that each trial to define them brings me more toward closure than openness. It is as if the large possibilities which resonate in these pieces prevented me from fixing their representation.

Table, shelf, box, console, lamp, vase: each of these objects is inhabited by a presence. Enigmatic, these forms—black or white—are at the same time rigid and sensual, and show off their uselessness quietly. Whether they are lying down or standing straight, they exist in front of us without revealing any information about their origins or provenance. They seem to be washed up like objects on the shore due to the never-ending flux of the sea. Smooth and polished, we can't see exactly what they are made of. They are pure forms, pure colors, before being materials. These forms attract our attention, prod our imagination. They put in perspective our relationship with objects, offering a more poetic and spiritual answer. These forms, presences, diffuse their strength to the objects, turning them into a presence of their own. This presence can be the only thing that is above signification, and at least above all justification.

The series of objects distinguishes itself from the rest also by their rigorous design. More than ever, to simplify, for me, is to propose an exemption of meaning. It is to propose forms which are not quite full, but full of meaning. It is to propose objects as receptors and not signifiers. When it comes to the title *Ignotus Nomen*, it indicates in an explicit way that this series has a name, but this name is unknown to us, or that it hasn't revealed itself to us just yet.

Pierre Charpin, August 2011

b

c

d

e

a Invitation card

b Unit Tower 5-6, 2011
Plaster, h. 5 ft. 6 in. × diam.
1 ft. 10 ½ in. (h. 163 × diam.
57 cm)

c Unit Shelf 10, 2011
Plaster, transparent or
black opaque doors. Each
module: h. 1 ft. 5 ½ in. ×
w. 5 ft. 7 in. × d. 1 ft. 3 ¼ in.
(h. 44.4 × w. 166.8 ×
d. 39 cm); shown here
11 modules: h. 7 ft. 3 in ×
w. 27 ft. 4 in. × d. 1 ft.
3 ¼ in. (h. 222 × w. 834 ×
d. 39 cm)

68

a

The Unit Shelves can be accumulated and stacked at will—without dimensional limits: from 5 ½ ft. (160 cm) to infinity. This typical unit form allows a great deal of flexibility: a well-ordered construction or an irregular composition as well as a multiplicity of forms. Its scale can be related to both furniture and architecture. Each module is the result of a cast of liquid plaster in its mold. The matte white plaster used is highly technical and of incomparable density. The weight of each module has been precisely calculated to ensure the stability of the stacked units, without having to use a mechanical process. Transparent and opaque doors can be added to slide between the modules. Unit Towers are round towers of drawers, which allow a 360° use.

Martin Szekely, August 2011

b

c

My intention is to consider only the nature of the object: its use. Without necessarily exposing a signature, craftsmanship, the beauty of a material or a pattern. The object appears in its strict form. By stretching to the limit materials and their application, the act of drawing self-destructs. The result is an aesthetic dimension that exists outside of intention.

Martin Szekely, 2011

2012

TANDEM

François Bauchet
Ronan & Erwan Bouroullec
Pierre Charpin
Front Design
Konstantin Grcic
Hella Jongerius
Naoto Fukasawa
Julia Lohmann
Radi Designers
Studio Wieki Somers
Ettore Sottsass
Martin Szekely
Maarten Van Severen

a Invitation card:

Maarten Van Severen
Wall-mounted bookshelf,
2001
Sanded and lacquered
aluminum, h. 1 ft. 2 in. ×
w. 12 ft. 5 in. × d. 1 ft. 3 ¾ in.
(h. 37 × w. 358 × d. 40 cm)

Martin Szekely
Low Cork bench, Cork
collection, 2009
Natural waxed cork, h. 1 ft.
4 ½ in. × w. 4 ft. 4 in. ×
d. 1 ft. 3 ¼ in. (h. 42 ×
w. 132 × d. 39 cm)

a

A free association of furniture and objects. This is not a rhetorical demonstration, but a play of association, pairs: either literal, conceptual or empirical, which shines a new light on existing works. Nine couples or "tandems" formed by affinity, analogy, or chosen for their apparent contradiction—all sharing a radical approach to design. For instance: the T2 shelf by Martin Szekely and the PC2 carpet by Pierre Charpin, where verticality and horizontality conflict; one being the shadow of the other. A bookshelf in 4G aluminum, known to be used in aeronautical engineering, with an extremely thin structure (¼ in./5 mm). A carpet, from which colors unfold, as though stretched to their limits. Or else the Wall-mounted bookshelf by Maarten Van Severen and the Low Cork bench by Martin Szekely. A formal complicity. Two parallelepipeds open and close, both support and contain: bookshelf/console and bench/storage. But the two pieces are produced in contradicting materials: one in aluminum, an industrial composite, and the other in cork of natural essence.

Press release, January 2012

2012

March 8–May 2, 2012—31, rue Dauphine, Paris

CHRIS KABEL, *WOOD RING*

Born in 1975, Chris Kabel lives in Rotterdam.

a Invitation card: Wood Ring, 2010

b Wood Ring, 2010
FSC-certified wood (here: mahogany), metal belt, h. 1 ft. 4 ½ in. × diam. 9 ft. 10 in. (h. 42 × diam. 300 cm)

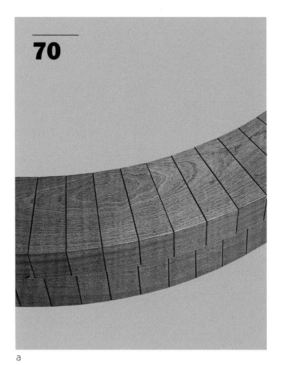

70

a

Wood Ring, a circular wooden bench of around 9 ft. (3 m) diameter, is composed of wooden elements carved in a trapeze shape from a single tree trunk which can reach over 30 ft. (10 m) tall. Placing the different elements side by side Kabel reproduces exactly the wood grain, which strengthens the majesty and the organic quality of the work. No glues are added to hold the pieces together, but a large metallic ring clinches them in a circular form. This spectacular piece raises the issue of space and, more specifically, how we share this space. The round-shaped bench represents an environment which is both public and intimate, inviting users to share their space, meet and bond, cut off from the world like a cocoon. Or they may decide to isolate themselves, by facing outwards.

Press release, March 2012

b

b

It's a bit like sharing a bath in the sauna but without the nakedness and the wetness.

Chris Kabel, March 2012

2012

May 23–July 28, 2012—31, rue Dauphine, Paris

TECHNIQUES MIXTES
ET DIMENSIONS VARIABLES

Ronan & Erwan Bouroullec
Pierre Charpin
Hella Jongerius
Alessandro Mendini
Adrien Rovero
Studio Wieki Somers
Ettore Sottsass
Martin Szekely

---

a Invitation card:
Hella Jongerius
Mini Swatch coffee table,
2009
American walnut,
multicolored resin blocks
with matte and glossy
finishes, h. 15 ¾ × w. 23 ½ ×
d. 18 ½ in. (h. 40 × w. 60 ×
d. 47 cm)

71

a

Through the pieces
of the exhibition,
the confrontation
between materials,
dimensions, and
techniques encourages
a new perspective.

Press release, May 2012

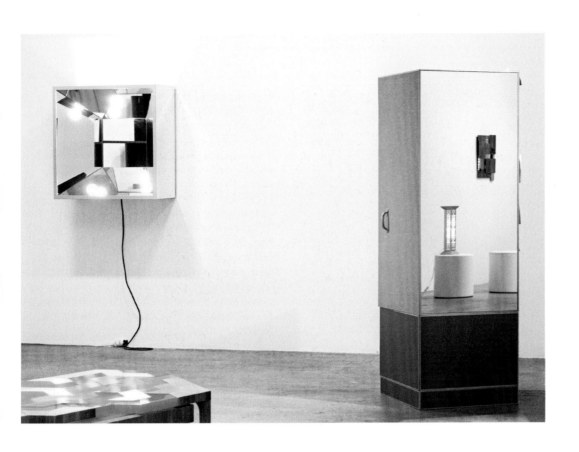

2012

October 12–November 24, 2012—31, rue Dauphine, Paris

ENSEMBLE

Exhibition conceptualized
with Marcel Brient, with
Antonin Artaud
Miquel Barceló
Ronan & Erwan Bouroullec
Andrea Branzi
Maurizio Cattelan
Pierre Charpin
Wim Delvoye
Urs Fischer
Fischli/Weiss
Alberto Giacometti
Konstantin Grcic
Hans Haacke
Carsten Höller
Hella Jongerius
Sherrie Levine
Nate Lowman
Michel Majerus
Alessandro Mendini
Jasper Morrison
Bruce Nauman
Marc Newson
Cady Noland
Ed Paschke
Paul Rebeyrolle
Arthur Rimbaud
Adrien Rovero
Gino Sarfatti
Studio Wieki Somers
Martin Szekely
Paul Verlaine

a Invitation card:

Michel Majerus
Burned Out, 2000
Acrylic on canvas, h. 8 ft.
2 ½ in. × w. 14 ft. 9 in.
(h. 2.50 × w. 4.50 m)

Konstantin Grcic
PODIFY table, 2011
Lacquered aluminum, glass,
h. 2 ft 5 ½ in. × w. 8 ft. 10 in. ×
d. 3 ft. 3 in. (h. 75 × w. 270 ×
d. 100 cm)

b Exhibition view:

Gino Sarfatti
3026/S ceiling light, 1954
Lacquered metal, neon tubes,
h. 8 in. × w. 5 ft. 10 in. × d. 8 in.
(h. 20 × w. 178 × d. 20 cm)

Bruce Nauman
*Hanging Heads #1 (Blue
Andrew Mouth Open/Red
Julie With Cap)*, 1989
Wax, wire, variable dimensions

72

Il n'y a pas de
vents favorables
pour ceux qui
ne savent pas
où aller·

a

Prior to being a simple display of works, the
exhibition *Ensemble* was a meeting point. An
encounter between contemporary art and design,
where poetry was a guest of honor. An encounter
between a collector and a gallery sharing mutual
admiration. An encounter centered on aesthetic,
and friendship cemented by the taste of the
collector and his vivid curiosity. An encounter with
the public to which Marcel Brient revealed a
chosen selection of his collection. Comprising
thirteen "mood rooms"—a reference to "period
rooms" in decorative arts museums—this
exhibition brought together and confronted, among
others, the lithe design of the PODIFY table by
Konstantin Grcic with the graphic power of *Burned
Out* by Michel Majerus, or the geometric and
surrealist forms by Sherrie Levine and Pierre
Charpin. But these associations, whether formal,
historical, conceptual, physical, or simply
unexpected, were not entirely due to coincidences;
they derived from the many years of collecting by
Marcel Brient, a cutting-edge art and design lover,
the same kind the Galerie kreo stands for—he was
one of the first visitors when the gallery opened its
doors in 1999, leading to a camaraderie and
uninterrupted dialogue materialized by this

exhibition. Already in 2008 for the exhibition *16
New Pieces* Marcel Brient wrote, "A marriage is,
for example, putting a Naoto Fukasawa coat-
hanger with my portrait by Felix Gonzalez-Torres,
in other words, 90 kilos of sweets. This proximity
will change the meaning and destination of the
works. The coat-hanger loses its function." At
home Marcel Brient lives with a Sam Francis print
and binders of photographs of his entire collection:
"it is all here, in my head," he says. At their home
Clémence and Didier Krzentowski live with their
collection of contemporary art, design, lights, and
memories from former collections. It is also the
encounter of the ascetic and the prolific, reunited
by one state of mind: to attach more importance to
the next piece of the puzzle rather than the one
recently acquired.

At the Galerie kreo, works of art, design, and
poetry were shown in unison. This was the
singularity of the proposition. It was not only
about seeing but also reading and telling, to fill the
exhibition space following a poetic route. And the
poets assembled were the ones that generations
of amateurs and lovers are eternally devoted
to: Arthur Rimbaud with his *Lettre du Voyant*,
Paul Verlaine with his *Sagesse*, Antonin Artaud
with his *Cahiers d'Ivry*. From the first day of his
meeting with Louis Clayeux, Marcel Brient has
shared his passion for original autographs. For
Louis, past and contemporary poetry; for Marcel,
autographs and portraits of writers. And one writer
in particular, Susan Sontag in *The Volcano Lover*
(1992) writes with accuracy about collecting:
"Collections unite. Collections isolate. They unite
those who love the same thing. (But no one loves
the same as I do; enough.) They isolate from
those who don't share the passion. (Alas, almost
everyone.) Then I'll try not to talk about what
interests me most. I'll talk about what interests
you. But this will remind me, often, of what I can't
share with you. Oh, listen. Don't you see. Don't you
see how beautiful it is." There is no doubt we will
all see how beautiful it is.

Clément Dirié, press release, September 2012

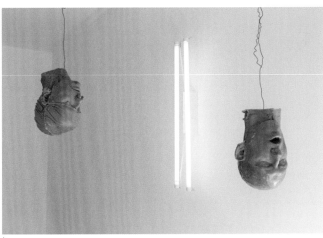

On first impression, certain character traits separate me from Marcel Brient. He finds the future captivating, and this gives him this vitality, this youthfulness, and this talent to bring together both art and design in his prodigious collection. I, on the other hand, am more inclined to let myself be carried by the current that continuously throws us back to the past. And yet I only need to be in the presence of this collector to feel that we are on a level. He leaves you, after a first encounter, with an impression of truthfulness and complete freedom. His voice is shot through with a certain Parisian banter, reminding you that he is not a snob. He has remained the young man who arrived in Paris from Brittany, "his only wealth being the tranquility of his own eyes," (as Paul Verlaine wrote), attending evening classes before he met the person who would change his life, Louis Clayeux, the director of the Galerie Maeght and friend of Giacometti.

Patrick Modiano, November 2012

b

a Invitation card:
   Lee Ufan
   Frémissement, 2012

b Exhibition view (left and
   right sides):

   Mike Kelley
   Memory Ware Flat #5,
   2001
   Papier-mâché, acrylic,
   buttons, jewels, wood panel,
   h. 5 ft. 11 in. × w. 3 ft. 9 ¾ in.
   (h. 180 × w. 116 cm)

   Azzedine Alaïa
   Concert dress for Tina
   Turner, 1989, for her
   1990 European tour
   Loan from the Fondation
   Azzedine Alaïa

c François Bauchet
   Tarquinia, 2012
   18-carat yellow gold, diam.
   16 ½ in. (diam. 42 cm)

d Constance Guisset
   Swing, 2012
   18-carat yellow gold,
   precious or semi-precious
   stones (onyx, blue
   chalcedony), chains:
   l. 13 ¾ in. and 17 ¾ in.
   (l. 35.3 and 45.3 cm)

e Martin Szekely
   Untouched Diamond, 2012
   Uncut diamonds, glass,
   18-carat yellow, rose, or
   white gold, diam. 16 ½ in.
   (diam. 42 cm)

f Dominique Modiano
   Cou de Foudre, 2012
   18-carat yellow gold, diam.
   16 ½ in. (diam. 42 cm)

g Élisabeth Garouste
   Mina, 2012
   Brass, 18-carat yellow gold,
   black netting, l. 10 × w. 8 ×
   d. 21 ½ in. (l. 25 × w. 20 ×
   d. 55 cm)

h Jaime Hayon
   Muñeco, 2012
   18-carat yellow gold
   Necklace: l. 27 in.
   (l. 69 cm); pendant:
   h. 2 ½ in. × w. 1 ½ × d. ³⁄₃₂ in.
   (h. 6.5 × l. 3 × d. 0.3 cm);
   chain: l. 2 ¼ in. (6.1 cm)

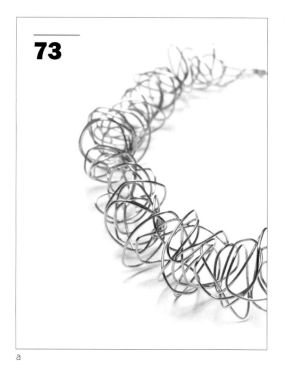

73

a

The neck sets off the face and separates it symbolically from the body. Designers, artists, and friends of the Galerie kreo were confronted by this challenging theme, resulting in unique objects. Each gave us their vision of the necklace with various materials: gold, onyx, marble, coral, hemp, wood, pearls, and rough diamonds. A few subjects are explored: flexibility, movement versus rigidity, original composition (threads, articulation), proportion and features of the jewel, as well as the symbolic usage of the necklace itself.

Press release, November 2012

The work had to be concentrated on one part of the body, so the proposals had to focus on that. We decided on the neck, which means the piece can be worn to be fully or partially seen, or not seen at all. The neck has a strong erotic power and the piece will underline this essential part of the body. Without a neck, there is no head—an elementary physiological point, because the neck is not one of the body's extremities, except in exceptional circumstances, but can be one of its most beautiful endings. The neck brings together different parts of the body in a symbolic and paradoxical manner— by multiplying them (the eye sweeping from top to bottom), or by unifying them (an examination from bottom to tip, inverting the hierarchy of importance).

The idea is strategic: to reach a sublime frontier with this piece. That of the object itself, in its equivocal and indomitable values. To also reach the frontier in an ideal sense, leaving the possibility for a return by concentrating on the neck. The piece, with its lightness and mobility, adds to the value of a freely consensual frontier, all the more desirable as it is uncertain. The neck cuts off the face from the rest of the body: the face is the human body's most fertile aspect in the way it makes

complex information accessible to the outside. The piece will frame the face and underline the emotions it inspires. It confirms or contradicts them, it broadens them. The ambiguity of the object/jewelry unfolds in this confrontation with the face. It rests on the neck, but evokes another place: around the neck the necklace is above all a detour. These pieces are so many translations. Neck detours.

Pierre Doze, December 2012

b

i   David Dubois
    Geometric, 2012
    Walnut, diam. 31 ½ in.
    (diam. 80 cm)

j   Ronan & Erwan Bouroullec
    Perles de jaspe, 2012
    Red jasper, diam. 17 ¾ in.
    (diam. 45 cm)

k   Fabrice Hyber
    Flèche-Flesh, 2012
    18-carat yellow gold, diam.
    16 ½ in. (diam. 42 cm)

l   Andrea Branzi
    La Vita, 2012
    18-carat yellow, sapphire,
    ruby, diam. 16 ½ in. (diam.
    42 cm); pendant: h. 3 ⅛ ×
    w. 2 ⅜ × d. ³⁄₃₂ in. (h. 8 ×
    w. 6 × d. 0.3 cm)

m   Lee Ufan
    Frémissement, 2012
    18-carat yellow gold
    threads, diam. 17 in.
    (diam. 43 cm)

n   Naoto Fukasawa
    Chaos, 2012
    Polished black onyx, diam.
    16 ½ in. (diam. 42 cm)

o   Dominique Perrault and
    Gaëlle Lauriot-Prévost
    Brisé, fer à béton, 2012
    Solid silver, diam. 16 ½ in.
    (diam. 42 cm)

p   Annette Messager
    Mon kreanet, 2012
    Agate, 18-carat yellow
    gold, diam. 22 ½ in. (diam.
    57 cm); pendant: h. 1 ¾ in. ×
    w. 1 ¾ × d. ⅝ in. (h. 4.5 ×
    w. 4.5 × d. 1.5 cm)

q   Hella Jongerius
    Knotted Pearls, 2012
    Solid silver pearls,
    18-carat yellow gold, silk
    threads, diam. 17 ¾ in.
    (diam. 45 cm)

r   Tatiana Trouvé
    Panta Rhei, 2012
    18-carat rose gold
    Chain: diam. 21 ½ in. (diam.
    55 cm); pendant: l. 2 ½ in.
    (l. 6.3 cm)

s   Fernando and Humberto
    Campana
    La Corde au cou, 2012
    Yellow gold and linen rope,
    two 18-carat yellow gold
    rings, l. 3 ft. 1 in. × d. ⅝ in.
    (l. 94 × d. 1.5 cm)

c

Tarquinia, or the recall of two wonderful memories: the magnificent Etruscan remains of the Italian city, but also the holidays in Marguerite Duras's famous novel *Les Petits Chevaux de Tarquinia*.

d

Swing is a necklace that brushes against the neck without resting on it. Carefully attached to the ears, it hangs and swings in rhythm with the movements of the body. Falling delicately, it brings out the oval shape of the face. C.G.

e

A caressing object in the palm of the hand, a pendulum level with the heart. And deep within, a few precious stones, unique and virgin, for the girlfriend, for love, the other, and myself. M.S.

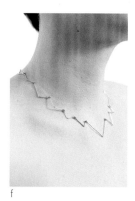

f

I called my necklace Cou de Foudre because to me it looks like an electric current bursting across the lines before solidifying to adorn the neck of the woman wearing it or to pierce the heart of the one who gives it to her. D.M.

g

My necklace is called Mina. That's the pet name of my granddaughter. In Bram Stoker's story, Mina is seduced by Dracula who casts a spell over her. I thought if Mina had worn that necklace she would have been protected from her predator. E.G.

h

Inspiration for this piece came from traditional pull-string toys, which I have always found magical because of their simplicity and liveliness. I love the simple engineering and the playfulness of the system of the piece. Wouldn´t it be lovely to wear jewelry that can bring a smile? J.H.

i

Adaptable in form, the construction principle behind this necklace encourages constant manipulation. With its imperfect outline, the asymmetry of this "generous" shape when placed around the neck interacts with the lines of the body. D.D.

j

Beads occupy a perfectly logical place in our work: they are a simple module that can be repeated. And together they bring about a new situation. There is also our penchant for stone, linked to a fascination with certain primitive jewels, that is, something direct that nonetheless strives for great delicacy in how things fall and relate to the body. E. & R.B.

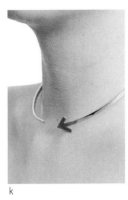

k

A simple golden arrow wraps itself around the neck. As close as possible to the skin: *flèche-flesh*. A.M.

l

Accompanying the joy of living with the caress of death and the joy of death with the caress of life. A.B.

m

Three golden threads as if entangled by a breath of wind. A quivering of gold around the neck.

n

Do we find beauty in an "orderly" world? Or do we find it by being immersed in a random world? "Orderly" is a human desire and "chaos" is reality. N.F.

o

The alchemy of rust to silver, shifting perceptions, rebar, construction materials thoughtlessly left outside, coated in rust, poorly finished and coarse transcended into unalterable jewelry, soft to the skin and fitted to the shape of the neck. Harshness transforms into sensuality. D.P.

p

I wanted to nest an embryo within the cleavage. It's a warm, welcoming, protective, and very sexy zone for me.

q

Golden beads that expose a silver interior. The irregular-shaped beads are pierced and crisscrossed by hand-knotted threads, a feat of skill typical of Hella Jongerius's work.

r

This piece of jewelry takes up the famous saying of Heraclitus and endows it with form. "Everything flows": starting with the bronze from which the form is cast. From the flow whence emerges this female bust that could hardly be guessed at. From this bust of a woman in the making to the bust of the woman who will wear it. T.T.

s

The Campana brothers slip a rope around our necks. Literally, with a rope braided from gold and hemp worn across the body.

a Invitation card:
  Cellae desk, 2013

b Cellae H3-3, 2013
  Technical felt, fiberglass,
  epoxy resin, h. 3 ft. 7 in. ×
  w. 6 ft. × d. 1 ft. 3 in.
  (h. 109 × w. 184 × d. 39 cm)

c Exhibition view:

  Cellae H6-1, 2013
  Technical felt, fiberglass,
  epoxy resin, h. 7 ft. 1 ½ in. ×
  w. 2 ft 2 ¼ in. × d. 1 ft.
  3 ¾ in. (h. 217.2 × w. 67 ×
  d. 40 cm)

  Cellae desk, 2013
  Technical felt, fiberglass,
  epoxy resin
  Large model: h. 2 ft. 5 in. ×
  w. 7 ft. 10 ½ in. × d. 2 ft.
  7 in. (h. 74.5 × w. 241 ×
  d. 79.5 cm); small model:
  h. 2 ft. 5 in. × w. 5 ft. 10 in. ×
  d. 2 ft. 7 in. (h. 74.5 ×
  w. 177 × d. 79.5 cm)

  Cellae coffee table, 2013
  Technical felt, fiberglass,
  epoxy resin
  Large model: h. 1 ft.
  4 ½ in. × w. 5 ft. 9 in. ×
  d. 2 ft. 9 ½ in. (h. 42 ×
  w. 175 × d. 85.5 cm); small
  model: h. 1 ft. 4 ½ in. ×
  w. 3 ft. 7 ½ in. × d. 2 ft.
  9 ½ in. (h. 42 × w. 110.5 ×
  d. 85.5 cm)

  Cellae H2-2 and Cellae
  H2-6, 2013
  Technical felt, fiberglass,
  epoxy resin
  Four modules: h. 2 ft. 5 in. ×
  w. 4 ft. 1 ¼ in. × d. 1 ft.
  3 ¾ in. (h. 73 × w. 125.5 ×
  d. 40 cm); twelve modules:
  h. 2 ft. 5 in. × w. 11 ft.
  10 in. × d. 1 ft. 3 ¾ in.
  (h. 73 × w. 360 × d. 40 cm)

  For all pieces in this series,
  dimensions are flexible and
  adjustable.

74

a

François Bauchet is showing nine pieces. The series is called Cellae, it is a composition of storage units, tables of different heights, and shelves. A clear-colored felt regularly punctured and soaked in a polymer-tinted resin constitutes the unique material of this collection. The unity of the material echoes the unity of the design and its rhythm. The formal vocabulary repeats itself in an identical manner, following a single modular logic. Only dimensions change, in response to the scale of each piece, while remaining attentive to its function. Cellae is a line anchored with repetition and marked by its fracture. A pace and discontinuity governed by variations: the clear concentration of vocabulary reinforces its strength, while provoking an emotional response. It is within these self-inflicted constraints—material, drawing, number, functions—that the force of this collection persists.

The characteristics of tension and release (possibly the most fascinating side of what design and architecture have developed) guide its lines. These characteristics drive the dynamic rigor of each piece. With a complex technical display, the work maintains a feeling of ease, lightness, simplistic elegance, and strength.... For Bauchet, the first steps of the creative process can be compared to monoliths—working from the mass of the material to the refinement of the piece, a process of subtracting not adding. This coherence is played out in the wonderful mass of the pieces, where austerity is just another challenge.

Throughout the collection Bauchet uses a modern approach, playing with angles and positioning the partitions of the modules in a slightly slanted manner. It's a refusal to comply with the general and physical order of orthogonality. Unbalance ensues. Cellae is like a shadow cut with a sharp blade. A rhythm can be found in each of the nine pieces. This rhythm is brought forward by a rupture in the dynamic of each piece's thematic variations. Cut and sever: the truth of the series lies in its steep slices, in which can be found violence and therefore movement. A peculiar energy comes from the collection, edging us closer to the void, inspired by multiple perspectives.

Pierre Doze, press release, January 2013

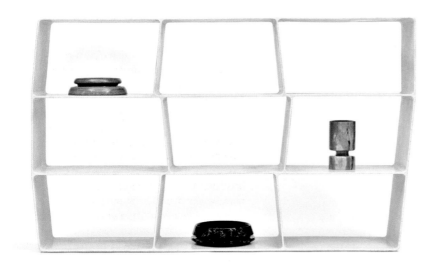

b

c

François Azambourg
François Bauchet
Ronan & Erwan Bouroullec
Pierre Charpin
David Dubois
Jean-Baptiste Fastrez
Hella Jongerius
Brynjar Sigurðarson
Studio Wieki Somers
Michael Young

a Invitation card:
   Jean-Baptiste Fastrez
   Totem console, 2013

b Exhibition view:

   Michael Young
   Money Clock, 2013
   Paper, aluminum
   Large model,
   4480 banknotes: diam. 3 ft.
   3 in. × d. 4 in. (diam. 100 ×
   d. 10.3 cm); small model,
   1440 banknotes: diam.
   21 ½ × d. 3 ¾ in. (diam. 55 ×
   d. 9.5 cm)

   François Azambourg
   Goat tables, 2013
   Wood, goatskin
   Large model: h. 12 ½ ×
   w. 31 × d. 23 in. (h. 31.5 ×
   w. 78.6 × d. 58.6 cm);
   medium model: h. 15 ¾ ×
   w. 24 ¾ × d. 18 ½ in.
   (h. 40 × w. 63 × d. 47 cm);
   small model: h. 10 × w. 20 ×
   d. 14 ¾ in. (h. 25 × w. 50.5 ×
   d. 37.6 cm)

c Exhibition view:

   Jean-Baptiste Fastrez
   Totem console, 2013
   Acetate, Hi-Macs, h. 2 ft.
   9 ½ in. × w. 4 ft. 11 in. ×
   d. 1 ft. 3 ¾ in. (h. 85 ×
   w. 150.3 × d. 40 cm)

   Dogon mirror, 2012
   Acetate, mirror, h. 31 ×
   w. 20 ¾ × d. 3 ⅛ in. (h. 79 ×
   w. 52.3 × d. 8.1 cm)

   Stromboli coffee table,
   2013
   Heat-tempered glass,
   anodized aluminum rings,
   acetate, h. 1 ft. 1 ¾ in. ×
   diam. 3 ft. 11 ½ in. (h. 35 ×
   diam. 120 cm)

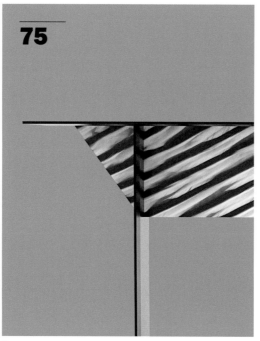

a

The title of the show *O.K.* stands for "Oll Korrect" according to the Bostonian interpretation of the famous nineteenth-century abbreviation. This exhibition presents completely new pieces conceived outside the ideas of thematic and monographic exhibitions. The pieces are important and meaningful, consecrated in the line of work of each of the designers. Each piece has never been seen before, is out of the ordinary, and created from materials as diverse as leather, mosaic, wood, and acetate.

François Azambourg redesigns the idea of "nesting tables" with his trio of Goat tables. The goat's skin is stretched to its limit, enveloping the birch structure of the coffee table. This unveils the table's "skeletal" interior and reveals its almost animal-like form. A literal demonstration of the proverb "Time is Money," Michael Young's Money Clock is composed of one dollar bills which are folded using traditional origami techniques. The clock is formed from 1.440 bills, which correspond to the 1.440 minutes in a day.

Press release, March 2013

b

The Totem console and the Stromboli coffee table are created mostly from acetate and follow after Fastrez's Masks mirror collection. Acetate, often used in the making of artisanal eyewear, is usually resized into many small pieces. Here, the acetate plates are used directly as constructive elements of the furniture pieces, which emphasizes their synthetic and organic aspects. This use of acetate evokes a stepping point between what is natural and what is artificial, what is chosen and what is by chance. The warmly graphic acetate contrasts with the cool monochromatic materials it's associated with: the resin of the console or the glass and anodized aluminum of the coffee table.

Press release, March 2013

c

a Invitation card: CHUUGI (Devotion), 2013, detail

b Drawings for the *Mitate* exhibition, 2019

c MEIYO (Honor), 2013 Shade in copper-plated oxidized stainless steel, cord binding, anodized aluminum, LEDs; pole in copper-coated aluminum, cord binding, h. 7 ft. 2 in. × w. 1 ft. 10 ¼ in. × d. 3 ft. 3 in. (h. 220 × w. 143.5 × d. 99 cm)

d MAKOTO (Truth), 2013 Shade in anodized aluminum with printed reflection foil, LEDs; pole in brass, cord binding, h. 6 ft. 9 ½ in. × w. 3 ft. 7 ½ in. × d. 1 ft. 7 ½ in. (h. 207 × w. 110 × d. 49.5 cm)

e REI (La Bonne action), 2013 Shade in Kozo paper with white gold leaf, waxed cord, coated aluminum, LEDs; pole in anodized aluminum, cord binding, h. 8 ft. 6 in. × w. 4 ft. 10 in. × d. 1 ft. 6 ½ in. (h. 261 × w. 148 × d. 77 cm)

f JIN (Compassion), 2013 Shade in Nuno fabric, fiberglass, carbon steel, aluminum, feathers, LEDs; pole in anodized aluminum, cord binding, h. 6 ft. 9 ½ in. × w. 3 ft. 7 in. × d. 1 ft. 7 ½ in. (h. 207 × w. 110 × d. 49.5 cm)

g Exhibition view (foreground): GI (Right Decision), 2013 Shade in Perspex, cord fringe, stainless steel, LEDs; pole in anodized aluminum, cord binding, h. 5 ft. 11 in. × w. 2 ft. 7 ½ in. × d. 12 in. (h. 242.5 × w. 80 × d. 30 cm)

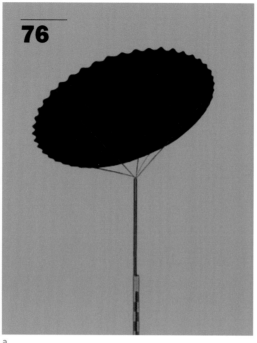

76

a

The new lighting collection of Studio Wieki Somers (Rotterdam) brings the pleasure of its evidence and oddity. As we move closer to the collection, the glowing figures become familiar—a familiarity in which we recognize the other. This sensation is not conjured by our everyday lives or background, but by our imagination and fascination for the otherness of a foreign culture, which seduces us as well as subdues our judgment. It is not the easiest form of seduction. Larger than us, the seven floor lamps united under the name "Mitate" fill and protect the gallery space, acting as flamboyant samurais. In Japanese, "mitate" refers to the perception of an object in a non-habitual way, to contemplate an object as if it were something else in order to renew its meaning and experience. An essential part of Japanese culture, the "mitate" principle is a cornerstone of ikebana art.

Since 2003, Studio Wieki Somers has personalized this philosophy in order to invent a breathtaking design practice, reworking the concept of "magic realism." Often inspired by ancient or mundane customs, its creativity imbues fantasy into the most common objects, promoting an enchanted perception of our everyday life.

With the Mitate collection, a game is played between the simplicity of the lamps and the sophistication of their Japanese forms, inspired by several trips to Japan in 2011 and 2012. From this travel and through research of local craft knowledge, Studio Wieki Somers collected sensations, materials, and images, such as the enigmatic sixteenth-century samurai flags, whose designs identified clans and demonstrated their unique powers, the production and use of which was a highly ritualized affair (*jin*). Wieki Somers writes, "We wanted to create a contemporary equivalent of sixteenth-century samurai flags translated into 'light poles'—a family of lamps." Other inspirations for the Mitate collection include the fabric used by geishas to protect their skin from the the sun (*chuugi*); the stone gardens re-enacting for the pleasure of the eyes the intensity of the world (*gi*); or the traditional doll who seems to be juggling with her hats (*rei*). Shown together and reflecting off one another, each of these lamps possesses its own identity, displaying its specific surface, shape, and chromatic colors while proposing a unique combination of technology and artisanal craft. What's more, each of these light totems illustrates one of the seven principles of the samurai bushido code of honor, from which they are named. The materials of each lamp are chosen with care. Whether reflective or mirroring, absorbing or translucent, each material creates a distinct lighting style. The lamps are created from two different kinds of bases. The first is a wooden base resembling a traditional *tokonoma* altar, creating space for the organization of different objects; the second is made from polyester concrete with its edges carefully sliced, revealing the texture of the stone.

Clément Dirié, press release, June 2013

b

c

d

e

f

"I was immediately and profoundly touched by the poetic sensitivity and narrative impact of Wieki Somers's pieces. *Chuugi*: a black sunshade with perfect pleats. A delicate evocation of a Japanese woman visiting a Niwaki garden. This *chuugi* (black hole) is definitely not gloomy! *Gi*: the 'correct decision' is this monstrance. This 'very beautiful stone' supporting the banner of a white sun."

Bruno E. Borie, collector, Château Ducru Beaucaillou, Bordeaux, 2019

g

Exhibition conceptualized
with Marcel Brient

Étienne Carjat
Alberto Giacometti
Félix González-Torres
Mike Kelley
Ross Laycock
Arthur Rimbaud
Ed Ruscha
Paul Verlaine

a Invitation card

b Display case dedicated
to Paul Verlaine; above:
photograph after Henri
Fantin-Latour, *Un coin
de table*, 1872

c Exhibition view: in the center:
Laurel et Hardy, gift from
Félix González-Torres to
Marcel Brient, c. 1992; Félix
González-Torres, *Untitled
(Portrait of Marcel Brient)*,
1992, candies, weight: 200 lb.
(90 kg), variable dimensions

d Display case dedicated to
Félix González-Torres and
Ross Laycock, 1990s

77

« ce passant considérable »

a

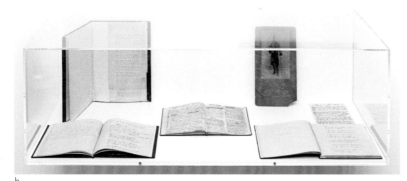

b

Suggestions abound as to who is worthy of being glorified at the National Pantheon, of exemplifying the values of the French nation and living up to the motto: "To these great men, the grateful homeland." This exhibition arose from that premise. For Marcel Brient, lover of art and poetry, and for those who believe in the notions of genius and competition, the names in this exhibition seem destined to be included.

They come in couples: the French poets Arthur Rimbaud and Paul Verlaine, and the American conceptual artists Félix González-Torres and Ross Laycock. Separated by a century of literary history and artistic creation, they can nevertheless be brought together under an epitaph borrowed from surrealist poet Stéphane Mallarmé: "ce passant considérable." This provisional memorial is the equivalent of a nineteenth-century literary elegy, but it is not in any way mournful or sorrowful: quite the opposite. On its frontispiece resound the verbs: live, celebrate, and bestow.

This exhibition brings together two visionary, absinthe-loving giants of the world of poetry with two artists whose fates were sealed by AIDS: Félix González-Torres, one of the most influential artists of the twentieth century and his life companion, who inspired some of his most moving artworks. This exhibition is a hymn to love, life, creation, and death—a love song. It is also a hymn to the gaze that each of us, mere mortal beings, can cast upon the works of these shooting stars in order to enrich one's own life and pursue, as must be, the fight for freedom, generosity, and the respect of difference, whether sexual, political, or related to identity.

Poems, original manuscripts, photographs, and letters of striking beauty by Arthur Rimbaud, Paul Verlaine, and their peers, including Rimbaud's early writings and his *Lettres au Voyant* (1871), interact with works and documents from Félix González-Torres, most notably the candy portrait of Marcel Brient, accomplished in 1992.

Clément Dirié, press release, October 2013

c

d

Born in 1986, Brynjar Sigurðarson lives in Berlin.

---

a Invitation card:
Side Table, 2013 (detail)
Ash wood, metal, rope, nylon string, and various materials including feathers, fur, leather, printed fabric, chains, hooks, h. 25 × w. 19 × d. 13 ¼ in. (h. 63.5 × w. 48 × d. 33.5 cm) (total height); tabletop: h. 21 ¼ in. (h. 54.5 cm)

b *High Shelf Long Version*, 2013
Ash wood, metal, rope, nylon string, and various materials including feathers, fur, leather, printed fabric, chains, hooks, h. 7 ft. 10 in. × w. 5 ft. 11 in. × d. 1 ft. 10 in. (h. 240 × w. 180 × d. 58 cm)

c Images from *The Silent Village*, 2013

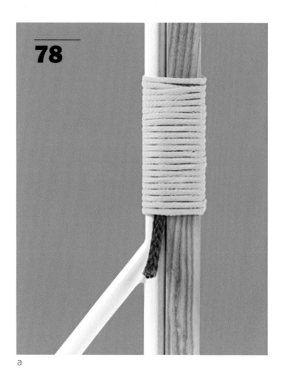

a

b

Brynjar Sigurðarson's work is an explosion of freshness in a lackluster world. Constructed using classical assembly techniques, the pieces of furniture featured in this exhibition nonetheless have something of the air of mystery of ritual objects. They step outside our world to tug upon powerfully evocative memories. These pieces of machined wood are held together by brightly colored ropes that also firmly bind a clutch of feathers, a tuft of fur, or some other detail taken from the natural world, in total contrast with the polished smoothness of the wood. These assemblies speak of a strong cultural identity, harking back to primitive cultures, the world of the Inuit. Fur hints at the icy landscapes of the designer's homeland.

Brynjar Sigurðarson was born in Reykjavík. On a trip to the village of Vopnafjörður, in northeastern Iceland, the young designer happened to meet an old man by the name of Hreinn, a former shark-hunter, who taught him a remarkable technique of rope lashing: "When I began to learn this method in his workshop, it felt as if I connected to a hidden Icelandic craft. Even though I had no specific ideas in mind on how to use it, when I began experimenting with ropes I found they offered enormous aesthetic variety."

The harmony in all these pieces flows from the dissonance between the work of the hand and the product of manufacturing. The craftsman's skill revives emotions linked to traditional forms and crafts now lost. Some might argue that these tufts of fur have no function, that they are superfluous. Yet what makes them so right is the freedom they take for themselves, the poetry they express. Their very lack of usefulness is a sign of special attention, of generosity. As Andrea Branzi would say, "What is truly fundamental is knowing when to add a gift, a flower, to what already exists." Brynjar Sigurðarson's Silent Village takes shape within an imaginary landscape, in order to re-engage with the "objects of hospitality."

Press release, November 2013

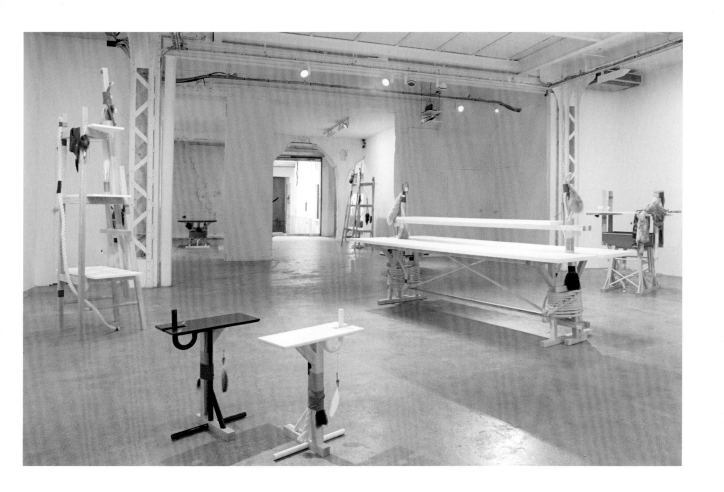

c

a Invitation card:
   Chair, 2014

b Vitrine, 2014
   ⅜ in. (10 mm) float glass,
   silicone, pneumatic pistons,
   h. 4 ft. 11 in. × w. 1 ft. ×
   d. 1 ft. (h. 150 × w. 30 ×
   d. 30 cm)

c M Table, 2014
   Securit glass top, ⅜ in.
   (10 mm) float glass, silicone,
   pneumatic pistons, h. 2 ft.
   4 ¼ in. × diam. 3 ft. 7 ¼ in.
   (h. 72 × diam. 110 cm)

d M Smoke Table, 2014
   Securit glass top, ⅜ in.
   (10 mm) float glass, silicone,
   pneumatic pistons, h. 2 ft.
   4 ¼ in. × diam. 3 ft. 7 ¼ in.
   (h. 72× diam. 110 cm)

e Exhibition view:

   Chair, 2014
   ⁵⁄₁₆ in. (8 mm) float glass,
   silicone, pneumatic pistons,
   h. 2 ft. 8 ½ in./3 ft. 2 in. ×
   w. 3 ft./3 ft. 7 ¼ in. ×
   d. 1 ft. 5 in. (h. 83/98 ×
   w. 93/110 × d. 43 cm)

   L Chest, 2014
   ⅜ in. (10 mm) float glass,
   silicone, pneumatic pistons,
   h. 1 ft. 3 in./2 ft. 9 ¾ in. ×
   w. 5 ft. 3 ¾ in. × d. 1 ft.
   8 in. (h. 38/86 × w. 160 ×
   d. 50 cm)

   XL Table, 2014
   ⅜ in. (10 mm) float glass,
   silicone, pneumatic pistons,
   h. 2 ft. 4 ½ in./3 ft. ×
   w. 8 ft. 2 in. × d. 3 ft. 3 in.
   (h. 72/90 × w. 250 ×
   d. 100 cm)

   S Chest, 2014
   ⅜ in. (10 mm) float glass,
   silicone, pneumatic pistons,
   h. 1 ft. 3 in./3 ft. 1 ½ in. ×
   w. 3 ft. × d. 1 ft. 11 ½ in.
   (h. 38/95 × w. 90 ×
   d. 60 cm)

   Shelf, 2014
   ⅜ in. (10 mm) float glass,
   silicone, pneumatic pistons,
   oak book ends, h. 3 ft.
   5 in. × w. 4 ft. 3 in. × d. 12 in.
   (h. 104 × w. 130 × d. 30 cm)

79

a

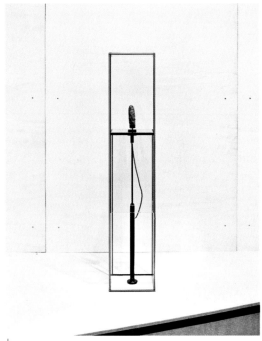

b

c, d

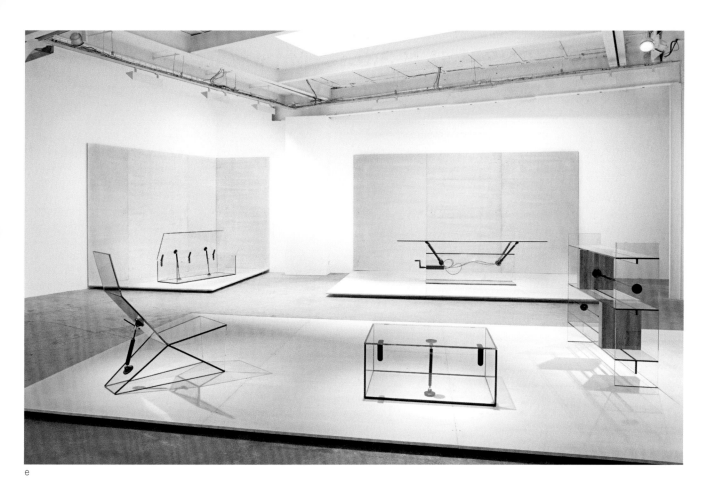

e

With *Man Machine*, Konstantin Grcic proposes nine moving pieces. With their engineered elements—pistons, pneumatic pumps, hinges—each one of them can be activated: the M Table unfolds to fit its use, the Chair can be adjusted to read or rest, the Side Table follows the movements of the body.

Clearly, Konstantin Grcic is a designer who thrives on challenges—whatever the technical constraints or time required for a project to unfold. For his new furniture collection Man Machine—taken from the name of the 1978 album by legendary group Kraftwerk—he has worked exclusively in glass, a common enough material, and yet one rarely seen in the field of contemporary design.

In collaboration with a workshop established in Frankfurt in 1829, Konstantin Grcic has developed an ingenious collection of glass furniture—made from industrial float glass identical to that used in architecture. Each piece is operated by a simple mechanism that not only meets contemporary design's demand for scalability but also truly performs its function. By means of pistons, hinges, cranks, and knobs, and through the use of black silicone that allows plates of glass to move while highlighting their design, each piece is dynamic and lends itself to human movements and mechanical strength—a reminder of the designer's penchant for the world of automobiles, already manifest in his CHAMPIONS collection exhibited at Galerie kreo in 2011. Nonetheless, there is nothing cold, distant or "electronic" about this association of the transparent and the mechanical. Although Man Machine is firmly bedded in the industrial design approach characteristic of Konstantin Grcic's work, here the glass—like Kraftwerk's electronic music—takes on sensual and porous notes. Yet, in 2008, with his Karbon chaise-longue, the designer was examining the tension between reality and appearance, and for this piece, between the lightness of a design and the sturdiness of a structure.

Exploring the relationships between exterior and interior, fragile appearance and real practicality, potentialities and tautology, human mechanics and the power of air, the Man Machine collection, stripped of all artifice, also seems to toy with the current questionings of design, elaborating on the issues addressed by the Light and Space movement in 1960s America—and Larry Bell, in particular—or those raised by Jeff Koons with his cabinets in the early 1980s. Once again, Konstantin Grcic pushes back the boundaries of the domestic stage by creating a radical collection poised between hi-fi aesthetics, a fascination with transparency, and a reflection on his own practice.

Clément Dirié, press release, February 2014

François Azambourg
Ronan & Erwan Bouroullec
Joschua Brunn
Pierre Charpin
David Dubois
Jean-Baptiste Fastrez
Naoto Fukasawa
Konstantin Grcic
Pierre Guariche
Hella Jongerius
Olivier Mourgue
Julie Richoz
Adrien Rovero
Brynjar Sigurðarson
Studio Wieki Somers
Maarten Van Severen

a Invitation card:
   David Dubois
   Reflect coffee table, 2013

b David Dubois
   Reflect coffee table, 2013
   Safety-glass top with
   mirrored silver, wood base,
   aluminum frame, h. 10 in. ×
   w. 4ft. 3 in. × d. 2 ft. 7 ½ in.
   (h. 25.8 × w. 130 ×
   d. 80 cm)

a

Different areas designated in wood are arranged
in the gallery like the rooms of an apartment or
an open-plan house, which the visitor is invited
to walk through. The exhibition presents different
combinations of pieces, showing all new editions
by young designers with a selection of significant
vintage lighting, including the Reflect coffee table
by David Dubois. This coffee table is composed
of a series of large sections of wood, arranged
in parallel with subtle spacing between, provoking
a sense of a visual rhythm. This feeling is further
enhanced by the reflection of the mirror on
the upper surface of the slices of black wood,
all visible through the glass top of the coffee table.
The asymmetry of the lines combined with the
transparent and reflective elements disrupt the
geometry of the table and enhance its uniqueness.
Press release, May 2014

b

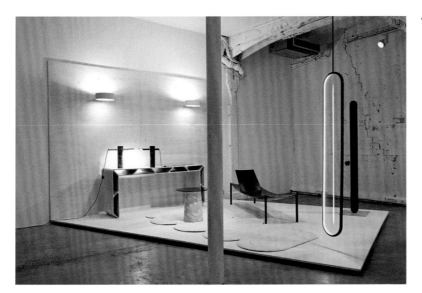

"From bookshelves by Maarten Van Severen to an exquisite desk signed François Bauchet, through a superb table by Marc Newson and a spectacular lamp by Studio Wieki Somers, it has been more than thirty years since I have had the chance and pleasure to accompany Didier and Clémence Krzentowski in their exploration of contemporary design. I don't care about it. I am still enthusiastic about it and fortunately they are too. Long live Galerie kreo!"

Christophe Durand-Ruel, collector, Paris, 2019

François Bauchet
Ronan & Erwan Bouroullec
Pierre Charpin
Jean-Baptiste Fastrez
Alessandro Mendini
Jasper Morrison
Studio Wieki Somers
Michael Young

a Invitation card

b Exhibition view:

Studio Wieki Somers
GI (Right Decision) floor
light, 2013
Shade in Perspex, cord
fringe, stainless steel,
LEDs; pole in anodized
aluminum, cord binding,
h. 7 ft. 11 in. × w. 2 ft.
7 ½ in. × d. 1 ft. (h. 242.5 ×
w. 80 × d. 30 cm)

Pierre Charpin
Mini Eclipse floor light,
2012
Lacquered and polished
resin, metal, h. 4 ft. 3 in.
(h. 131 cm); bowl: diam.
8 ½ in. (diam. 22 cm)

Ronan & Erwan Bouroullec
Bells floor light, 2004
Bell and base in metallic
blue-lacquered copper,
metal tabletop covered
with leather, h. 6 ft. 1 in. ×
w. 2 ft. 2 ½ in. × d. 2 ft. 2 ½ in.
(h. 185 × w. 67 × d. 65 cm);
bell: h. 17 ¼ × 23 ½ in.
(h. 44 × d. 60 cm)

Alessandro Mendini
Lampada, 2002
Gold mosaic, h. 7 ft. 7 in.
(231 cm); base: h. 26 ×
w. 31 ½ × d. 31 ½ in. (h. 66 ×
w. 80 × d. 80 cm)

Studio Wieki Somers
Frozen Lantern floor light,
2010
Fabric, resin, metal, wood,
UV topcoat, h. 5 ft. 9 in. ×
diam. 2 ft. 5 in. (h. 175 ×
diam. 73 cm)

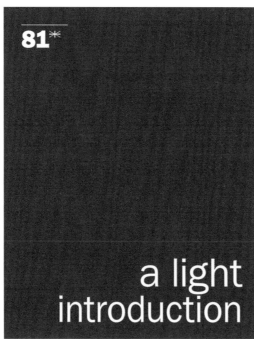

81※

a light
introduction

a

Galerie kreo's move to open a space in London is a significant one. This Paris gallery is highly respected and a prolific commissioner of design, working with both established practitioners and emerging designers. It also has a reputation for its vintage pieces and founder Didier Krzentowski's unrivalled collection of Gino Sarfatti lights. Its arrival in London should bolster the city's design scene, which has previously been served by a limited number of galleries specialized in contemporary design.

Johanna Agerman Ross, "Galerie kreo opens in London," *Disegno* (London, May 14, 2014)

b

François Bauchet
Ronan & Erwan Bouroullec
Joschua Brunn
Pierre Charpin
Konstantin Grcic
Hella Jongerius
Muller Van Severen
Jerszy Seymour
Studio Wieki Somers

a Invitation card:
Joschua Brunn
Grand Central and Petit
Central lights, 2014
Nero Marquina marble
structure, black-lacquered
aluminum stem, LEDs,
rubber ring, h. 3 ft.
11 ½ in. × w. 2 ft. 1 ½ in. ×
d. 6 ¾ in. (h. 120 × w. 65 ×
d. 17 cm) and h. 14. × w. 16 ×
d. 3 ½ in. (h. 35.5 × w. 40.5 ×
d. 9 cm)

b Exhibition view:

Ronan & Erwan Bouroullec
Stool, 2007
Tinted and varnished
sculpted oak, h. 10 ½, 11,
and 14 ¼ in. (h. 28, 30, and
26.5 cm)

Ronan & Erwan Bouroullec
Red Screen, 2008
Painted steel, painted
aluminum, wool, steel cable,
h. 6 ft. 7 in. × w. 8 ft. 6 in. ×
d. 1 ft 5 ¼ in. (h. 200 ×
w. 260 × d. 44 cm)

a

This group exhibition proposes a visual game, with pieces which greatly differ in size. Placing the large and small together gives us another reading of the purpose of the designer and brings a new perspective on the pieces. We will show for the first time the Crescendo dining table by Pierre Charpin, the Cellae dining table by François Bauchet, the Niebla coffee table and dining table by Hella Jongerius, as well as the Grand Central floor light by Joschua Brunn.

Press release, September 2014

b

a Invitation card

b Exhibition view:

Doshi Levien
Squarable Lune mirror,
2014
Lacquered MDF structure,
tinted mirrors, h. 4 ft. ×
w. 6 ¼ in. × d. 2 ⅜ in.
(h. 122 × w. 16 × d. 6 cm)

Studio Wieki Somers
Aoyama floor light, 2014
Silkscreened Tyvek,
fiberglass, anodized
aluminum, polyester,
concrete, brass, LEDs,
h. 8 ft. 4 ½ in. × w. 7 ft.
4 ½ in. × d. 2 ft. 7 ½ in.
(h. 255 × w. 225 ×
d. 80 cm)

Ronan & Erwan Bouroullec
Geta Black coffee table,
2014
Black-stained oak,
h. 10 ½ in. × 3 ft. 11 in × 2 ft.
10 in. (h. 27 × w. 119.6 ×
d. 86.4 cm)

c Exhibition view:

Hella Jongerius
UN Lounge Chair, 2014
Leather, fabric, metal,
rubber, h. 31 × w. 25 ×
d. 21 in. (h. 79 × w. 65 ×
d. 54 cm)

Pierre Charpin
Univers mirror, 2014
Mirror with gold-leaf
edge, Krion frame, h. 4 ft.
3 in. × w. 3 ft. 3 in. ×
d. 1 ½ in. (h. 130 × w. 100 ×
d. 3.9 cm)

Konstantin Grcic
London Calling steps, 2014
Solid oak, h. 6ft. 10 in. ×
w. 3 ft. 2 in. × d. 2 ft.
(h. 210 × w. 97 × d. 60 cm)

d Exhibition view
(on the floor):
Jasper Morrison
DOOW4L desk, 2014
Oak, h. 2 ft. 5 in. × w. 6 ft.
7 in. × d. 2 ft. 11 in. (h. 74 ×
w. 200 × d. 90 cm)

83 ✳

François Bauchet
Ronan & Erwan Bouroullec
Pierre Charpin
Nipa Doshi & Jonathan Levien
David Dubois
Konstantin Grcic
Jaime Hayon
Hella Jongerius
Alessandro Mendini
Jasper Morrison
Studio Wieki Somers

a

For the inauguration of the Galerie kreo in
London, we are pleased to offer a group exhibition
of the most emblematic designers in our gallery.
Brand-new pieces were created for the occasion,
including a desk by Jasper Morrison, mirrors
by Doshi Levien and Hella Jongerius, a staircase
by Konstantin Grcic, and a coffee table by Ronan
and Erwan Bouroullec. London Calling by
Konstantin Grcic: five spiral steps made of oak
take you to a height of 3 ft. (90 cm), in a semi-
circle around their central pole, and allow you to
reach the highest bookshelves. These steps
remind Konstantin Grcic of his first stay in London,
in the early 1990s, especially of the famous stairs
of the red buses. A piece conceived of to be mobile
and freestanding.

Press release, September 2014

b

c

d

François Azambourg
François Bauchet
Pierre Charpin
Doshi Levien
Jean-Baptiste Fastrez
Garouste & Bonetti
Hella Jongerius
Alessandro Mendini
Marc Newson
Studio Wieki Somers

---

a Invitation card:
 Alessandro Mendini
 Perugia coffee table, 2014
 Fiberglass, Bisazza mosaic,
 h. 17 ¾ in. × w. 5ft. 11in. ×
 d. 3ft. 7 ¼ in. (h. 45 ×
 w. 180 × d. 110 cm)

b Exhibition view:

 Jean-Baptiste Fastrez
 Papou mirror, 2012
 Acetate, lacquered resin,
 mirror, h. 20 × w. 18 ¼ ×
 d. 2 ⅜ in. (h. 50.6 ×
 w. 46.3 × d. 6.6 cm)

 François Bauchet
 Cellae desk, 2013
 Technical felt, fiberglass,
 epoxy resin, h. 2 ft. 5 in. ×
 w. 5 ft. 10 in. × d. 1 ft.
 7 in. (h. 74.5 × w. 177 ×
 d. 48 cm)

 Marc Newson
 Komed chair, 1996
 Steel structure, leather
 seat, h. 33 ¼ × w. 19 ¾ ×
 d. 19 ¾ in. (h. 84.5 × w. 50 ×
 d. 50 cm)

c Hella Jongerius
 Gemstone M side tables,
 2013
 Plywood, tinted resin,
 h. 17 ¾ × w. 26 ½ × d. 15 in.
 (h. 45 × w. 67.2 × d. 38 cm)

a

Reproducing the natural beauty of stones like agate, rose quartz, and malachite, Hella Jongerius's Gemstone side tables are composed of layers of transparent and opaque jewel-toned resin and wood.

Press release, October 2014

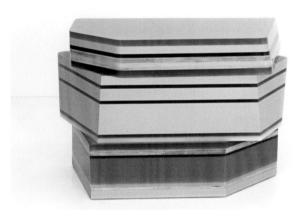

c

b

François Bauchet
BIG-GAME
Ronan & Erwan Bouroullec
Pierre Charpin
David Dubois
Naoto Fukasawa
Konstantin Grcic
Chris Kabel
Jasper Morrison
Marc Newson
Martin Szekely

a Invitation card:
Jasper Morrison
DOOW4L desk, 2014
Oak, h. 2 ft. 5 in. × w. 6 ft.
7 in. × d. 2 ft. 11 in. (h. 74 ×
w. 200 × d. 90 cm)

a

The group show *Only Wood* presents a selection of works in wood. Oak, white beech, mahogany: each finds their unique expression through the eye of the designers.

Press release, November 2014

Tito Agnoli
Arredoluce
Arteluce
Sergio Asti
Jacques Biny
Renato Forti
Bruno Gatta
Pierre Guariche
Ugo la Pietra
Jean-Boris Lacroix
Angelo Lelli
Vico Magistretti
Robert Mathieu
Monix
Joseph-André Motte
O'Luce
Giuseppe Ostuni
Philippe Parreno
Pierre Paulin
Charles Ramos
Alexander Rodchenko
Gino Sarfatti
Gaetano Sciolari
Stilnovo
Vittoriano Vigano
Nanda Vigo

a Invitation cards:

Gino Sarfatti/Arteluce
3026/40 wall/floor light,
1954
Lacquered metal, neon
tubes, h. 8 in. × w. 4 ft.
1 in. × d. 8 in. (h. 20 ×
w. 125 × d. 20 cm)

1063 floor light, 1954
Lacquered metal, neon
tube, h. 7 ft. ½ in. × w. 1 ft.
3 in. × d. 1 ft. 5 ½ in. ×
diam. 2 in. (h. 215 × w. 38 ×
d. 44 × diam. 5 cm)

3026/S wall light, 1954
Lacquered metal, neon
tubes, h. 8 in. × w. 5 ft.
10 in. × d. 8 in. (h. 20 ×
w. 178 × d. 20 cm)

2042/9 wall light, 1963
Lacquered aluminum,
frosted glass, h. 17 ×
w. 29 ¾ in. (h. 43 ×
w. 73 cm); spheres: diam.
8 in. (20 cm)

a

A life dedicated to lights is the uniting factor that brings these designers together, thanks to a passion that Didier Krzentowski has been fueling for thirty years. Gino Sarfatti and Arteluce, the lighting production company he founded and then ran from 1945 to 1973, are the emblems of this period. Gino Sarfatti dedicated his life to creating and producing lights, and understanding how to combine the bulbs, their medium, and space harmoniously. For this reason, his creations are at the core of this large selection of more than one hundred and twenty lights (ceiling, wall, floor, and desk lights).

This overview of the history of lighting design is placed in the context of previous significant exhibitions: *Lumières, je pense à vous* (Centre Pompidou, Paris, 1985) and *Gino Sarfatti. Il design della luce* (Triennale Design Museum, Milan, 2012). It presents the evolution of the technical and plastic innovation of lighting design from the 1950s (the use of colored lampshades, the rise of the fluorescent light, and the study of structural and spatial limitations) to the changing forms of the 1960s (narrative will and the Space Race) and the technical experimentations of the 1970s (the creation of the halogen bulb and the introduction of plastic into functional design).

La Luce Vita brings together French and Italian creations like Pierre Guariche's G23 light (1951) and Vittoriano Vigano's 1049 light (1952) around an experimentation with mobility through the new use of counterbalance, such as the innovations of Gino Sarfatti—with the articulating 1050/2 light (1951)—or Robert Mathieu (1955–56). The research and development of lampshades and bulbs, integral to the work of these designers, bands together various families of lights. Most importantly, 237, 238, 239, and 2042 by Gino Sarfatti, for which the diameter of the globe increases consecutively.

Designed like a landscape with various heights and volumes, a bright cave where stalactites and stalagmites reflect upon one another, this exhibition celebrates the taste for experimentation, formal and technical creation, and the functional success of these designers who wrote one of the most important chapters in the history of design.

Clément Dirié, press release, January 2015

"1063 is the name Gino Sarfatti gave to the most radical, masterful, and sculptural luminous object of all. A lamp he designed in 1954. Just a neon tube and a metal armature that allows it to exist there, standing in front of us, a pure, joyous line extending skywards. A neon sculpture that can be used as direct or reflected light and that precedes Dan Flavin's works by several years."

Marin Karmitz, film producer and collector, Paris, 2019

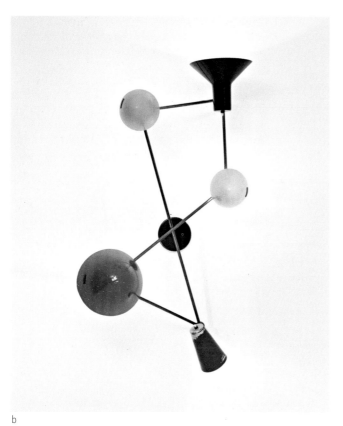

b

c

b Gino Sarfatti/Arteluce
   191 wall light, c. 1951
   Metal, h. 3 ft. 5 in. ×
   w. 24 ½ in. × d. 16 ½ in.
   (h. 105 × w. 62 × d. 42 cm)

c Philippe Parreno
   Happy Ending light, 2014
   Blown crystal, variable
   dimensions

"Gino Sarfatti's 2109/24 ceiling light: my
starry sky! A soft light and an object full
of presence that asserts itself powerfully.
An unexpected contrast. Thanks to the eye
of my friend Didier I've learned how to look
at light, to tame it, to love it, and to take risks.
Discovering Gino Sarfatti changed everything.
The structure and presence of such lighting
become an uncompromising dance."
Dominique Lévy, collector and gallerist, New York, 2019

2015

SHADES OF VARIETY

François Azambourg
François Bauchet
Ronan & Erwan Bouroullec
Joschua Brunn
Achille Castiglioni
Pierre Charpin
Joe Colombo
Doshi Levien
David Dubois
Jean-Baptiste Fastrez
Garouste & Bonetti
Konstantin Grcic
Fabrice Hyber
Hella Jongerius
Robert Mathieu
Dominique Modiano
Alessandro Mendini
Jasper Morrison
Marc Newson
Giuseppe Ostuni
Julie Richoz
Daniel Rybakken
Gino Sarfatti
Ettore Sottsass
Stilnovo
Studio Wieki Somers
Superstudio

a

a Invitation card:
Jasper Morrison
TOOW4L table, 2015
Black stained and waxed
oak, h. 2 ft. 4 ¾ in. × w. 9 ft.
2 in. × d. 3 ft. 6 ½ in.
(h. 73 × w. 280 ×
d. 108 cm)

We design the display for each
exhibition—solo ones in close
collaboration with the designer
or collective—differently each time.
Nevertheless, both in London and
Paris, we like our "cabinet-of-
curiosities" space, where making
connections between periods and
designers seems more natural,
more homely.
Clémence Krzentowski, 2019

JAIME HAYON, *GAME ON*

Born in 1974, Jaime Hayon lives in Valencia.

a Invitation card:
Basket side table, 2015
Black-lacquered ceramic, copper lacquer, h. 17 ¾ × diam. 15 ¾ in. (h. 45 × diam. 40 cm)

b Exhibition view:

Ping Pong table, 2015
Oak, metal, h. 2 ft. 5 ½ in. × w. 9 ft. 10 in. × d. 3 ft. 9 ¾ in. (h. 75 × w. 300 × d. 116 cm)

Racket mirror, 2015
Solid oak, lacquer, mirror. Small model: h. 3 ft. 11 ½ in. × w. 2 ft. 3 in. × d. 3 ⅛ in. (h. 120 × w. 68.5 × d. 8 cm)

c Sketch for *Game On* exhibition, 2015

d Exhibition view:

Racket mirror, 2015
Solid oak, lacquer, mirror. Large model: h. 5 ft. 9 in. × w. 3 ft. 3 in. × d. 4 ½ in. (h. 175 × w. 100 × d. 11 cm)

Ice Skating daybed, 2015
Solid oak, wood, chrome-plated metal, Kvadrat fabric, colored yarn, h. 17 ¾ in. × w. 6 ft. 7 in. × d. 3 ft. 3 in. (h. 45 × w. 200 × d. 100 cm)

Trapeze floor light, 2015
Lacquered wood, leather, neon, burnished brass, h. 21 × w. 27 ½ × d. 1 ¾ in. (h. 54 × 70 × 4.5 cm)

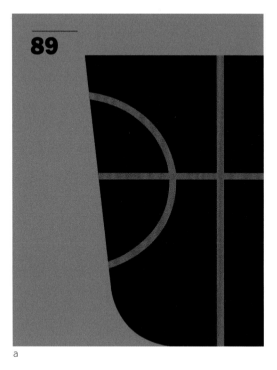

89

90 *

a

For his first collaboration with Galerie kreo, following the Carnival collection of mirrors in 2014, Jaime Hayon has created a collection inspired by sports—a theme in tune with Galerie kreo's DNA as Clémence and Didier Krzentowski both come from this industry, having participated in the production of the Albertville Olympic Games in 1992. In a similar manner when Hayon stages fauna, flora, games, or the circus, the inspiration of sports allows the Spanish artist and designer to bring to life cartoon-like pieces that play with themes of metamorphosis, scale, and disguise. The visual theme of sports also allows Hayon to play with forms, colors, and patterns—graphic lines of sports fields, aerodynamic curves, ergonomic structure. For example, the Golf side table mimics the pattern and texture of a golf ball in precious Carrara marble.

"What matters is participation," declared Pierre de Coubertin, founder of the International Olympic Committee. "What matters is imagination," claims *Game On* at Galerie kreo. Here the Sledge Sofa plays on its resemblance to a sled or bobsleigh, conveying speed and recklessness only to invite sleep and relaxation, an oxymoron, if you will. The Podium cabinet suggests we hierarchize the way we store our goods, and the Ping Pong Hanger mirror seems to spring from a hallucinatory experience of Olympic proportions. But the pieces are much more than an invitation to a dream-like state, and reveal a precise technique of design allied with the vocabulary of the sports industry: research, efficiency, technical demands ... and it is with a perfect knowledge of metamorphosis that Jaime Hayon successfully meets the expectation of functionality. The many disciplines invoked: gymnastics for the Trapeze light, ping-pong for the Ping Pong table, collective sports for Sports lights and Basket side table—bring coherence to the collection. Furthermore, Jaime Hayon decided to give the collection a final twist: the use of artisanal and traditional materials (his favorites: ceramic, wood, marble, hand-blown glass, leather) instead of the obvious high-tech and composite materials preferred today. As always crossing the line.

Clément Dirié, press release, May 2015

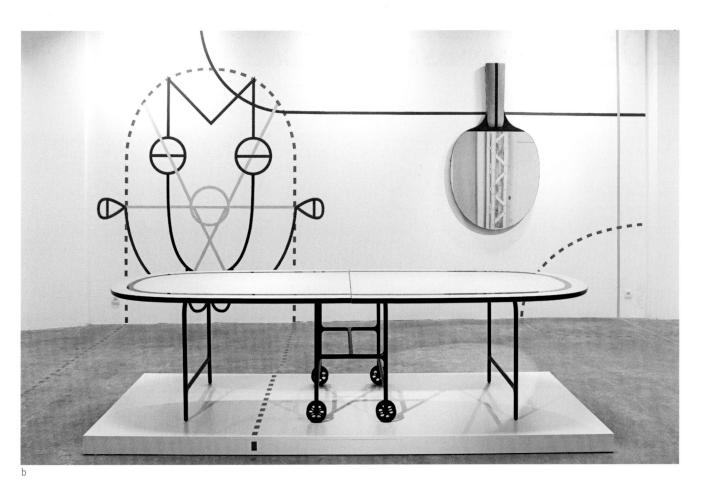

b

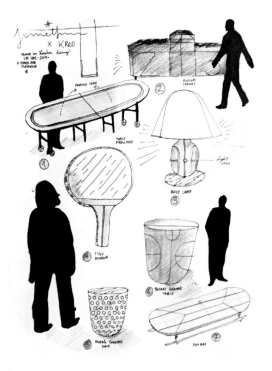

c

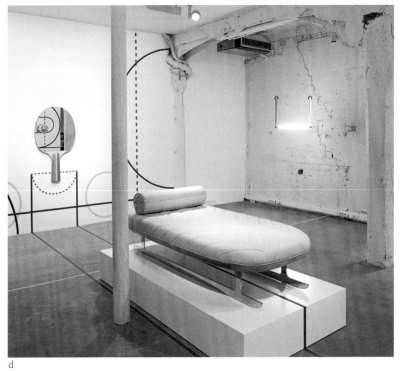

d

2015

PIERRE CHARPIN, *MARBLES & CLOWNS*

a Invitation card:
Alex vase, 2015

b Zippo vase, 2015
Alex vase, 2015
Kiko vase, 2015
Pepi vase, 2015
Clopin vase, 2015
Achille vase, 2015
Oleg vase, 2015
Joseph vase, 2015
Pipo vase, 2015
Nello vase, 2015
Pieces made at the
Manufacture de Sèvres
Handmade painted
enameled porcelain, string,
h. 19 × d. 9 ¾ in. (h. 48 ×
d. 25 cm)

c Exhibition view:

M & C high console, 2015
Marquinia marble, h. 3 ft. ×
w. 4 ft. 7 in. × d. 1 ft. 2 in.
(h. 90 × w. 140 × d. 36 cm)

M & C low console, 2015
Bardiglio marble, h. 1 ft.
3 in. × w. 4 ft. 7 in. × d. 1 ft.
2 in. (h. 38 × w. 140 ×
d. 36 cm)

91 ✳

a

b

Marbles & Clowns: as titles go, this one couldn't really be any clearer about what lies in wait at this exhibition. First up, the marbles. These come in the form of consoles and low tables. And then there are the clowns. Or, to be more precise, ten clown faces, which appear on the immaculate porcelain sides of the vases—the so-called "Charpin vases"—that I designed several years ago for the Manufacture Nationale de Sèvres, one of France's best-known ceramic factories. I say "appear," but what the faces really do is inhabit or adorn these pieces, like make-up fit for the stage.

So there we have it: *Marbles & Clowns*. And in that order ... it just sounds better, and you can never underestimate the importance of a title. But also because that's the order they arrived on the page: the marbles simply came to me first. The clowns followed later ... they weren't part of the program, not least because there never was a program. Once again, the only entities were the unknown—the unexpected. So that's how they made their entrance: no drum rolls or pre-show announcements, but flying in the face of the perfect, impassive solemnity and elegance of the marbles, which unsurprisingly remain stonily indifferent, as the expression goes. Marble is

shapeless when it exists in the landscape, in its mountainous origins, and only really becomes marble when it has been extracted. Once it has taken on the form of large, plane-parallel blocks, with more or less even sides, its qualities as a material ripe for sculpture are clear to see. After that, the block must be molded patiently, either by hand or by machine (or sometimes even by digital means), the material subtracted—emptied—to create the finished work. Some people claim that truth lies hidden in these blocks, waiting to be chipped away, but there's every reason to doubt this, because the fact is that truth comes in so many various and fortuitous forms. Whatever the case, marble is all about removal. Even the finishing and polishing processes involve removing a matte surface to reveal—in all its shiny brilliance—the inner beauty of the material. Just by looking at the collection's console tables, whose middles have literally been emptied, this idea of removal is fully in evidence.

Clowns, on the other hand, won't hear a word said about removal or subtraction. Quite the opposite, in fact. Theirs is a different way of being, singled out by a desire for addition, excess, transformation, hocus-pocus and make-up—known

as *trucco* in Italian (images from Federico Fellini's *I Clowns* spring to mind). Whether they are feigning joy or sadness, their grotesque character hinges on the make-up tracing the contours of their eyes, mouths, and sometimes their cheeks, not forgetting the addition of the obligatory red nose. This make-up is not about showcasing virtuosity, but all the same, you have to aim straight to avoid following in the clownish footsteps best left to the Commedia dell'arte or the carnival.

Now that the finishing touches have been put to the make-up—and without paying too much attention to the fact that Pipo, Nello, Zippo, and the others are only vases—the show is ready to begin. *Marbles & Clowns* is a show in which each component plays its role with assurance, and where the "&" represents the intersection of everything that is created.

Pierre Charpin, June 2015

c

2015

SIGNES DES TEMPS

Works by A.R. Penck, McDermott & McGough, and Fabrice Hyber—chosen by Didier Krzentowski and Jérôme de Noirmont—exhibited in dialogue with selected pieces by the gallery's designers

a Invitation card:

Alessandro Mendini
Poltrona di Proust
armchair, 1990
Bronze, h. 3 ft. 5 in. ×
w. 3 ft. 4 in. × d. 2 ft. 7 ½ in.
(h. 104 × w. 101 × d. 80 cm)

A.R. Penck
K. im Blickfeld, 2001

b Exhibition view:

Angelo Lelli
Cavalletto floor light,
c. 1950
Varnished and polished
copper, metal, h. 6 ft.
9 ½ in. × w. 1 ft. 10 ½ in. ×
d. 2 ft. 3 ½ in. (h. 207 ×
w. 57 × d. 70 cm)

A.R. Penck
K. im Blickfeld, 2001
Acrylic on canvas,
h. 35 ¼ in. × w. 27 ¼ in.
(h. 89.5 × w. 69.5 cm)

c Exhibition view
(on the wall):
A.R. Penck
Ich Anders in London, 1982
Oil on canvas, h. 3 ft.
4 in. × w. 4 ft. (h. 101.8 ×
w. 122 cm)

d Exhibition view
(on the wall):
A.R. Penck
Gleichgültigkeit 1, 1983
Oil on canvas, h. 6 ft.
10 in. × w. 9 ft. (h. 210.2 ×
w. 275.5 cm)

e Exhibition view
(on the wall):
A.R. Penck
Ohne Titel, 1982
Oil on canvas, h. 4 ft.
11 in. × w. 6 ft. 7 in. (h. 150 ×
w. 200 cm)

a

b

The history of taste is a perpetually evolving and reimagined concept where past, present, and future are all intertwined. Discoveries, forgotten memories, disappearances, reassessments, landmarks, and contradictions all take part in its complex elaboration; and each artist, designer, and creation is consistently compared and appreciated at the mercy of evolving gazes, sitting in the history of their discipline which they simultaneously alter.

As a result, the art and design lover always asks the same questions: this piece that I am confronted with for the first time— with what other pieces can I compare it? How does it fit into my mental puzzle of other pieces that I own or have already seen? What will I think of it in the future, when its reality will have been buried in technical innovations and successive aesthetic inventions? What power will it hold for my contemporaries? What does it say of our time?

Signes des Temps acts like an exhibition of meetings—a venture so often pursued by Galerie kreo—and moreover represents the joint response of Didier Krzentowski and Jérôme de Noirmont to the questions asked above. In the form of a rebus, the show juxtaposes emblematic pieces

by designers who have been a part of Galerie kreo for many years, and others who have recently joined the gallery, with works by contemporary artists chosen by Jérôme de Noirmont, including a substantial number of pieces by A.R. Penck, a central figure within the German arts scene. The exhibition's geographical and conceptual horizon is further expanded with the addition of some of Azzedine Alaïa's soft "archisculptures" and Jean-Christophe Charbonnier's collection of war masks from Japan's eighteenth-century Edo period.

Each piece has been carefully curated into an ensemble that acts on various aesthetic, chromatic, conceptual, and playful levels. The works reflect each of our times, acting symbolically as the archaeology of contemporary creation. Bringing together works created between the beginning of the 1980s (for some of A.R Penck's paintings) and the beginning of 2015, *Signes des Temps* proposes a journey through contemporary art and design thanks to the dedication of the two collectors, who have been friends for more than twenty years. When Didier and Clémence Krzentowski founded their gallery in 1999, Jérôme de Noirmont was one of their first followers, convinced of the strength of their project....

c

Several iconic works by A.R. Penck create an all-over forest of instantly recognizable inscriptions. Penck's stylistic self-evidence is further complemented by a constant effort to achieve precision and to go on innovating. "I always imagine my own work to be like visual search. The most important experience: the contemplation of the piece by the viewer," explained A.R.Penck, emphazising his desire to create a direct dialogue with the viewer thanks to an expressive and universal iconography, a familiar vocabulary that is pared down and graphic. In a word, manifestly his vision materialized in three dimensions.

This visual expression, a marker of the timelessness for creativity, has also spread to the entire ensemble of pieces included in *Signes des Temps*, a new chapter of the eternal history of taste, a chapter that has been deliberately formed thanks to the subjectivity and freedom of two serial collectors and all of their ensuing viewers.

Clément Dirié, press release, October 2015

d

e

2015

ECLECTIC MATCHES

François Azambourg
François Bauchet
Roger Capron
Pierre Charpin
Garouste & Bonetti
Jaime Hayon
Hella Jongerius
Jasper Morrison
Joseph-André Motte
Pierre Paulin
Studio Wieki Somers

———————

a Invitation card:
   Jaime Hayon
   Game On vase, 2015
   Ceramic, h. 25 ¼ × d. 11 in.
   (h. 64 × d. 28 cm)

a

**Drawing
is my oxygen.
I spend
my entire time
drawing.**

Jaime Hayon, 2019

2015

November 20, 2015–January 30, 2016—31, rue Dauphine, Paris

RÉUNIONS DE FAMILLES

Ronan & Erwan Bouroullec
Pierre Charpin
Jaime Hayon
Hella Jongerius
Alessandro Mendini

a Invitation card:
   Alessandro Mendini
   Firenze dining table, 2015
   Wood, wood marquetry,
   h. 2 ft. 5 ½ in. × w. 9 ft.
   2 in. × d. 4 ft. (h. 75 ×
   w. 280 × d. 120 cm)

b Pieces by Alessandro
   Mendini

c Pieces by Jaime Hayon

d Pieces by Ronan & Erwan
   Bouroullec

e Pieces by Pierre Charpin

f Pieces by Hella Jongerius

94

a

I like all these interconnections. It's the same with designers. It's good to recall how we've gathered around the gallery a family of designers and that they almost all know each other, that some are friends, that others collaborate on projects or exhibitions, that our young designers have sometimes studied and worked with those we've been representing since they started out.... Over these twenty years, a kind of "family" of about twenty people has formed with whom we remain in almost constant contact. With them, we keep thinking things through and having almost daily discussions.

Didier Krzentowski, 2019

b

c

d

e

f

January 29–March 24, 2016—14A Hay Hill, London

THE ENLIGHTENED 1950S: ICONIC FRENCH LIGHTING FROM A MODERN DECADE

Jacques Biny
Pierre Disderot
Pierre Guariche
Jean-Boris Lacroix
Luminalité
Robert Mathieu
Michel Mortier
Joseph-André Motte

———

a   Invitation card:
    Jean-Boris Lacroix
    Floor light, 1953
    for Robert Caillat
    White-lacquered cast
    iron, perforated lacquered
    metal, lacquered aluminum
    circular reflector, glass
    lens, h. 6 ft. × w. 2 ft. ×
    d. 2 ft. 3 in. (h. 182 ×
    w. 60 × d. 68 cm)

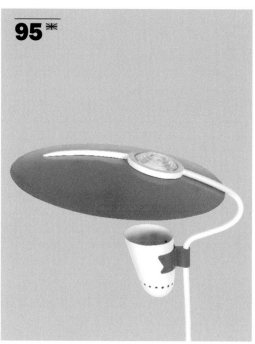

95 ✳

a

The 1950s marked a jubilant period of reconstruction and renovation in war-torn France. Indeed, one might say that innovation in lighting during this decade emerged as a reaction against the darkness of the previous years. For architects, designers, and manufacturers, the diffusion of light became an essential focus of research. The austerity and formalism of the prewar era was replaced by a more organic design, fit for everyday use. Functionality and flexibility became central concerns and gave way to forms that had not been seen before: articulated arms, pivots, and interchangeable stems to reach the farthest corners. The group of young designers that gave rise to this innovative movement—Pierre Guariche, Michel Mortier, Joseph-André Motte, and Jacques Biny—shared a desire to re-think shapes and introduce color in interiors. Their creative vision, alongside the introduction of new materials like aluminum and steel in lighting design, was fostered by brave manufacturers such as Pierre Disderot, Luminalité, and Robert Mathieu, thus enabling them to reach a wider market. It is this very modernity that Galerie kreo wants to celebrate with this exhibition dedicated to twentieth-century lighting designers: a modernity that is still inspiring and relevant today.

Press release, January 2016

Tito Agnoli
Joe Colombo
Joe and Gianni Colombo
Leonardo Ferrari and
Franco Mazzucchelli
Tartaglino
Bruno Gatta
Ugo La Pietra
Angelo Lelli
Vico Magistretti
George Nelson
Angelo Ostuni and Renato
Forti
Giuseppe Ostuni
Pierre Paulin
Gino Sarfatti
Gaetano Sciolari
Stilnovo
Vittoriano Vigano
Nanda Vigo

a Invitation card:
Gino Sarfatti/Arteluce
1079 floor light, 1960
Aluminum, Perspex, h. 4 ft.
10 in. × diam. 1 ft. 3 ¾ in,
(h. 148 × diam. 40 cm)

96

a

Galerie kreo pays
homage to a decade
that was unique in its
abundant creation, equally
diverse and modern.
The exhibition highlights
pieces that were both rare
and intelligent and which,
like all masterpieces,
are timeless.

Press release, February 2016

After the war, Italian culture was still largely affected by the austerity of the 1930s and several decades of dictatorial regime. Many artists and architects moved to the United States, where culture was being rapidly industrialized. They discovered products with rich forms that were opulent, aerodynamic, and shown to best advantage by frequent advertising. It was in this entirely new spirit that the Italians entered the 1950s. Industrial production of design, especially lighting, developed largely thanks to numerous architects/designers: among them Giuseppe Ostuni, Tito Agnoli, Joe Colombo, and, of course, the greatest of all, Gino Sarfatti. Italian homes were brightened, forms became rounder, and color increasingly found its way into designs. Designers began to consider different possibilities for lighting: indirect, by projection. Lights began to have more arms, branches, ball joints, allowing them to move in all directions. The materials used also began to evolve. The 1950s welcomed the arrival of Plexiglas and aluminum: both were less fragile, more malleable, and easier to produce industrially. The publications (*Domus*, *Casabella*, *Stile Industria*) and exhibitions such as the Triennale of Milan helped establish the influence of Italian design on an international scale. Similarly, designers such as Gino Sarfatti, Angelo Lelli, and Vittoriano, gained status as the reference point for their contemporaries.

Press release, February 2016

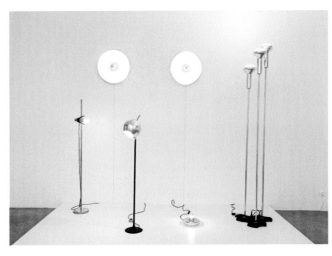

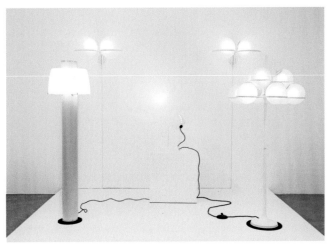

a Invitation card:
  Hieronymus Wood, 2016
  Walnut, h. 2 ft. 5 ½ in. ×
  w. 3 ft. 1 in. × d. 2 ft. 8 in.
  (h. 75 × w. 94 × d. 82 cm)

b Hieronymus 3D Printed,
  2016
  3D-printed resin and
  sand, h. 3 ft. 9 in. ×
  w. 7 ft. 4 ½ in. × d. 6 ft.
  4 ¾ in. (h. 115 × w. 225 ×
  d. 195 cm)

c Hieronymus Marble, 2016
  Carrara marble, h. 4 ft.
  3 in. × w. 3 ft. × d. 2 ft. 4 in.
  (h. 130 × w. 90 × d. 71 cm)

d Hieronymus Minero, 2016
  Minero (composite material
  especially developed for
  this piece in concrete
  and resin), h. 3 ft. 5 in. ×
  w. 3 ft. 5 in. × d. 2 ft. 3 ½ in.
  (h. 105 × w. 105 × d. 70 cm)

e Hieronymus Metal, 2016
  Anodized aluminum, 5 ft.
  3 in. × diam. 2 ft. 3 ½ in.
  (h. 160 × diam. 70 cm)

97

a

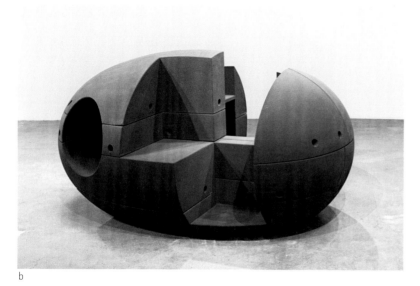

b

In this ensemble of five new pieces, Konstantin Grcic confronts the fundamental issue of space in design. Grcic first encountered Antonello da Messina's masterpiece *Saint Jerome in his Study* (1475) at the National Gallery in London, when he was in his early twenties. What struck him then and has remained with him ever since, was the elaborate architecture of the saint's study and the way it created a space in itself. In this series, he takes the design of the study as a question to be rearticulated: what makes a space intimate? How should one experience a particular space? Drawing from a variety of materials, from marble to aluminum and fiber cement, combined with the use of 3D printing, he builds upon the fifteenth-century study furniture and develops it into a principle for contemporary life. One of the pieces, designed to potentially seat two people, explores the potential for dialogue; another separates the sitter from his surroundings; a third requires one to be aware of bodily tension; and in a fourth, one must actively define one's position on the seat, and therefore in the world; the fifth piece epitomizes it all, as the sitter is required to decide between several positions in which to sit on the furniture. In engaging with the monumentality of the original furniture depicted in the painting, Grcic renders it mobile, and fluid. He invites us to find a new type of modern comfort, one that would be our own that is of both body and mind; not laziness, but study; just as the Italian master did for the scholarly saint who translated the Bible from Greek for the world to read for more than fifteen centuries. We ourselves are now able to enter into the reflective space of these architectural pieces in order to redefine the structure of our lives.

Donatien Grau, press release, March 2016

c

d

e

Pierre Charpin
Jean-Baptiste Fastrez
Jaime Hayon
Studio Wieki Somers

---

a Invitation card:
Jean-Baptiste Fastrez
Ra vase, 2016

b Exhibition view:

Jean-Baptiste Fastrez
Ra vase, 2016
Ceramic, h. 26 ¼ × diam.
15 ¼ in. (h. 67 × diam.
39 cm)

Jean-Baptiste Fastrez
Osiris vase, 2016
Ceramic, h. 17 ¼ ×
w. 17 ¼ × d. 9 ¾ in. (h. 44 ×
w. 44 × d. 25 cm)

Jean-Baptiste Fastrez
Anubis vase, 2016
Ceramic, h. 22 ½ × diam.
15 in. (h. 57 × diam. 38 cm)

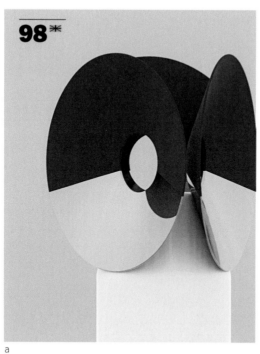

a

Super-Natural Geometry explores the relationship between geometry, nature, and tradition.

Press release, April 2016

b

The newly designed vases by
Jean-Baptiste Fastrez continue
the dialogue between functional
object and ritualistic origins that
commenced with his Masks mirror
collection (2012). Inspired by
the canopic jars used in Ancient
Egyptian burial rituals, the similar
bodies of the vases are distinguished
by different lid ornaments evoking
the Egyptian divinities guarding
their contents. The figurative
representation has been abstractly
reinterpreted through geometric
shapes more attuned with
contemporary visual language:
the solar disk for Ra, the pointy ears
of the jackal for Anubis, and the
royal crook and flail for Osiris.
The juxtaposition of ancient and
contemporary references blurs
the temporal and functional origin
of the object.

Press release, April 2016

2016

SUMMER SOLSTICE

Pierre Charpin
Garouste & Bonetti
Jaime Hayon
Doshi Levien
Hella Jongerius
Alessandro Mendini
Gino Sarfatti

———

a Invitation card:
Pierre Charpin
M & C side table, 2015
Marquina marble,
Rosso Francia marble,
h. 16/19 ¾ × w. 17 ¾ ×
d. 15 in. (h. 41/50 × w. 45 ×
d. 38.5 cm)

b Exhibition view:

Hella Jongerius
Bead Bulb light, 2005
Fiberglass, embroidered
fabric, Plexiglas, bead
knitting, h. 15 ¾ × diam.
16 ½ in. (h. 40 × diam.
42 cm)

Pierre Charpin
M & C coffee table, 2015
Antigua marble, h. 1 ft.
3 in. × w. 3 ft 7 ¼ in. × d. 2 ft.
7 ½ in. (h. 38 × w. 110 ×
d. 80 cm)

Alessandro Mendini
Poltrona di Proust
armchair, 1990
Bronze, h. 3 ft. 5 in. × w. 3 ft.
3 ¾ in. × d. 2 ft. 7 ½ in.
(h. 104 × w. 101 × d. 80 cm)

Garouste & Bonetti
Lanterne ceiling light, 1995
Gold leaf, metal, and yellow,
turquoise, and pale pink
glass, h. 11 ft. 6 in. × diam.
1 ft. 1 ¾ in. (h. 349 × diam.
35 cm)

99 ✳

a

b

Alessandro Mendini originally designed this iconic model for Studio Alchimia in 1978. In creating the Poltrona di Proust he succeeded in uncoupling design from its solely functional objectives and shifting it to a new paradigm brought about by a world in constant flux. He rethinks the famous baroque Proust armchair, produced on a very large scale, and thus raises questions of tradition, the production of design, and how it is perceived.

Press release, May 2016

Ron Arad
François Azambourg
François Bauchet
BIG-GAME
Camille Blin
Ronan & Erwan Bouroullec
Andrea Branzi
Joschua Brunn
Fernando and Humberto Campana
Pierre Charpin
Doshi Levien
David Dubois
Jean-Baptiste Fastrez
Delphine Frey
Front Design
Naoto Fukasawa
Olivier Gagnere
Élisabeth Garouste
Konstantin Grcic
Jaime Hayon
Hella Jongerius
Alessandro Mendini
Jasper Morrison
Muller Van Severen
Marc Newson
Verner Panton
Pierre Paulin
Radi Designers
Julie Richoz
Adrien Rovero
Daniel Rybakken
Gino Sarfatti
Jerszy Seymour
Brynjar Sigurðarson
Studio Wieki Somers
Martin Szekely
Lee Ufan
Maarten Van Severen
Michael Young

a Invitation card:
Konstantin Grcic,
Hieronymus Wood, 2016,
walnut, h. 2 ft 5 ½ in. ×
w. 3 ft. 1 in. × d. 2 ft. 8 ¼ in.
(h. 75 × w. 94 × d. 82 cm)

Verner Panton, Wire lights,
1969, for J. Lüber

b Exhibition view (on the wall):
Andrea Branzi
Figure #5, 2000
Acrylic on wood and
aluminum figurines,
h. 5 ft. 7 in. × 9 ft. 10 in. ×
4 ¼ in. (h. 170 × w. 301 ×
d. 10.5 cm)

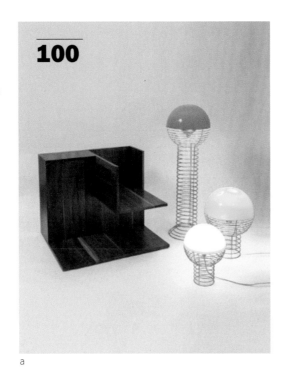

a

For its one-hundredth exhibition, in a nod to that of its first exhibition, the invitation card echoes the inaugural composition, replacing the Colombo piece with Konstantin Grcic's iconic Hieronymus Wood (2016), one of the most recent pieces produced by Galerie kreo.

Press release, September 2016

For its one-hundredth exhibition, Galerie kreo has gathered together approximately a hundred pieces of contemporary and vintage design. They have one thing in common: all have already been presented in one of the ninety-nine previous exhibitions, between 1999 and 2016. Together, they form the history of the discipline of kreo design, even as they question its materials and forms, or its hybridization with other fields of creativity. As a retrospective of seventeen years in the business, *Une pièce par jour* (One Piece a Day) is a panorama of design made in kreo, a journey documenting what makes the gallery unique: that of offering designers a space that allows them to shape both their everyday intuitions and their visions of the extraordinary. Galerie kreo is a laboratory that produces, exhibits, and disseminates today's design, rooted in the history of modernity that has formed since the 1950s, and questioning the future of our relationships to objects and our habits.

The first exhibition was held in May 1999; the hundredth in September 2016, which adds up to one amazing number. As per the title, this amounts to "one piece a day," the average for the number of pieces produced over the past seventeen years. Make no mistake, however—this is no Stakhanovite mantra. "Exhibitions are presented only when they are ready, when production has been finalized, when certain pieces have been eliminated and others perfected," explains Didier Krzentowski. So not a stale formula, but a sign of vitality, to remind us of the irreplaceable contribution made by designers exposed to the recent history of design. A piece a day keeps the monotony away.

Press release, September 2016

b

a Invitation card

b Ruutu Green 37, 2015
   Hand-blown glass,
   h. 14 ½ × w. 16 ¼ × d. 9 in.
   (h. 37 × w. 41 × d. 23 cm)

c Ruutu Brown 54 (#7), 2015
   Hand-blown glass,
   h. 21 ¼ × w. 16 ½ × d. 9 in.
   (h. 54 × w. 42 × d. 23 cm)

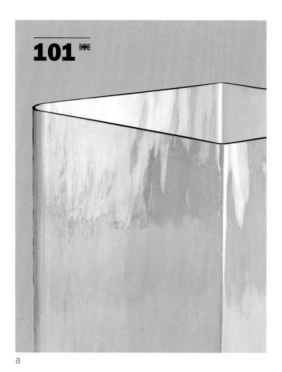

101 ✳

a

b, c

Ronan & Erwan Bouroullec's new collection: fourteen unique vases in hand-blown glass made by Iittala, the renowned Finnish manufacturer of the iconic Alvar Aalto vases. The shape of the vases, combined with their considerable sizes challenges the material to its limits and unveils the highest level of glass-blowing expertise. These grand vases, produced in three different colors, fully expose the qualities, translucency, and purity of such a living material.

Press release, September 2016

a Invitation card:
  White Mineral Chain, 2016
  Plaster, detail

b Ceramic Multiple Chains,
  2016
  Enameled ceramic, h. 7 ft.
  8 in./8 ft. 2 in./8 ft. 6 in.
  (h. 2.35/2.50/2.60 m)

From October 28
to December 17, 2016,
Galerie kreo hosted,
in one of its windows,
the Apprentissages project
by Sheila Hicks for the
Festival d'Automne à Paris,
curated by Clément Dirié.

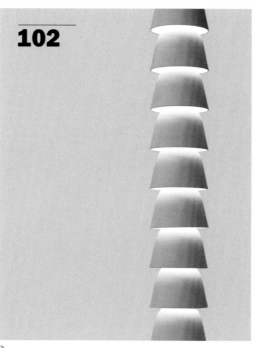

102

a

b

The Chains collection by Ronan & Erwan Bouroullec
represents a continuation of the formal vocabulary which
the brothers have been developing for many years. Module,
assembly, and the relationship with the surrounding space—
central aspects of their research—characterize this new
work. The collection is composed of a series of lampshade-
like modules that can be endlessly joined together. Whether
they are made of white plaster—where the immaculate
matte skin seems to materialize the light—or anodized
aluminum in azure blue, pale green, or pale gold, the light
shows off their substantial bell shapes and glitters over
each curved surface. Also in the collection are a series
made from ceramic, glazed in glossy red, without light,
which can be mounted either as an installation or as a set
of screens. The glossy glaze confers an organic dimension,
almost as if the pieces were alive.

Press release, November 2016

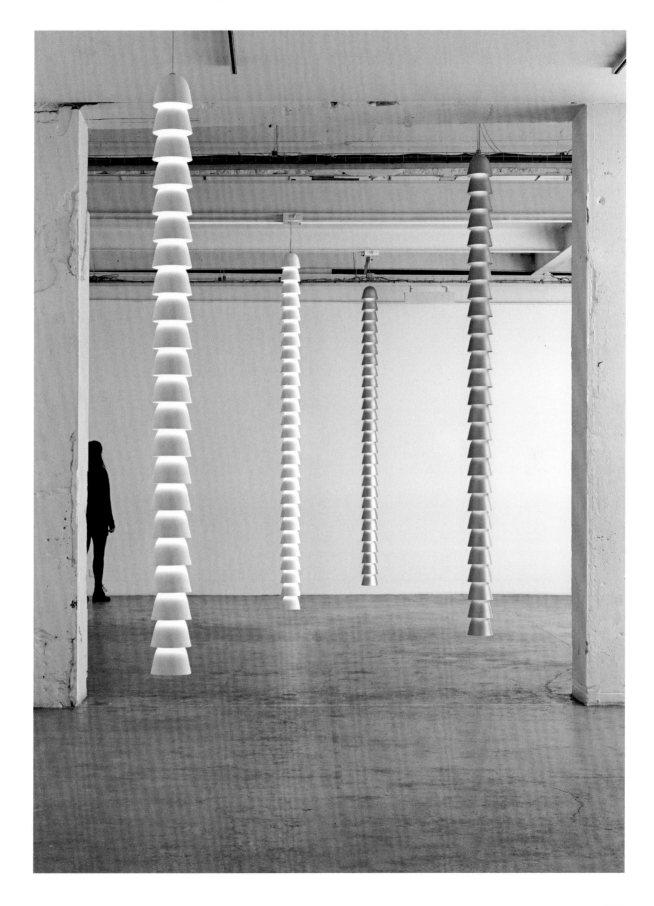

François Bauchet
Camille Blin
Ronan & Erwan Bouroullec
Fernando and Humberto
Campana
Pierre Charpin
Jacques Dumond
Delphine Frey
Konstantin Grcic
Jaime Hayon
James Irvine
Julia Lohmann
Roberto Lucci and
Marcello Pietrantoni
Angelo Mangiarotti
Alessandro Mendini
Jasper Morrison
Dominique Perrault
Martin Szekely
Vittoriano Vigano

a Invitation card:
Jaime Hayon
Game On side table, 2015
Carrara marble, h. 17 ¾ ×
d. 15 ¾ in. (h. 45 ×
d. 40 cm)

103

a

Monobloc, i.e., "made of one piece" is the common thread of this exhibition, which presents seats and vases as well as contemporary and vintage lights. Jaime Hayon's Game On side table is shaped in one single block of Carrara marble. The Ignotus Nomen coffee table by Pierre Charpin appears as a solid piece: the white object, leitmotif of the eponymous collection, is an integral part of the work, "inhabiting" it and bestowing its singularity. Hieronymus Marble by Konstantin Grcic is made of a single material: white Carrara marble. The piece contains various functions: it can serve as seat, writing desk, pedestal. Through the Hieronymus collection, Konstantin Grcic explores the different ways of taking possession of a seat and how these stimulate our concentration. For the Cellae collection, François Bauchet uses an innovative material combining technical felt, resin, and fiberglass. Each work is composed of different cells to create a unique piece.
Press release, January 2017

François Azambourg
François Bauchet
Ronan & Erwan Bouroullec
Fernando and Humberto Campana
Pierre Charpin
Jean-Baptiste Fastrez
FontanaArte
Konstantin Grcic
Pierre Guariche
Jaime Hayon
Hella Jongerius
Harri Koskinen
Alessandro Mendini
Muller Van Severen
Pierre Paulin
Gio Ponti
Samy Rio
Daniel Rybakken
Gino Sarfatti
Ettore Sottsass
Stilonovo
Oscar Torlasco
Nanda Vigo

a Invitation card:
Samy Rio
Totem mirror, 2016
Solid ash wood, mirror, ropes, h. 3 ft. 3 in. × w. 1 ft. 5 in. × d. 7 in. (h. 100 × w. 43.4 × d. 18.2 cm)

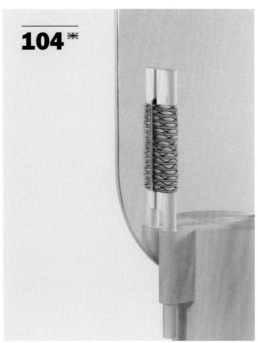

104 ✳

a

This mirror is part of the same collection as the Vases Composés. Made of natural ash wood, the mirror contains the same types of joins as the vases, creating a tension between the precision of the craftsmanship and the regularity of an industrial object. Its assembly—of a mirror posted within a wooden trunk and bound by ropes— looks primitive at first sight, but it demands advanced manufacturing methods. There are cultural traces in this totemic aesthetic, evoking a reflected mask. However, the result arises more from the demanding production and mechanical assembly (also an homage to the cabinetmaker's skills) than from the desire for an exotic figuration.
Samy Rio, 2016

Sergio Asti
Joe Colombo
Tartaglino and Leonardo
Ferrari
Bruno Gatta
Angelo Lelli
Michele de Lucchi
Franco Mazzucchelli
Gino Sarfatti
Ettore Sottsass
Stilnovo
Oscar Torlasco

---

a Invitation card:
Gino Sarfatti/Arteluce
536 table light, 1966
Black-lacquered metal,
h. 12 × w. 17 ¾ in. (h. 30 ×
w. 45 cm)

b Gino Sarfatti/Arteluce
2066 ceiling light, 1952
Varnished brass, black
perforated metal, h. 7 ft.
10 in. × diam. 1 ft. (h. 240 ×
diam. 30 cm)

c Joe Colombo
Shu desk light, 1971,
for Forma e Funzione
Black-lacquered aluminum,
chromed metal, h. 17 ¾ ×
diam. 9 in. (h. 45 × diam.
23 cm)

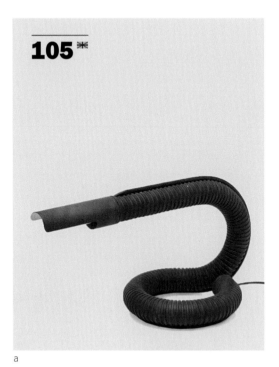

105 ✳

a

b

c

Switched On presents a selection of postwar Italian vintage lights—desk lights and floor lights by the great Gino Sarfatti and Gae Aulenti, Joe Colombo, Bruno Gatta, Angelo Lelli, and many others. Among the lights on display is the 2066 ceiling light (1952) by Gino Sarfatti, shown in Paris on the occasion of the exhibition on Italian decorative arts in 1952. This ceiling light epitomizes one of the innovations that Sarfatti brought about in lighting design. The counterweighted adjustable chandelier leaves the work environment to find its place in the house and fulfill the needs of the changing postwar lifestyle. Also adjustable, the 566 table light (1956) was one of the first in Italy to use the Cornalux bulb, the best to illuminate the workstation, according to the designer. The Shu (1976) by Joe Colombo represents another great example of a desk light intended for the workstation. The swiveling arm, as well as the adjustable lampshade, makes the piece adaptable to diverse requirements. Every detail is perfectly studied, including the base, which is split into two parts to allow the cable to be wrapped and unwrapped in order to find the desired length and hide the remaining portion.

Press release, March 2017

Barber & Osgerby
François Bauchet
Ronan & Erwan Bouroullec
Konstantin Grcic
Alessandro Mendini
Jasper Morrison
Giuseppe Ostuni
Pierre Paulin
Gino Sarfatti

a Invitation card:
   Barber & Osgerby
   Hakone table, 2016

b Barber & Osgerby
   Hakone table, 2016
   Oak, h. 2 ft. 5 in. × w. 9 ft.
   6 in. × d. 3 ft. 7 in. (h. 73 ×
   w. 290 × d. 110 cm)

c Alessandro Mendini
   Umbria table, 2015
   Fiberglass, Bisazza mosaic,
   h. 2 ft. 5 ½ in. × w. 9 ft.
   2 in. × d. 4 ft. (h. 75 ×
   w. 280 × d. 120 cm)

d Jasper Morrison
   DOOW4L desk, 2014
   Oak, h. 2 ft. 5 in. × w. 6 ft.
   7 in. × d. 2 ft. 11 in. (h. 74 ×
   w. 200 × d. 90 cm)

106

a

This first collaboration of the London-based design duo and Galerie kreo, the Hakone table signed by Jay Barber and Edward Osgerby is inspired by the sobriety of Japanese carpentry. Its forms are reminiscent of the curved lines of the Hakone sanctuary's architecture.

The mosaic, Alessandro Mendini's preferred material, is used once more in the design of his Umbria table. The many shades of green—from the darkest, almost gray, to the lightest—recall Umbria, the famous region in central Italy, well known for its verdant landscapes, vineyards, and olive trees.

Press release, April 2017

b

c

d

a Invitation card:
Tile coffee table, 2017
Wood, porcelain, h. 13 ¾ ×
w. 12 ½ × d. 23 in. (h. 35 ×
w. 32 × d. 58 cm)

b Knots and Bead Curtain,
2016
Ceramic pearls, cotton
ropes, h. 9 ft. 10 in. ×
w. 3 ft. 3 ¼ in. (h. 3.00 ×
w. 1.00 m)

c Artificial Vases, 2009
Mixed media, h. 7 ft. ×
w. 6 ft. × d. 2 ft. (h. 213 x.
w. 185 × d. 60 cm)

107 ✳

a

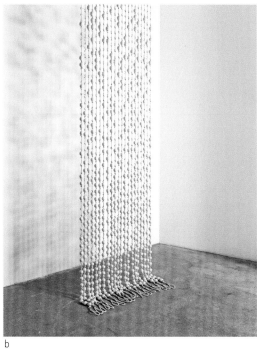

b

c

Chromatic Sequences features distinctive works by Hella Jongerius which highlight her masterful use and understanding of colors, materials, and light. Shown for the first time, the Tiles collection reveals the result of an extended color research in ceramics, using a limited palette of clay and glaze colors. New and unexpected colors emerge by layering the glaze on colored clay, a technique also seen in early oil paintings to achieve a wide range of colors with a limited range of pigments. The color of the ceramic tiles is made by the material itself. On each tile, the glaze partially covers the clay, contrasting the natural clay color with the glaze layering on the other part of the tile.

Originally designed for the United Nations Delegates' Lounge in New York in 2013, the Knots and Beads Curtain is composed of handcrafted half-glazed beads handknotted along cotton ropes. The rhythm of the beads becomes more and more dense as the curtain reaches the floor, yet it is softened by irregularities, which make each of the works in this limited edition even more unique.

Press release, July 2017

"An animal. An object. A sculpture. Living with the Turtle Coffee Table brings surprises every day. An adventure, a dialogue. On encountering it, I was fascinated by the sensuality of the materials and its courageous mixtures. The beauty of the object is purely the result of Hella Jongerius's unbelievable talent."
Dominique Lévy, collector and gallerist, New York, 2019

DIDIER LAVIER

An exhibition of works
by Bertrand Lavier
in dialogue with designers
from the gallery

a Invitation card:
Dean, 2017
Teddy bear, h. 20 × w. 7 ×
d. 6 in. (h. 52 × w. 17 ×
d. 15 cm). In Konstantin
Grcic's Vitrine, 2014

b Exhibition view (center):
Colonne Lancia, 2017
Carved stone, car light,
h. 5 ft. 7 in. × w. 11 ¾ in. ×
d. 11 ½ in. (h. 170 ×
w. 29.7 × d. 29 cm)

c Exhibition view (on the left):
Paulin/Kind, 2017
Seat on horizontal filing
cabinet, h. 4 ft. 4 in. ×
w. 4 ft. 5 ½ in. × d. 3 ft.
3 in. (h. 132 × w. 136 ×
d. 100 cm)

d Exhibition view (on the wall
and on the right):

Rue Saint-Séverin, 2004
Laser print on canvas,
h. 5 ft. 11 in. × w. 7 ft. 6 in.
(h. 181 × w. 228 cm)

Eames Armchair, 2017
Acrylic on armchair,
h. 30 ¾ × w. 25 × d. 25 in.
(h. 78 × w. 63 × d. 63 cm)

e Exhibition view
(on the wall):
*Walt Disney Productions
1947–2013 n° 13*, 2013
Acrylic and laser print on
canvas, diam. 7 ft. 7 ½ in.
(diam. 2.33 m)

f Exhibition view (on the
wall):
Montagne Sainte-Victoire,
2017
Acrylic on road signage,
h. 4 ft. 7 in. × w. 7 ft. 10 in.
(h. 1.40 × w. 2.40 m)

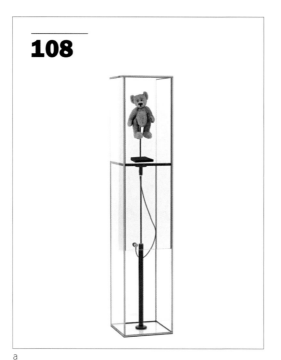

108

a

b

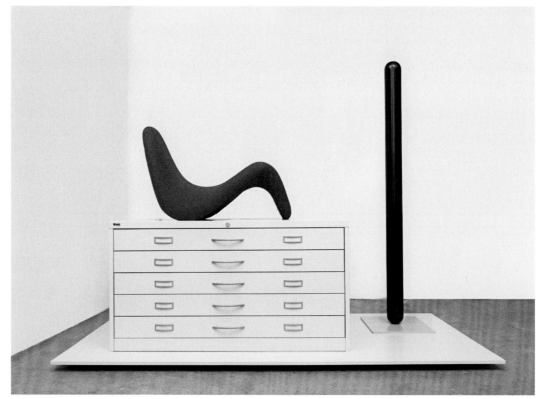

c

The exhibition *Didier Lavier* reflects the long-standing conversation between Bertrand Lavier and Clémence and Didier Krzentowski, founders of Galerie kreo in 1999. In 2002, on the occasion of an exhibition dedicated to Marc Newson, they presented Lavier's work *Embryo,* showing the iconic chair by the Australian designer rotated ninety degrees and resting on a plinth. The piece was thus added to the French artist's playful series of artistic gestures which earned him the title "happy postmodernist" coined by Michel Gauthier, curator at the Centre Pompidou, Paris. For this exhibition, conceived as a game of dominoes, Bertrand Lavier and Didier Krzentowski combine historical and new works by the artist from all his important series (the painted objects "à la Van Gogh," the Walt Disney Productions, the "superposed objects," the Frank Stella neon-ized paintings etc.) with vintage and contemporary design pieces by, among others, François Bauchet, Ronan & Erwan Bouroullec, and Gino Sarfatti.

The resulting dialogues retain the strength of the self-evident and the promise of joyful accumulations: it is indeed the first time that Bertrand Lavier displays his works so closely to pieces of design, a discipline which he "cannibalizes" as soon as he appropriates a Verner Panton chair, a highway sign by Jean Widmer, an armchair by Pierre Paulin, and all those consumerist goods (fridge, Ferrari, skateboards etc.), for which he reveals their "sculptural dreams." A playful sequence juxtaposing formal, colorful, narrative, and oneiric short-circuits, *Didier Lavier*, with its title reminiscent of horticultural grafting—a beloved method of Bertrand Lavier, inherited from his studies of botany—wants to sow confusion and harvest your astonishment.

Press release, September 2017

d

e

f

Born in 1952, Olivier Gagnère lives in Paris.

a Invitation card:
Cabochon Ancient Greece, 2017
Enameled ceramic,
h. 21 ½ × diam. 13 in.
(h. 54.5 × diam. 33 cm)

b Ring Black and White, 2017
Enameled ceramic, h. 15 × diam. 8 ½ in. (h. 38 × diam. 22 cm)

c Tuxedo Ancient Greece, 2017
Enameled ceramic, h. 15 × diam. 8 ½ in (h. 38 × diam. 22 cm)

109 ⚹

a

If there is one area in the decorative arts in which Olivier Gagnère excels, it is ceramics. With each new adventure, he innovates, transcends the material, imprints his style: the clear and joyful line.... The new models presented testify to his ability, so specific to him, to control the material and to endow it with all its expressivity, and by this fact, to follow in the footsteps of great contemporary artists and designers such as Ettore Sottsass and Gio Ponti, whose ceramic oeuvre he admires. Like them, Olivier Gagnère loves rigor and the constant shifting back and forth between tradition and modernity.

David Caméo, Director General of Les Arts Décoratifs (2014–2018), Paris

b

c

For well on thirty years, Olivier Gagnère has been working with the greatest ceramicists from around the world: from the faience factories of Quimper to that of Fukagawa in Arita, Japan, collaborating on a long-term basis with Claude Aiello in Vallauris and the Bernardaud porcelain manufacture. *New Works* presents a new series of vases and cups made of ceramic, his preferred material.
The pieces here were crafted in Sergio and Mauro Parigi's workshops at Siesta Fiorentino, near Florence. Composed of four models in a range of different color schemes and ornaments, including cabochons, full rings, facets, and flat rings, the collection gives form to a melodic suite where the ancestral knowhow of the ceramic art meets the geometric and elegant practice of Olivier Gagnère.

Press release, November 2017

a Invitation card:
   Losange vases, 2017
   Enameled ceramic, two
   colors, h. 15, 23, 26 ¼, and
   33 in. (h. 38, 58, 67, and
   84 cm)

110

a

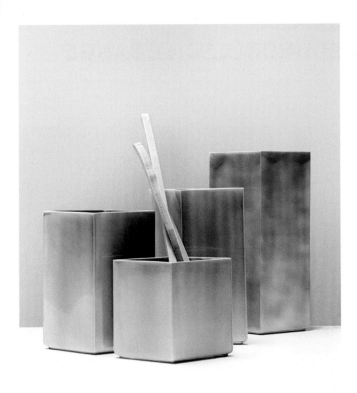

One diamond, two diamonds, three diamonds, four blue diamond-shaped vases.

Four diamonds, three diamonds, two diamonds, one green diamond-shaped vase.

All serve to contain—why not flower water? All are ceramic.

Each of them is higher or lower than all the others. Each of them bears the name of its geometric form.

All come after the Combinatory vases (1997), the Torique vases (1999), the Honda vase (2001), and the Cloud vases (2015). All recall that the vase object is one of Ronan & Erwan Bouroullec's favorite territories of formal and material research.

Each of them is unique, combining the regularity of a generic form, of its angles and bevels, with the organic variety of craft production. Each of them reflects the light differently, depending on your vision, your distance from it, and its lighting.

All produce for me the *sfumato* effect, between the vaporous evanescence of the glazes and the depth of chromatic field. All, thanks to the science of enamels, seem to issue from magic: vibrations that escape and complement each other. (Some wink at me with their ceramic marshmallows, their baked-clay supports.)

Each of them has the crystallized fragility of paper architecture. Each of them evokes for me the static compositions of Giorgio Morandi.

All of them remind me of the diamond shapes of the Ruutu vases (2015)—that difference and unity are two sides of the same coin. All of them extend the exhibition *Seventeen Screens* (2015) in which Ronan & Erwan Bouroullec experimented with multiple modes of ceramic assemblage and enameled renderings.

Each of them specifically associates the blurry and the sharp, the shadow and the light.

All of them make up a diamond-shaped and oscillating atmosphere.

Clément Dirié, press release, November 2017

FRANÇOIS BAUCHET, *AZO*

a Invitation card:
  Azo rectangular coffee table, 2018
  Composite mineral material (sand, concrete, resin), h. 1 ft. 3 ¾ in. × w. 5 ft. 9 ½ in. × d. 2 ft. 8 ¼ in. (h. 40 × w. 176 × d. 82 cm)

  Azo bench, 2018
  Composite mineral material (sand, concrete, resin), h. 1 ft. 6 in. × w. 5 ft. 11 in. × d. 1 ft. 8 in. (h. 46 × w. 180 × d. 50 cm)

b Azo round table, 2018
  Composite mineral material (sand, concrete, resin), h. 2 ft. 5 in. × diam. 5 ft. 11 in. (h. 74 × diam. 180 cm)

c Azo oval coffee table, 2018
  Composite mineral material (sand, concrete, resin), h. 1 ft. 3 ¾ in. × w. 7 ft. 2 in. × d. 3 ft. 11 ¾ in. (h. 40 × w. 220 × d. 120 cm)

d Exhibition view:

  Azo high side table, 2018
  Composite mineral material (sand, concrete, resin), h. 34 ½ × diam. 17 ¼ in. (h. 88 × diam. 44 cm)

  Azo side table, 2018
  Composite mineral material (sand, concrete, resin), h. 18 × diam. 17 ¼ in. (h. 46 × diam. 44 cm)

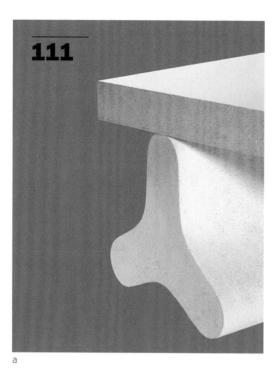

111

111 ✳

a

b

"With its imposing central leg and its resistant texture, which is so pleasant to the touch, François Bauchet's Azo table is for me an example of great functionality. Accompanied by Franz West's Doku Chairs, it is a daily pleasure to sit around it."
Émilie Pastor, collector, Monaco, 2019

c

d

For his Azo collection, François Bauchet continues his research on forms and materials, having developed an innovative composite material of sand, resin, and concrete. This endows the pieces with a mineral facet which is proposed in two colors: intense brick red and very pale gray. The pieces are composed of two main elements: a "clover"-shaped column, used vertically or horizontally as legs, and substantial surfaces of variable shapes and sizes. This new vocabulary of pure and simple forms—a recurring feature in Bauchet's work—is very graphic and sensual.
Press release, November 2017

a Invitation card
Volume M, 2018;
Volume U, 2018

b Exhibition view:

Volume T, 2018
Bleu de Savoie marble,
h. 23 ½ × w. 15 × d. 15 in.
(h. 60 × w. 38 × d. 38 cm)

Volume U, 2018
Bleu de Savoie marble,
h. 35 ½ × w. 17 ¾ × d. 15 in.
(h. 90 × w. 45 × d. 38 cm)

Volume L, 2018
Bleu de Savoie marble,
h. 35 ½ × w. 15 × d. 15 in.
(h. 90 × w. 38 × d. 38 cm)

Volume W, 2018
Bleu de Savoie marble,
h. 31 ½ × w. 25 ¼ × d. 15 in.
(h. 80 × w. 64 × d. 38 cm)

Volume M, 2018
Bleu de Savoie marble,
h. 23 ½ × w. 15 × d. 15 in.
(h. 60 × w. 38 × d. 38 cm)

Volume P, 2018
Bleu de Savoie marble,
h. 31 ½ in. × w. 15 × d. 15 in.
(h. 80 × w. 38 × d. 38 cm)

112

a

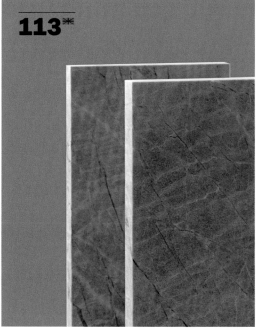

113＊

"The set of
VOLUMES by
Constantin Grcic
is a highlight of our
collection. The subtle
lines of the marble
make the shapes
of letters. Whether
used as functional
pieces or just
floating in space,
these pieces remind
me of the genius of
Grcic. The fine line
between purpose and
abstraction."

Jay Franke, collector
and patron, Chicago, 2019

There is a small but significant detail on Achille and Pier Giacomo Castiglioni's Arco lamp, which Konstantin Grcic admires. A hole runs through the solid rectangular marble base, wide enough for a broomstick to fit through such that two people can then use it to lift the stone. It's a humorous contradiction—the suave and luxurious marble making room for such a humble device to add something to the lamp's functionality. This detail is one that Grcic has applied to the six objects in the new Volumes collection. Executed in solid Bleu de Savoie stone, the pieces all have the same circular void cut through their bases. But while Arco is a lamp, Volumes has no such straightforward domestic function. The floor-standing pieces instead remain open-ended propositions for speculative uses. While Grcic is well known for engineering his industrial designs down to the smallest detail, he saw this project as an exercise in simplicity, both in expression and construction. The idea was to create objects that could be made using a singular material, without added structures or supports—they are sculpted rather than constructed. "I instantly thought of these objects as made out of stone," says Grcic. "As such they are cut away from a solid block rather than built up from different elements and components, which is my normal way of thinking and doing." However, the execution is more complicated than it might first appear. After each block has been cut into its desired shape, the freshly cut surface has a smooth and unnatural finish. This is a state that, typically, is emphasized and further polished for domestic use. But in a gesture that runs counter to the collection's domestic intention, the stone surfaces of the Volumes objects have been sandblasted, recreating something akin to the stone's natural and grainy texture. There is an inherent contradiction in this manmade naturalness that is both appealing and mystifying, befitting the question around what these objects are designed to do. Volumes conjures up other equally mute and monolithic structures which hint at functions that are unfamiliar or unknown. Consider flint axes from the Stone Age, clearly shaped into tools but now worn down enough to be confused with small rocks weathered by nature. Or the monolith most of us carry in our pocket—a black, shiny tablet that reveals its content at the touch of a thumbprint. Used as a tool to access digital-only data, this device has a mostly mineral body and, in the hands of future generations, may come to seem as foreign as the black monolithic slabs in science fiction author Arthur C. Clarke's 1968 *Space Odyssey*, transformed into a cinematic masterpiece by Stanley Kubrick. In *Space Odyssey*, Clarke describes the monolith as a machine, but nobody remembers what for.

Grcic's monoliths have similarly ambivalent characters. They have six distinct forms, approximately of the same volume as a stool or chair, hinting at their suggested purpose, but not enough to reveal their exact functions. There is a novelty and daring in this non-prescribed use.... The abstraction of Volumes is, therefore, an intriguing turn away from the cerebral and towards the instinctive—towards making objects of uncertain use.

Johanna Agerman Ross, press release, May 2018

b

September 27–November 17, 2018—31, rue Dauphine, Paris

JEAN-MICHEL SANEJOUAND,
OPÉRATION CONTACT

An exhibition by
Jean-Michel Sanejouand
featuring pieces by
Ronan & Erwan Bouroullec
Pierre Charpin
Hella Jongerius
Julia Lohmann
Jasper Morrison
Studio Wieki Somers
Organized in collaboration
with Olivier Antoine, Galerie
Art Concept, Paris

a Invitation card:
*Châssis carré et croix
de tissu blanc*, 1964
Wood, canvas, pencil, h. 31 ½ ×
w. 31 ½ in. (h. 80 × w. 80 cm)

b Exhibition view:

*Planche à repasser
avec lacet*, 1966
Wood, canvas, metal, string,
h. 4 ft. 3 ¾ in. × w. 1 ft. 2 ¾ in. ×
d. 1 ³⁄₁₆ in. (h. 129.5 × w. 37.5 ×
d. 3 cm)

Jean-Michel Sanejouand
for Atelier A
Symétrique rocking chair
and foot rest, 1969
Steel, leather, h. 2 ft. 5 ½ in. ×
w. 3 ft. 1 ½ in. × d. 5 ft. 2 in.
(h. 75 × w. 95 × d. 157.5 cm)

c Exhibition view:

*Châssis, grillage plastique
rouge et grillage jaune sur
toile bleue*, 1965
Wood, canvas, plastic,
mesh, h. 8 ft. 1 in. × w. 2 ft.
(h. 248 × w. 60 cm)

Jeu de Topo, 1963

Monochrome bleu derrière,
1964
Fabric, wood, h. 3 ft. 3 in. ×
w. 2 ft. 8 in. (h. 100 × w. 81 cm)

d Exhibition view:

*Châssis encre noire
sur bâche à rayures*, 1966
Wood, tarp canvas, ink, h. 3 ft.
3 in. × w. 2 ft. 8 in. (h. 100 ×
w. 81 cm)

En losanges, 1964
Wood, plastic, h. 7 ft. 5 in. ×
w. 3 ft. 8 ½ in. (h. 226 ×
w. 113 cm)

114

a

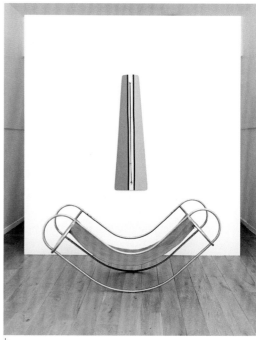

b

c

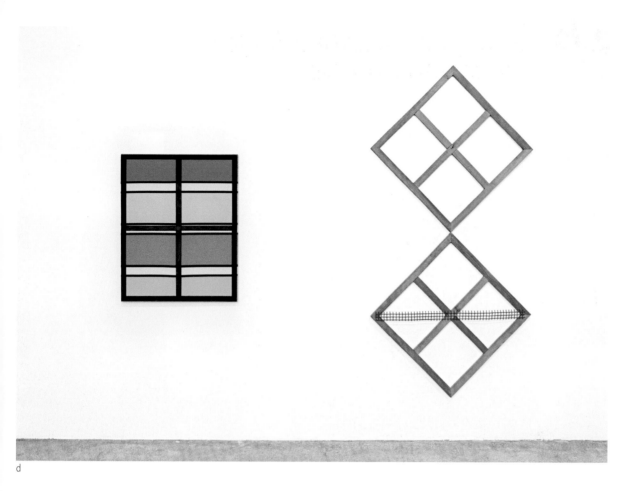

d

In 1964, in a Parisian gallery located in rue du Bac, Jean-Michel Sanejouand began his prolific artistic journey in which he established himself as an incessant pioneer, by revealing his "Charges-objets." Fifty-five years later, Galerie kreo is exhibiting these to highlight their historical importance. Conceived in the mid-1960s as a critical response to the promises of the *Trente Glorieuses* (the Glorious Thirty Years following the end of World War II) and the artistic expressions that accompanied them, the Charges-objets constitute a significant, and paradoxically rather unknown, milestone in the history of French and international contemporary art. By choosing a very singular way to stage the object—beyond Marcel Duchamp's readymade, divergent from the surrealists' practice, more scathing than that of the New Realists— Sanejouand realized an act of bravery: one of a pioneer for

whom experimentation is never as energetic as when it can also be mischievous.

What are these Charges-objets created between 1962 and 1967? There are many answers, as their relevance lies in their multiple and open nature. Here are some definitions, each one complementary to each other: subjective associations of "fascinating objects for nothing," according to the artist. Instruments to emancipate the gaze and disturb our relationship to objects—whether they are manufactured products used unchanged (ironing boards, wire mesh, linoleum), or old abstract paintings redeployed without affectation. Bitter aphorisms about the "system of objects," described by Jean Baudrillard in 1968. A series of works whose title sounds like a warning, each piece constituting an uncompromising portrait of our industrial, artistic,

and economic modernity. Proof of the artist's undeniable talent as a colorist. Exercises in irony toward the status of the artwork, the artistic movements of the postwar period, and the sacrosanct painting form. A French response to Donald Judd's "Specific Objects." A way of examining the organization of space and the relationships between things: "the Charges-objets responded to a sudden urgent need to experiment with concrete space and a violent desire to provoke this space," Jean-Michel Sanejouand recalled in 1986. This was one of his major concerns during his fifty years of creation, as illustrated by his fascinating *Jeu de Topo* (1963), in which the outcome of each game is determined by the agreement of the two players on the best possible arrangement of the pebbles turned-pawns.

Clément Dirié, press release, September 2018

2018

A PLACE TO DWELL

Franco Albini
François Bauchet
Ronan & Erwan Bouroullec
Pierre Charpin
Jaime Hayon
Hella Jongerius
Alessandro Mendini
Jean-Michel Sanejouand
Studio Wieki Somers

———————

a   Invitation card:
François Bauchet
Melancholia mirror, 2014
Printed and silvered mirror,
lacquered MDF, h. 30 ×
w. 23 × d. 1 ¾ in. (h. 77 ×
w. 60 × d. 4.5 cm)

b   Exhibition view (on the
wall):
Jean-Michel Sanejouand
8.10.84, 1984
Diptych, acrylic on canvas,
h. 7 ft. 10 in. × w. 6 ft. 3 in.
(h. 2.40 × w. 1.90 m)

a

Echoing the Paris exhibition, a work
from Jean-Michel Sanejouand's
series of *Espaces Peintures* (1978–
86) is presented in the midst of a
collection of furniture by Franco Albini
and Gino Sarfatti, representing the
masters of Italian design, and pieces
by Alessandro Mendini, Ronan &
Erwan Bouroullec, and Jaime Hayon,
for the designers of today.

Press release, September 2018

b

a Invitation card

b Exhibition view:

Jolly mirror, 2018
Mirror, lacquered wood,
h. 3 ft. 6 in. × w. 3 ft 7 ¼ in.
(h. 1.07 × w. 1.10 m)

HYMY coffee table, 2018
Marble, lacquered wood,
h. 13 ¾ × diam. 35 ½ in.
(h. 35 × diam. 90 cm)

HYMY table, 2018
Carrara marble, Marquina
marble, metal, h. 2 ft 5 ½ in. ×
w. 9 ft. 2 in. × d. 3 ft. 3 in.
(h. 75 × w. 280 × d. 100 cm)

Cheeky mirror, 2018
Mirror, lacquered wood,
h. 5 ft. 8 in. × w. 5 ft. 4 in.
(h. 1.73 × w. 1.63 m)

c Exhibition view:

Blueto vase, 2018
Murano glass, marble,
h. 15 ¼ × diam. 14 ¾ in.
(h. 39 × diam. 37.3 cm)

Oceanoz vase, 2018
Murano glass, marble,
h. 19 ¾ × diam. 11 in.
(h. 50 × diam. 28 cm)

Ropojom vase, 2018
Murano glass, marble,
h. 17 × w. 14 × d. 8 in.
(h. 43.4 × w. 35.9 ×
d. 21.5 cm)

Verdino vase, 2018
Murano glass, marble,
h. 21 ½ × w. 12 ½ × d. 8 ¼ in.
(h. 54.6 × w. 31.6 × d. 22 cm)

Pinkoz vase, 2018
Murano glass, marble,
h. 20 × w. 12 ½ × d. 8 ½ in.
(h. 50.8 × w. 31.5 × d. 22 cm)

Mentolato vase, 2018
Murano glass, marble,
h. 21 ½ × w. 13 × d. 10 ½ in.
(h. 56.4 × w. 33.2 ×
d. 27 cm)

Darkol vase, 2018
Murano glass, marble,
h. 21 ½ × w. 12 × d. 8 ½ in.
(h. 54.6 × w. 31.6 × d. 22 cm)

Jolly mirror, 2018

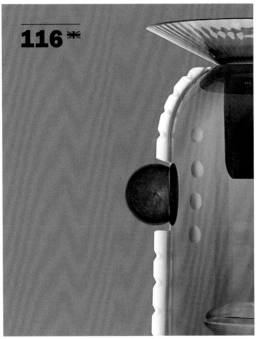

116 ✳

a

117

There are two main subjects in this body of work,
each focused on a different noble material.
In London the show is devoted to a colorful group
of vases made in hand-blown Murano glass.
In 2018 Hayon first designed a special set of
vases for the Milwaukee Art Museum Collection
(Afrikando), using the rough finish of the
handmade African masks as a starting point,
giving an utterly different approach. For Galerie
kreo, he pursues this inspiration. He is interested
in the colorful side of Africa, its crafts, its
textures… and he adds his personal playful touch
to these delicate works. The contrast between the
strong power of the African world and the use of
glass as a material— a liquid way of working that
adds flexibility and freedom—results in a range of
pieces full of joy and sophistication. He has used a
mix of strong colors like golden reds, greens, or
oranges with very subdued ones in contrast.
The bases are made in precious marbles in
delightful tones like Rosa Portogallo or Giallo
Siena, which complete the works and give them
physical and emotional stability.

   The Paris gallery is exhibiting a group of
works which shows the same interest in material
and color, but in this case, devoted to marble.

The central theme of the collection is the work
in stone marquetry, a traditional craft that is part
of our Mediterranean culture, a subject that Hayon
is always eager to explore with rigor and respect
for techniques and materials. It consists of a range
of tables of all sizes made in Vicenza and Verona
marbles, in which the hard material has been
domesticated by Hayon through his signature soft
lines and curves, giving each piece its own unique
character. The pared-down geometric patterns
of the tabletops employ Hayon's characteristic
iconography, an abstract appearance with
a figurative touch: the winking eye, the smile.…
Again, the colors of the marbles are central to
these pieces: from the classic black and white
combination to a mix of bold shades of greens,
reds, and yellows, all reinforced with lacquered
wood bases, sometimes striped for a greater
impact.

Ana Domínguez Siemens, December 2018

"A sublime marble marquetry made to perfection.
The soothing evocation of Italy, of clowns. Jaime evokes
in me, with joy, with humor, delicacy, and mischief,
the heartbreaking memory of the Way of the Cross
of Gelsomina from *La Strada* by Fellini. *Grazie.*"
Bruno E. Borie, collector, Château Ducru Beaucaillou, Bordeaux, 2019

b

c

RONAN & ERWAN BOUROULLEC, *DRAWINGS*

a Invitation card

b Exhibition view:
Series of drawings by
Ronan Bouroullec, 2018
Felt pens on paper, each:
h. 29 ¾ × w. 29 ¾ in.
(h. 76 × w. 76 cm)

c Erwan Bouroullec
Terrain 1, 2018
Digital drawing, h. 5 ft.
1 in. × w. 4 ft. 2 in. (h. 1.55 ×
w. 1.27 m)

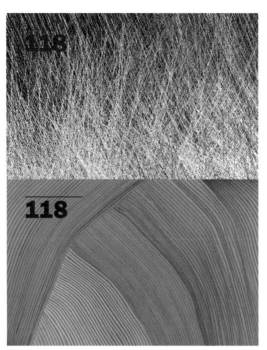

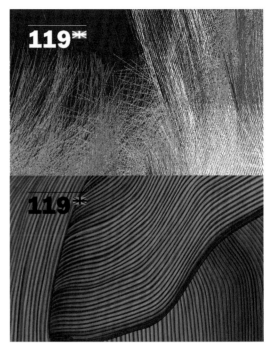

a

Let us first and foremost look at what we see: two series of drawings showing distinct compositions, formats, modes of production, and universes of evocation. Both share the same generous use of color, mastery of space, taste for combining elements, and a rigorous and informed approach to the physicality of drawing.

The first series by Ronan Bouroullec includes work in five different formats, all dated 2018, in which each element is only referenced by its place of creation. Covering the walls of the gallery, it shows a set of ink and Japanese brush pen drawings on glossy paper. The hand gesture, always similar yet always novel, organically deposits a trajectory of color on the glossy surface. Made on a daily basis, the drawings accompany the designer day after day, like a diary. Suspended moments in time, they express a great fluidity, a frank simplicity. Forms and furrows pass from one sheet of paper to another in an almost infinite continuum. Colors are rarely mixed, dialogueuing through recurrences and similarities. The gesture is sometimes ample and sometimes more constrained, saturating the paper with more or less intensity. All express colorful sensations, spontaneous compositional

intuitions, without a single protocol ever being followed. An autonomous practice, made possible by the economy of means and by the freedom— that intimate plenitude—which Ronan Bouroullec allows himself when, outside of his studio, he is faced with a page waiting to be tested. Are these drawings meant to be read and interpreted? Or should they be encountered, as we would a familiar tune? It is up to each of us to decide, according to our own references—surrealist, contemporary, or idiosyncratic.

The second series by Erwan Bouroullec is composed of twelve drawings with descriptive titles, *Marché, Forêt, Chantier,* or *Pile.* These drawings are digital in a double sense: they are not only produced by digital printing, but also conceived using a specially developed software, which processes the photographs chosen for their structure and color compositions. The result is a series of "translations": from the eye to the lens, from pixel to digital coding, from software to printing, from figurative to abstract, from the chosen subject to the image produced—all this gives birth to complementary optical games, simultaneously macroscopic and microscopic. Each drawing reminds us that every image

b

is the result of a process and a succession
of choices: framing, format, color saturation,
considerations of perspective and depth....
All of them testify to a tension between contact
and contrast, between the life of each line and
its encounter with all the others, between the
amplitude of its radiation and its ability to blend
into a network. Through their appearance and their
mode of production, these digital drawings are
both mental exercises—how to show the shapes,
structures, and colors in movement that make
up the bare thread of our reality—and aesthetic
reveries, sometimes melancholic, sometimes
chaotic, sometimes joyful, always fascinating.
It is up to each of us to exercise our sagacity in
the face of a reality which has thus been redrawn.

The brothers, Ronan and Erwan Bouroullec,
have been working together since 1998. This
eleventh exhibition is therefore an event for them
as well as for the gallery. It is indeed the first
time they have exhibited together their respective
personal drawing practices.

Clément Dirié, February 2019

c

April 18–July 26, 2019—31, rue Dauphine, Paris

GUILLAUME BARDET

Born in 1971, Guillaume Bardet lives in Dieulefit, France.

a Invitation card

b Exhibition view:

Grande table, 2019
Bronze, h. 2 ft. 5 ½ in. × w. 15 ft. 4 in. × d. 4 ft. 3 in. (h. 75 × w. 468 × d. 130 cm)
Fondation d'entreprise Martell Collection

Tabouret n°1 à n°13, 2019
Bronze, various dimensions

120

a

At the nearby Barthélémy Foundry in Crest, Guillaume Bardet learned how bronze figures are initially made using wax. He bought 110 lb. (50 kg) of wax and began working. Through his decision to circumvent the process, he rediscovered "the power of his sketches in wax." The first object he created was an everyday cup from an impression of an Amora glass—fragile, uneven, sturdy. Then he shaped other models in wax, with polystyrene casings: a long table, stools, pitchers, benches, and lamps, always playing with different light. He listened to the radio station France Culture, read and wrote; as part of a ritual of direct and indirect thought, his actions became intertwined with the words and the world's workings. His pieces, which all evoke a particular usage, made their way around his workshop before finding their rightful place. And so a timeless and unchanging scene was created with a long table, stools, bottles, and glasses. He saw it as a metaphor for the Last Supper. The Last Supper? Guillaume Bardet was hesitant to use this religious and artistic symbol, which he saw as taboo. He's not religious and didn't want to offend anyone.

But having listened to René Girard, the religious anthropologist, he understood that the Last Supper can also represent faith in humanity. Slowly, he developed an idea for his own Last Supper. It would express what remains of the cyclical nature of mankind's humanity, with thirteen stools to represent the apostles, human beings in all their diversity, from redemption to betrayal. He gave himself permission to call this universal, earthly, and informal banqueting scene *La Cène* [the Last Supper]. Back at the foundry in Crest, a successful and welcoming organization, the time came for the most exciting stage of the process. His work became solid pieces of glittering bronze. He learned everything he could about the process. Most importantly of all, he witnessed the magical process of bronze being poured into molds, every Monday: the alchemy of the glowing metal inspired him to create a perfectly polished lamp. This was followed by the carving process, before he used various nitrates to create a patina finish. He spent hours polishing his enormous table, poured in six pieces, weighing almost 2,000 lb. (900 kg) and measuring 15 ft. 7 in. (4.75 m): a challenge within a challenge. He created a landscape of "wobbly and powerful, fragile and long-lasting" pieces. He lived in a bubble, between his workshop and the foundry, taking the time to create and to wait, a perfectionist on the hunt for just the right imperfection. Now, Galerie kreo is to exhibit part of his *Fabrique du présent* [Present-day Factory], *La Cène* [The Last Supper], already displayed in wax at Le Corbusier's Couvent de la Tourette in 2017. An oblong black table, uneven, huge but with a smooth tabletop, in bronze tones, with three solid and different table legs; thirteen expressive variations of black stools; black, dented, and damaged bottles and glasses, with flashes of gold and other colors. And an enormous lamp which balances out the physicality of the composition of this still life scene which is so full of life and harmonious, which illuminates this call to feast and creates a shared experience. At first glance, these pieces have an archaic feel, molded by the archaeology of so many recollections. But they also demonstrate the power of the transfigured, contemporary bronze in its brilliant shades of black and with its satin-finished brutality, its movement and asymmetrical shapes which reflect the faltering yet everlasting world in which he uncovers this "uniquely human tremor".... Guillaume Bardet has managed to forge and tame both the bronze metal and his soul, with a prolific disquiet all of his own which has become his strength.

Anne-Marie Fèvre, April 2019

b

Born in 1984,
Jean-Baptiste Fastrez lives
in Paris.

a   Invitation card

b   Jellyfish ceiling light, 2019
Aluminum, Perspex,
h. 55 in. × diam. 16 ¼ in.
(h. 140 × diam. 41 cm)

c   Crocodile coffee table,
2019
Marble and steel, h. 1 ft.
3 in. × w. 7 ft. 4 in. × d. 2 ft.
5 in. (h. 39 × w. 224 ×
d. 74 cm)

121✳

a

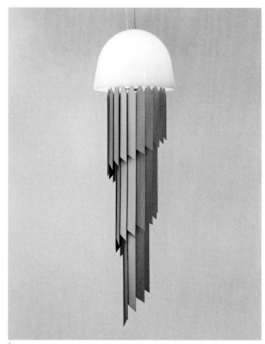

b

c

What is the missing link between the animal kingdom and the object? In his new exhibition *Vivarium*, Jean-Baptiste Fastrez offers a very personal response to this issue: eight works, comprising furniture and objects, presented like animals in a jar, within the London gallery. In this bestiary, the designer has invited only wild— sometimes dangerous—animals, which he has tamed and placed as if they were in a vivarium. In his subtle work of representation, which he approaches with a distant gaze, we recognize each animal by a clue, as so many enigmas to resolve in order to affirm a familiar but never obvious presence. The mirror's sinuous curve resembles a snake, the green marble from the Alps evokes crocodile skin, and the console's marble recalls the hide of an elephant. Fastrez, as always, mixes natural and synthetic materials. Corian is combined with natural stone; the anodized aluminum pendants and the polycarbonate lampshade of the Medusa lamp seem to have just risen from the waters. This synergy between form, technique, and narration guides his work. The

objects always recount a tale and animals constitute an inexhaustible source of inspiration, because they are loaded with symbolic power, referring to our human attachment to life. This work on animal textures follows the Masks mirror collection with frames in acetate looking like horn and tortoiseshell, which marked the first collaboration between Galerie kreo and Fastrez seven years ago. Since then, zoomorphism has continued to permeate his work as a designer, from his butterfly glasses to his Beetle vase, and he endeavors to synthesize animality without any folklore. *Vivarium* is rooted in the 1930s and especially in Jean Dunand's work, providing a more abstract and contemporary version. A rediscovered balance between rationality and free forms, abstraction and narration in which Fastrez navigates with humor and subtlety, indeed, with a certain welcoming irony.

Marie Godfrain, press release, May 2019

Barber & Osgerby
Guillaume Bardet
François Bauchet
Camille Blin
Ronan & Erwan
Bouroullec
Andrea Branzi
Joschua Brunn
Pierre Charpin
David Dubois
Jean-Baptiste Fastrez
Front Design
Naoto Fukasawa
Olivier Gagnère
Garouste & Bonetti
Konstantin Grcic
Jaime Hayon
James Irvine
Hella Jongerius
Chris Kabel
Julia Lohmann
Alessandro Mendini
Jasper Morrison
Muller Van Severen
Marc Newson
Radi Designers
Julie Richoz
Samy Rio
Daniel Rybakken
Gino Sarfatti
Jerszy Seymour
Ettore Sottsass
Studio Wieki Somers
Maarten Van Severen

a   Invitation card

122

20 ans

a

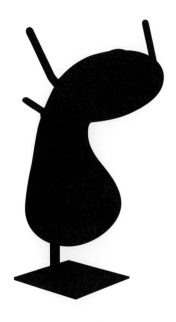

THE COMPANIONS

JOHANNA AGERMAN ROSS

GUILLAUME HOUZÉ

DONATIEN GRAU

BERTRAND LAVIER AND DIDIER KRZENTOWSKI

ALEX COLES

CHRISTIAN SCHLATTER

MARCO ROMANELLI

MARCEL BRIENT

JOHANNA AGERMAN ROSS

Curator of Twentieth-Century and Contemporary Furniture
and Product Design, Victoria & Albert Museum, London;
founder and director of the quarterly design journal *Disegno*

WHEN TYPOLOGIES CHANGE

"Let's buy a pipe that is really a pipe, let's fill it with real tobacco, light a match that looks like a match and works like a match, and apply it to the pipe-pipe. Let us have a cup of coffee in a cuplike cup on a table-table on our chairlike chair, and read a good book-book."

These words were written by Bruno Munari in *Design as Art* (1966), composed in reaction to objects that Munari had encountered which had been designed to look other than what they were: "An umbrella like a pagoda, a table lamp made of a clarinet (likewise, a trumpet), with a lampshade of sheet music." Munari felt nauseated by these kitsch suggestions. He called for design with more clarity and certainty.

In the half-century that has passed since Munari published *Design as Art*, definitions of objects have shifted drastically, as have our expectations of them. A phone is no longer just a *phone-phone*—it is a communication platform that we rely on for most of our interactions, information gathering, and entertainment. A lamp is not just a *lamp-lamp*—it can be equipped with motion sensors, charging pads, and data-capturing technology.

In light of technological advances, typologies always shift; they give birth to new forms and new ways of considering our relationship to objects. At the same time, those same objects become charged with meanings we may not previously have considered.

In this process of morphing typologies, design galleries and museums become crucial platforms for experimentation. They are spaces that enable the exploration of new uses. Without the constraints associated with mass manufacture, temporary exhibition spaces—and the financial support to develop ideas that they enable—allow for objects and their function to be pushed further, inviting discussion and critical discourse around the environments we want to live in and how we might best serve them.

Over the last twenty years, Galerie kreo has been one such space, pushing thinking around design—both its uses and manufacture—forward. But we have also

View of the exhibition
Ronan & Erwan Bouroullec, Galerie kreo, Paris, 2001
Center:
Parasol lumineux, 2001

Above, left
Julia Lohmann
View of the Cow Bench
collection in front of
the designer's studio,
London, 2005

Above, right
Pierre Charpin
Monolith, 8 ½
collection, 2008
Stand/hanger in
brilliant polished resin,
h. 5 ft. 10 in. ×
diam. 4 ⅜ in. (h. 178 ×
diam. 11 cm)

seen the rise of events such as the design biennale and spaces for more open-ended conversations around the designed object and its meaning in society. This is a welcome engagement with design as an autonomous form and it gives design a sense of importance that previously was reserved solely for art and architecture.

Open questions on ways to live

The first solo exhibition by Ronan & Erwan Bouroullec at Galerie kreo in the summer of 2001 contained object types that were difficult to place in relationship to existing furniture. The almost 6½ × 6½ ft. (2 × 2 m) light canopy Parasol lumineux was not so much a lamp as a way of dividing space without the use of physical structures. Instead, it let the light itself define an area. The same could be said for *Cabane*, a cage-like hub made from wide strips of felt that left one side entirely open to create an inviting, rather than restrictive, space.

"Our objects are tools which make their own solution, they are open questions on ways to live," said Ronan and Erwan at the time. Recognizing that where we live and work is shifting—from clearly defined spaces to more fluid interior landscapes—the studio's work has continued to explore these unknown territories through proposals for seating platforms, sofa boxes, draped lights, and textile room dividers that play on the visual language of airing rugs or hanging laundry. That fluidity and flexibility is now a common feature within design and the recognition that design needs to respond to more nomadic living patterns and open-plan spaces.

While the use of objects is crucial for our understanding of them, we tend to be less preoccupied with how things are actually made and what they are made from. This was something that Julia Lohmann questioned when working on the Cow Bench project in 2005, exhibited at Galerie kreo in 2006. Here, Lohmann created anything but a *bench-bench*, instead producing a seat in the shape of a stylized cow torso. If the clarinet lamps Munari observed were entirely nonsensical, Lohmann's cow

benches were a clear provocation—their final form mimicking the origins of the leather that covered the object. To add to this effect, Lohmann even gave the benches names typical of cows: *Rosel, Belinda, Raul, Eileen, Carla, Elsa, Radia*. "We don't want our food to remind us of the animal it is made of and, at the same time are able to create living materials through advances in bio-technology," said Lohmann at the time. "The Cow Bench explores the threshold between animal and material."

Lohmann's project became a commentary on our own distance from the source material of the objects we encounter and handle on a daily basis. Since the development of these "bovine memento mori"—as Lohmann called them—this discussion has been brought to the fore within wider design production. Social Label in the Netherlands is a project that itemizes both materials and labor used within design and production, mapping the true costs of both. Belgian fashion designer Bruno Pieters' Honest By initiative was founded on the premise that both the materials used and the people crafting those materials into garments should be clearly credited—a desire to use transparency to create a closer connection between consumers and often distant factories.

The psychology of an object, its ability to instill confidence or communicate its strengths and desirability within its form was a point of experimentation for Konstantin Grcic when he designed the CHAMPIONS collection in 2011. Each table in the series was emblazoned with names and tags more typically associated with performance-related equipment, such as skis or bicycles. "I want the tables to appear like they are Formula 1 cars lined up on the starting grid of a race track," said Grcic of the series. Rather than using transfer foils, which are custom-made for sports equipment, each table was painted by lacquer artist Walter Maurer. While the visual language resembled a fast-paced performance object, the artistic execution was more closely related, for instance, to the painted furniture of the nineteenth century. Consider architect John P. Seddon's own desk from 1861, in the Victoria & Albert Museum's collection. Its painted panels, which depict the medieval King René of Anjou, a notable patron of the arts, were executed by the artists Ford Madox Brown, Edward Burne-Jones, and Dante Gabriel Rossetti. The completed panels representing "architecture," "painting," and "sculpture" were intended to act as an inspirational aid for Seddon, in much the same way the user of Grcic's CHAMPIONS tables might feel spurred on by their visual language quoting the colors and wording of sports equipment. While this level of decoration is one that feels familiar from postmodern design and the work of Studio Alchimia or Memphis, the implication of the CHAMPIONS pieces is different. It's imperative, not passive.

Familiar but different

Object as provocation—that is probably the most accurate way of considering the pieces that have come out of Galerie kreo over the last twenty years. They are not forgone conclusions and they don't represent finite thinking. Neither are they prototypes or unfinished experiments. The works developed through Galerie kreo are highly refined and executed objects in their own right. In their accomplished craftsmanship we can decipher real possibilities for changing attitudes within the design industry—not just speculative ideas.

Galerie kreo's objects are highly functioning pieces intended for use. They are *lamp-lamps* and *table-tables* and *chair-chairs*, just not how Munari considered them. Here the work of Wieki Somers comes to mind—dreamy and surreal and almost otherworldly in execution. Somers creates the kinds of objects you might consider in wonder. The *Frozen in Time* exhibition from 2010 gave the illusion of being coated in a thin layer of ice, causing slight distortion and a feeling of the uncanny. Familiar but different. And that is a sensation that runs through much of the work that Galerie kreo presents, whether it's Hella Jongerius's Cupboards collection from 2005—so-called 3D sketches or object collages—or Pierre Charpin's totemic Monolith from 2008, they

all contribute to a feeling of something familiar that has been gently twisted to prompt us to look in a new direction.

While the monetary value of these limited-edition pieces can't be overlooked, it is also entirely possible to consider them as separate to the market. Their display can be appreciated without buying or engaging with them on a commercial level. In that regard they are also designed to suit platforms geared towards debate. These objects want to trigger thought, feeling, and action. Somers communicates this intention and potential particularly clearly when speaking about *Frozen in Time*: "I feel objects should convey the idea of memory, the idea of a world beyond bare functionality and beyond first appearances. We want to transfer the well known by asking unusual questions, in order to trigger the imagination of the user and discover the unknown."

That uncertainty is vital for pushing the debate around purpose, use, and manufacture forward. Even better is that it does not need to add to the cacophony of differing opinions; instead, it has the strength and ability to be non-verbal, taking place within the carefully considered form and surface of an *object-object*. One that you can *use-use*.

Top
John Pollard Seddon,
Ford Madox Brown,
Dante Gabriel Rossetti,
William Morris,
Edward Burne-Jones,
and Val Prinsep
*King René's
Honeymoon Cabinet*,
1861
Oak, inlaid with various
woods, with painted
metalwork and painted
panels, h. 4 ft. 4 ½ in. ×
w. 8 ft. 3 in. × d. 2 ft.
10 in. (h. 133.4 ×
w. 252 × d. 87 cm)
Victoria & Albert
Museum Collection,
London

Bottom
Konstantin Grcic
View of the exhibition
CHAMPIONS,
Galerie kreo, Paris,
2011

GUILLAUME HOUZÉ

President, Lafayette Anticipations–
Fondation d'entreprise Galeries Lafayette, Paris

BEING TWENTY
(YEARS AHEAD)

Twenty years is a mythical age, an ideal age, when one has the strength of one's convictions and mental clarity. It is both a happy yet serious age; an age of birthdays, of retrospectives, of assessments, but also a turning point.

Galerie kreo is twenty years old, twenty years spent at the vanguard—twenty years of design, suspended, literally, between the world of ideas and the world of forms. By the very nature of its stance and its history, Clémence and Didier Krzentowski's firm remains a venture, a project whose sole ambition is to shake up the world by catering for objects that live out on its margins. As such, and together with real talents, they have succeeded in redefining the practice of design, situating it in a broader relationship with being and having. Their research has led them to subvert the codes of the industry and to attain a new state, free of borders and authority. The choice of the Esperanto word "*kreo*" to designate design says a lot, it seems to me, about their vocation: to turn design into a vehicular language between different cultures, to create a unified zone of expression through use, and to take—as Francis Ponge does in *Le parti-pris des choses*—the "side of things."

Their gallery is one of a kind, a laboratory that fosters the unique thinking of all its creatives, allowing them to present to the world new figures that often *prefigure* it. Galerie kreo gives them carte blanche for their future endeavors, and it is there, in the future, that we find ourselves when amongst the gallery's designers, many of whom, in their own way, stood by my side for several years as part of the ongoing development of Lafayette Anticipations, the Galeries Lafayette corporate foundation, whose production aims so often to expand on work at Galerie kreo. A crazy but oh-so-telling project comes to mind: the pavilion of the *Extra National Assembly* #1 we helped Jerszy Seymour erect on the side of a Swiss mountain. Over two days in October 2014, philosophers, researchers, artists, and hikers climbed up in droves to discuss identity.

Facing page
Hella Jongerius
Views of the exhibition
*Interlace, Textile
Research*, Lafayette
Anticipations–
Fondation d'entreprise
Galeries Lafayette,
Paris, 2019

We experienced a similar act of forging new connections in 2019, literally, with Hella Jongerius's *Interlace*. The very structure of our foundation, designed by Rem Koolhaas, was treated as a total system for her work. As visitors looked on, materials were stacked up and power tools hummed to bring back to life a world of craftsmanship that globalization tends to obscure.

It is the reevaluation of gesture and memory that is, I am convinced, the hallmark of a great designer. I have observed this on several occasions, particularly with Ronan & Erwan Bouroullec, with whom we worked renovating the fountains at the rond-point des Champs-Élysées. Funded by the Fonds pour Paris, this unique commission demonstrates that design is not only the expression of time present: it also furthers a sense of our responsibility to the past.

If the tension between the historic and the contemporary strikes everyone in the creative industries, designers—and in particular those whose paths have crossed mine at Galerie kreo—remain the best placed to reflect on, express, and even celebrate this fact. I love seeing this in my everyday world; it is what drove me to become a collector. Not obviously so, to turn my environment into a museum, but to make it conscious, and to make *me* conscious, even in the most ordinary manifestations of existence, that the world has existed prior to all of us.

Sitting down, switching on a light, writing, eating are all acts freighted with archetypes, with references. Each time a designer tackles such an activity, however exalted or subtle his intentions might be, he deflects the course of events, opening the door to the possibility of something different.

Above
Jerszy Seymour
Extra National Assembly #1, Glarus, Switzerland 2014
Project produced by Lafayette Anticipations under the auspices of the Klöntal Triennale, Glarus, Switzerland
On October 11 and 12, 2014, the pavilion hosted a forum on questions such as nationhood, identity, and territoriality

Facing page
Ronan & Erwan Bouroullec
Champs-Élysées Fountains, rond-point des Champs-Élysées, Paris, 2019
Crystal and bronze aluminum alloy: h. 42 ft. 3 in. (h. 13 m)
Commission launched by the Fonds pour Paris—private capital fund of the City of Paris

DONATIEN GRAU

Writer and art critic

THE MEMBRANE
OF THINGS

Most of the time we do not question the categories of things. We encircle them in the rings of their definition, where they can be kept in place—locked up, some might even say. And we no longer have to think about their location, their identity, their relationship to the world and to the human. Of course, some thinkers have attempted to envision the freedom of things—things that would be able to be everything and nothing, without a fixed identity. Such an approach, however beautiful and poetic it may seem, risks calling into question all our systems of definition. A work of art is not a piece of furniture.

And yet, the space for play, of the becoming of things, this fluid space is the one that at once fascinates and alarms us the most: the space of objects with multiple identities, ever-changing, shimmering, altering according to the light of their denomination, and whose creators make transformation into a significant element of their presence. The risk of confusion is made even more complex by the ambiguities of their makers, whose identities sometimes allow them to produce forms on which they are not necessarily an authority, but whose appropriation further increases their charge. This is the world we live in.

Faced with this world, the Galerie kreo offers a ready antidote. The experience of this antidote has always enthralled me: as one is faced with the indeterminacy of things with respect to their denomination, and confronted with objects and makers that play both sides—such an expression is not meant to be pejorative—each with a dual identity, which, like a passport, makes it possible, at any time, to be on the right side of the border at the right moment, the gallery's exhibitions and projects allow one to experience the very membrane of things. They let us sense at once what is inside and what is outside—the frontier of a thing that is itself, that is none other than itself, that asserts itself as something else only as itself.

Everything that design is not, with everything that it is: Galerie kreo sets up encounters and fruitful confrontations in areas such as form, ethics, poetics.

Their very titles speak volumes, because they hint at confluences, at associations: "One thing can only really be known by comparing it to another," said Georges Dumézil. This is a principle of anthropology, of discernment, of all thought.

The *Ensemble* exhibition proposed a confrontation between design pieces and works and manuscripts from the collection of Marcel Brient, a friend of the gallery's with a sharp eye. Seeing manuscripts by Rimbaud next to works by Bruce Nauman, Michel Majerus, and Marc Newson opens us up to sharing in an ethics of things. Each remains absolutely, resolutely, uncompromisingly itself: no one incarnates poetry more than the poet Rimbaud, absorbing the entire history of poetry and its beauty and then abusing it in one supreme act of love. In Marc Newson's and Bruce Nauman's creations, the genealogies, the sources that mean that a thing never exists alone, that it invokes so many precedents and descendants, are clear for all to see: Richard Prince, Jasper Morrison, histories of technology—recent, less recent, archaic, about how the world is made. At its very end, the thing is complete: the membrane determines its unique form, allowing the thing, once its order has been established, to transform itself, to mutate inside until it exactly counterbalances the order it might have been restricted to by its limits. But if, after Rimbaud and Nauman, we turned our gaze on designer furniture, what would happen? Even in transition, they would remain themselves. Rimbaud and Newson, together: the membranes turn out real.

In 2017, *Didier Lavier* brought together works by Bertrand Lavier and a selection of design pieces by, among others, François Bauchet, Ronan & Erwan Bouroullec, and Gino Sarfatti. There we brushed against the very membrane of things, made visible, perceptible: where the artist's work, grasped as a counterpoint to the things of this world, appropriated, transformed, redeemed, and made manifest, merges into and runs counter to the objects of life, whose counterpoint is internalized, since they are quite literally things of the world. The question of use was redirected, being no longer asked from the point of view of design but from that of the confrontation with art. It was a conversation on the glory of objects. With the soft toy and its glass case (see p. 258, top left), each *exhibits* the other. Looking at Didier Krzentowski and Bertrand Lavier together illuminates both.

Among the designer pieces on display, so many could be described as art; but, for Clémence and Didier Krzentowski, the imperative of functionality affirms, with no possible contradiction, that the object is design and not art—a modern opposition that states where the game is to be played out. Yet this opposition also opens the door to experimentation: that of Konstantin Grcic, who created the Hieronymus collection, whose origin was distilled from a painting by Antonello da Messina, *St. Jerome in his Study* (c. 1474–75, National Gallery, London); or that of Ronan & Erwan Bouroullec, who showed drawings in the Galerie kreo to coincide with the unveiling of their public fountain on the Champs-Élysées. People tried to read these drawings as forms, these forms as furniture, already designed or for the future. It was not design, it was drawing: a contemporary manifestation of the *arte del designo*, which was at the same time, by design, both design and drawing. Fluid in status, the authorship of these graphic works was clearly demarcated: some were by Ronan and others by Erwan, and each possessed his own poetics, separate from that of his brother and co-designer. Were they artworks? Sketches? They were, first and foremost, drawings: so, there again, we return to functionality. The use of a drawing is to be a drawing. Categories are not boundaries: they ought to be the flexible yet firm membrane that marks the interaction and not the separation between things.

All the exhibitions in a gallery whose owners are passionate and exigent art collectors might thus be reread as one continuous examination of the relationship, the tension, between design and art. But this examination is not performed theoretically, in an abstract fashion. It is embodied in each object and still more so in the space between each of two objects presented at the same exhibition, or even in all the exhibitions: all these objects, all these works speak to one another. One would have to compile an exhaustive list, complete with all the images, with all their possible arrangements, and think about that place, unimaginable except in a dream, where all these things might coexist, interact, stand, shine. This dreamlike world, where all these things presented separately are gathered together, would demonstrate how to *feel* the life of objects among themselves.

Let us consider for a moment how we might look at all these things at the same time. From Artaud to Sarfatti, Lavier to Newson, Morrison to Alaïa, Bouroullec to Penck, the symphony of visions is anything but a pile of images. Such a vision is not *Instagrammable*. Today, there is a lot of talk about "curating," about the "curating of culture," the "culture of curating." But people rarely speak of "connoisseurship," a venerable term that has an experienced eye as its benchmark.

Galerie kreo is governed by this "connoisseurship": looking at masterpieces of postwar design cheek by jowl with the most cutting-edge objects, we think back to the eye of Apollinaire— who knew what to look for in Chardin, Picasso, and Duchamp—to those with an awareness of history, but who were not closed to the presence of the present. An assured eye also applies itself to the membrane of things: it caresses them, feels their roughness, smoothes them down. It perceives them for themselves, in the order of the creation of things. It respects them, it does not seek to alter them, and embraces them entirely, its ultimate aim being to reveal the thing in its completeness. There can be no experience of thinking more powerful than design, because it stands inside life and, especially, with art, that second life. Ranged against one another, the levels do not merge; they interlock, with friction, and from this friction thought arises.

All in all, it's never worth going against the world: to be against the world is to be entirely within it. The most transversal of all contemporary figures, the one who rethought and reconfigured the collage culture of the 1990s, Virgil Abloh, also forms part of this history. It is as *future* as it ought to be, said one writer: his exhibition will not appear in this book, but, when it is published, it will take place, it will have already taken place. To live at the membrane of things does not mean saying yes to disorder and confusion: it means making apparent at the interstices a potential for reflection, about things between themselves, on the contents between one another, and so foster the parallel and the secant construction of existences.

View of the exhibition
Didier Lavier, Galerie kreo, Paris, 2017
Featuring:
Walt Disney Productions 1947–2015 n° 2, 2015
Acrylic and print on canvas, h. 4 ft. 5 in. × w. 4 ft. (h. 136.2 × w. 120.5cm)

Embryo, 2002
Marc Newson chair on a pedestal, h. 4 ft. × w. 2 ft. 8 in. × d. 2 ft. 8 in. (h. 122 × w. 80 × d. 80 cm)

BERTRAND LAVIER

Artist

DIDIER LAVIER, OR BERTRAND KRZENTOWSKI

The following conversation between Didier Krzentowski and Bertrand Lavier, under the egis first of Éric Troncy and then of Clément Dirié, offers a reflection of their enduring companionship. Edited and updated, it is based on an initial interview conducted in spring 2010 on the initiative of Jeanne Brun, then curator at the Musée d'Art Moderne de Saint-Étienne Métropole,[1] and a second interview organized on the occasion of the *Didier Lavier* exhibition at the Galerie kreo in autumn 2017. It is further enriched by a third interview conducted in summer 2019.

Éric Troncy	Maybe we can start with a general question: when you two visit museums, do you take a look at the design collections?
Bertrand Lavier	Never. I never take a look at the design collections if I can help it. There is MoMA, where I don't have much choice—so I see them along the route the visitor has to take. Otherwise, no, I give them a miss.
E.T.	And yet you sometimes use household appliances and that sort of thing in your works, and I imagine you choose them very carefully.
B.L.	Let's say I go and look at the design collections at Darty [electrical goods store], i.e. before they become museum pieces. That is more how I go and see them.
Didier Krzentowski	Italian designer Achille Castiglioni (1918–2002) used to say that his favorite museum was the BHV department store.
B.L.	Exactly. I go and see things when they have just come out, and yes, I am interested in the household appliances, and furniture for that matter, in these stores.
E.T.	Didier, I guess you make systematic visits to the design collections in museums?
D.K.	No, I prefer to look at them in books. It has to be said that not many museums actually have a design collection.[2]
E.T.	Didier, I have already heard you say—you also work as a gallery owner who shows design—that design tends to disappear somewhat in the gallery setting. You put it rather neatly by saying that to show design, it has to be lived in, to be alive.

D.K. It strikes me that what has changed since the 2000s is that yes, design has become extremely fashionable. Marketing people have talked about "design-art" or that sort of thing, which for me is meaningless, because design is inextricably bound up with this notion of "use value." As regards galleries, you need to know that for the last thirty or forty years, in industry (the furniture industry, and industry generally), there has been technological progress, but very little creative work being done. This is because fifty or sixty years ago, business owners were product people, whereas nowadays you are dealing much more with financiers. So products now have to be an instant success. So things are remixed. Take cars for instance: they are making the FIAT 500 again, the Austin, they are making American cars again. They "revisit." This is also valid for jewelry: at Cartier's, they are revisiting the 1900s, 1930s, and 1950s. So there is only a new design when there is a new product, because all the same you do have to.... Otherwise you are revisiting. The same goes for furniture! It's actually very funny, many museums say they are only interested in "industrial" design, especially for furniture. What you need to know is that, with the exception of about fifteen companies— and this is where everyone has got it wrong—even in Italy, furniture and furniture companies are actually great craftsmen. The real industrialists are Ikea. Otherwise, when you go to find a chair of whatever make, at whatever shop, you are told you'll have to wait six weeks, meaning that it is not industrial. When you go to IKEA, you take the chair home. Ikea's place in a collection is a complex issue, because there we have the industrial representation of today, but with people who adhere to creation in a very brilliant way.

B.L. They are dealing in inspiration.

D.K. Exactly. They don't create, but they adhere to creation fantastically well, to the second. The kitchens they make are four times cheaper than any other kitchen. It is very close to what creation can do, and at the same time it is something else. Be as that may for a museum, it definitely stands as a moment in the history of design.

In many design museums today, we find, for example, the Carlton bookcase by the Italian designer Ettore Sottsass (1917–2007), eminently symbolic of the early 1980s. In 1980, in connection with what he does with his comrades from Memphis, he says, "We made industrial products, but there were no customers."

E.T. Didier, you mention Sottsass: I think he rather ties in with your personal story, that of your collection at least, since you became very interested in his work very early on.

D.K. As a collector. I have always enjoyed looking at, and have always been interested in things I didn't understand. I did indeed linger over these themes, notably launching into light fixtures about twenty years ago, and now I collect nothing else. Gino Sarfatti, for instance, is unbelievable. In 1954, he said to himself, "Once there is a light bulb, it is the light bulb that will make my object." And he made this neon lamp with the foot that serves as a mounting. This was maximum minimalism, way back in 1954! But to cut a long story short, before the lights, I was collecting shelves, and my collection begins in the 1950s, through the two-sided bookcase for the Maison du Mexique, made by Charlotte Perriand for the tiny bedrooms of the Cité Universitaire halls of residence in Paris. This tied in with my own story, linked to the mountains. Perriand lived in Méribel, and I was also collecting furniture from Jarus in Savoie, which was also so minimal before the word was used. I started out from that, and I went as far as Sottsass, with his bookcase by Rocca 6, directly connected to Perriand's, like the Bouroullecs with the Charlotte [bookcase], which is a tribute to her.

E.T. While we are on the subject of reinterpretation, you showed us, Didier, a rather interesting document that you use in your lectures. It is four Apple appliances, a computer (CPU), an iPhone, an iPod, and a monitor—compared with four items produced by Braun thirty years earlier, and which are unbelievably similar in terms of their shapes.

D.K. What really bothers me, in both art and design, and has shocked me for several years now, is the way people forget everything. When a piece is produced which is a perfect copy of something else, people forget its history. We see how there is an obvious reinterpretation of history that may or may not be admitted.

B.L. I who don't visit museums but go to Darty, when for my own reasons I pick this or that appliance, if I decide for example to become interested in electric kettles, in the relevant section I will find twenty-five or thirty different brands, which are nearly all the same—but it is the designer at Braun who sets the tone. Now that is what we are talking about.

D.K. I couldn't agree more; this is because for the kettle, just as for any electrical appliance, the market demand is for a new machine every six months.... On the other hand, it is obviously out of the question to go redoing the molds for the mechanical parts; all that is required is to freshen up the surface looks. Business needs these repetitions.

B.L. The amazing thing is that behind every item in a design collection there are, in reality, about thirty similar items that are not on view. The little transistor radio from Brionvega was done in at least twenty different versions, by other brands. If we want to carry on the parallel between the world of design and the art world—which I think is somewhat complicated—plainly pretty much the same kind of demonstration can be made in art.

D.K. It is even more complicated in the case of contemporaries. For Braun and Apple, we are talking about things made thirty years apart—so that can be simply called a rereading.

E.T. It is still an iterative reading.... Every time, Apple seems to be leafing through the Braun catalog for something to reread.

D.K. Absolutely. And it's Braun! But the lamp above you, which is by the Bouroullec brothers, was seen some years ago by the president of Flos, the biggest light company today, who came to see the gallery exhibition. He saw it as the lamp specialist he is and chairman of one of the biggest light companies, and apologized to the Bouroullecs, because Marcel Wanders did the same thing for Flos a year ago. That one was made four or five years back.... But people don't have time to see everything.

E.T. Didier, your phone rang just now. What type of object is it? What type of mobile phone does a design specialist carry around?

D.K. A very good question. Here's my answer: what strikes me as being of primary importance in design is the technology—whether it is a telephone you are choosing or anything else. For the telephone, for instance, there is the issue of the battery life. I noticed that, because I was very surprised when Thomson made all its TV sets with Philippe Starck (b. 1949), including the one with the wood molding (Jim Nature TV set, 1993), which looked really beautiful. They didn't sell, and I couldn't understand why. So I go to Darty, who had this set, and I was

told that commercially it wasn't doing well. As I was very surprised, I asked the salesperson why it wasn't selling, and he told me that for the same price, Sony was offering the Trinitron, where the screen covers 100 percent of the surface of the set. When this is what you are up against, design can do nothing. The first things that come into play are the technological advances. And the rest follows. To come back to my phone, I had a BlackBerry for a very long time. I used it as my office, as in life I have no office. It was the phone with the longest battery life. I now have an iPhone I renew regularly.

E.T. And yet all you probably find in museums' collections is the iPhone, because it marks an important "moment." How do you decide whether an object gets into the collection of a specialist museum?

D.K. It is extremely complicated. Of course there are movements large and small. But technology is moving so fast that museums are not able to buy everything. So we have to pick out the main highlights. If only because of its commercial success, the iPhone will have represented a period—I suppose—that is as important as the first Apple computer.

E.T. Listening to Bertrand just now talking of the chair and of MoMA, I was wondering if, basically, given that the furniture is placed on pedestals and paintings have decorative value, if it was still very honest to hold art and design exhibitions that were not model apartments. You would understand the use value of all this....

B.L. Now you see at art fairs reconstructions of collectors' apartments, with artworks, so that people passing through can imagine their homes being like that, too!

D.K. I agree with you, dear Bertrand, design works are very complicated to show in a museum or even in a gallery since they are made to be used.

E.T. Basically, what would you keep from today's design? Would you rather keep a very successful chair, like Starck's Louis Ghost chair (2002), or that Zaha Hadid sofa, because there are in fact many architects doing design these days—which is presented rather literally as a collector's item, as an item intended to end up in a museum?

D.K. Concerning collections, a collector builds up his imaginary jigsaw puzzle, which is a kind of self-portrait, and museums will have a more methodical approach.

E.T. Anyway, concerning Zaha Hadid's sofa, it is designed almost exclusively to get into a museum.

B.L. That is how we know it is not going to stay there. As for the Starck chair, the Louis Ghost…. It is one of the most produced things, isn't it?

E.T. It is every designer's dream. To create the equivalent of the Louis Ghost would stop you going out of business…

B.L. I ground it into powder. Twenty artists were given this chair for a charity auction. Each artist had to interpret, do something with the Starck chair. John Galliano I think glued feathers on it, and I ground it into powder, so that the chair would fit inside a small plastic bag.

D.K. If I'd known I would have bought that piece! I would have loved to have had it!

B.L. I was then told: it's a success, the powder is selling well! I think Starck must have got to hear about it, and I think he was very unhappy. He was wrong, it was a homage after all!

  You were asking me just now if I went to visit museums. The only thing that has made me take a close look at design in general was just one gesture, the pedestal effect at MoMA, in New York. The day it was decided to put a Panton chair on a white wood pedestal. It was just that gesture, which by extension might be termed Duchampian, but it goes beyond that; the idea was to tip this functional object over into the field of sculpture, by giving it the showcase and the most equivocal display instrument. And I fell for it, I said to myself, ultimately if they wanted it to be a sculpture, I would do whatever it took to make it one. Dual punishment, basically. After that, by extension, I became interested in this design, because I did notice—and Didier is a witness to this and involved in this—that the boundary became more porous. There were some very enriching comings and goings, and other more alarming ones.

D.K. There was also some weird stuff! I am thinking for instance of when Franz West made his first chairs, he wasn't really expecting them to be used much.

E.T. They are comfortable though, although it is a truism to say so.

D.K. Yes, they are! They work very well. I had a discussion with someone who worked for a museum, and they told me it wasn't a chair. I said, "Listen, if you put it out on the street, someone will feel like sitting on it. It is a chair."

E.T. Ultimately you never know how you end up in a museum. Well, in any case as an object, maybe not a museum object, but as evidence of one's times. You, Bertrand, at a café in Avignon, you replaced all the things that could have been found in a "country" café, slightly overdoing the typicalness—old saucepans, old rakes—with ordinary contemporary design items.

B.L. I replaced them with their contemporary equivalent. That is, the old coffee-makers were turned into the latest coffee-maker collections—Braun, Miele, Seb, whatever. The old rake I replaced with a small Hoover vacuum cleaner, and so on. And so we were in a kind of nostalgia for the future. You could have imagined going into a bar in Avignon in fifty years' time and finding decorations of that sort. Now, at skiing resorts, we are beginning to see skis from the 1970s on the walls. Whereas twenty years ago they had old wooden skis with leather straps. It is all moving along nicely.

D.K. Paradoxically, industrial stuff, which is generally hugely mass-produced, is getting rare. And hence becoming not necessarily design museum pieces but just generally museum pieces. Meaning that the 1932 Coca Cola bottle is definitely a great curiosity. There were millions of them made, and there are only three left.

  I want to come back to what Bertrand said earlier about the porous border between design and art. On this subject, I'd like to recall what Donald Judd (1928–1994) used to say when he started out designing furniture. He said he realized that he could not think as an artist for design works, but had to think differently to draw these pieces of use. Regarding artists who create furniture, the example of Atelier A is often given, with François Arnal, Arman, César, and Jean-Michel Sanejouand, who for a short time, from 1968 and 1974, produced furniture, but as artists. Atelier A, in my view, was a moment, but there is not much. When we look at the activities of someone like Ugo La Pietra (b. 1938), he perhaps develops a practice one might describe as "artistic," but always with design issues in mind. He is one of the first to ask, "Should we carry on consuming objects?" He was highly critical, but his subject is design.

E.T. I think the priority issue is: "Is Judd's furniture interesting from the design historian's standpoint?" Is Van Lieshout's furniture, or Franz West's we were talking about earlier, interesting from the design historian's standpoint?" That is the real issue. When you try to tackle some discipline, it is hard to avoid being judged in that discipline, on the basis of that discipline's criteria.

D.K. I haven't given any thought to what you are saying. But as to Judd and Van Lieshout, I would say yes. For Franz West, I don't think so, but I am comfortable sitting in it! It's amazing.

Let me tell you a story. It's about Van Lieshout, I bought some of his pieces years ago. I also exhibited him in the 13th *arrondissement* gallery, and I took this piece which was a Van Lieshout washbasin. I had bought it at Roger Pailhas's. So I had this wash-stand installed but—he wasn't a designer, this clinched it—the surface on the bottom was flat, and so the water wouldn't drain off out of the basin. So it is bad design, because it just doesn't do the job, but still a good art work.

We discuss many of my designers' proposals with them. I've even gotten angry, or rather had a long discussion with one of my designers because he made a piece I found really went too far, because the object was made out of human ashes. Nevertheless, I like to consider the space of the Galerie kreo as one for debate on contemporary design, where designers can try things out, even if it means pushing the limits.

You know, designers have very few propositions from the furniture industry, besides Vitra, Kartell, Magis, Flos—the others being craftlike. So the designers have very few possibilities for their research. They have commissions to produce. In the 1960s to 1980s, Italian manufacturers were just small producers, it was not industrial at all.

B.L. It was craft work.

D.K. It was entirely craft work. Designers made the research pieces, which were loss leaders, to sell other stuff, and the gallery was their laboratory. The Bouroullecs' *Lit clos*, for instance, was produced by Capellini but none was sold. When they made it, they got worldwide press coverage, and it helped them sell other things. With the Bouroullecs' pieces currently on show at the gallery (the Liana lamps),

the idea is really—and confirms with Flos—for some industrialist in the background to make it differently. If there hadn't been these pieces, there would not have been an industrialist. But as regards pure research, designers have nowhere to go. But, as we all know, the costliest part of any undertaking is the prototype prior to making the mold. When they began to limit the number produced, it wasn't to sell them at a higher price, it was because they couldn't make more of them. And the tremendous thing is that the image—since the image makes the world go round these days—circulates so much that it gets into all the trends journals, and in this world of design, it will lead to loads of industrial things, that will use it differently.

E.T. Meaning that, if I follow your reasoning correctly, designers produce, invent forms, techniques, research, and take kindly to the prospect of industry latching onto it all, with no reference to them.

D.K. Yes. And what can also happen—and I have examples with many of our designers and a big Japanese company—is that the products by the designers are accepted by industry only if they accept them to be remixed to their convenience (and of course, without their signature).

Let's take, for instance, the Rowenta line by Jasper Morrison. Here is a collector's item that is going to become expensive, because in France only a very small number from this line were produced. It is indeed a magnificent design, but the technology used for that in those days—it wasn't his fault— meant that it was a flop.

E.T. But one might also imagine that these researcher-designers—let's call them that, whoever they are—also feel like creating more ordinary products more directly.

D.K. But these researcher-designers do create in other ways as well. Martin Szekely, for instance, designed the Perrier glasses, there are about twenty-five million of them, and these twenty-five million Perrier glasses mostly come free. Likewise, the Bouroullecs' idea of re-architecturing places; or Naoto Fukasawa and Jasper Morrison's talk of the "Super Normal." When I say that these researcher-designers create in other ways, I am thinking of designers who direct their research towards new materials, new technologies.

E.T. You are telling me that, I am listening, but it does not go without saying. For the moment I am almost facing someone telling me, "Invention in art today is the hologram, it's 3D, it's Avatar goggles." I don't think so, and so I fail to see why it would be true in design, but you say so, and I hear you. But I would tend to think that the real invention today is creating an armchair with wood and fabric. I am willing for you to explain the opposite to me.

D.K. Then I'll explain the opposite to you, absolutely.

B.L. It is about inventing regardless of the material, in actual fact.

D.K. Agreed. But it turns out today, and while we are on the subject of use, that in two thousand years of chairs, the comfortable chair or the comfortable armchair has been worked on over and over so often that they are knowns, and among the things that have ever existed, we know what works. The Eames armchair, in this folded wood system, we know that there has never been anything better. I agree, in the visual arts, the technology and what it is used for don't really matter; I won't have anyone telling me otherwise. But for design, it is different. Carbon, for instance, is an extraordinary material in design because it is ultra-light and ultra-tough, basically it has all the qualities, it has dream qualities. At the time when one of the very first carbon chairs was made, there were two companies working on this subject, because it was very expensive and there weren't many outlets: aircraft, Formula One … let's say there were about thirty because the processing and working of this material were so costly. Today, a lot more applications for use exist.

B.L. In other words, it's better.

D.K. Exactly.

B.L. And that is the interesting thing about design: progress. People often say, "There is no progress in art." It is surely true.

D.K. You who are keen on cars, for instance, if you get into a 1950s car and drive it for three hundred miles, you see how you are not in the same system.

B.L. I would go even further than that: the 2020 Ferrari is better than the 1950 Ferrari. This is beyond debating. It is indisputably better.

E.T. I would prefer a 1970 Jaguar, a Sovereign, to a present-day Jaguar.

B.L. That's because you haven't used either enough!

E.T. It's because the present-day one is ugly.

B.L. No, there is one that is really beautiful. The big saloon car is very ugly.

D.K. Where I would agree with Eric is in saying that a designer today has all the ingredients for it to be better. But there is room for progress now and again. Cars today, technically, are definitely better, but overall they are all clones in design.

E.T. Even so, this thing about invention and technology is weird. I, of course, understand this story about cars. But basically, whenever for instance, at your gallery, Didier, I have seen things that really struck me, I think it was the least technological things. Hella Jongerius's Office Pets and sofas, Julia Lohmann's Cow Benches.

D.K. Yes, but as you are also very keen on Sottsass, think for example of the Valentine, there is a funny story about it. Mr Olivetti had asked Sottsass to work on a typewriter—there is one of them at the museum in Saint-Étienne—and Sottsass realized that someone working with a typewriter spent fifteen hours a day at it. Before there was the black Remington…. So Sottsass said to himself, "You want to add a colour to it, to brighten up your whole day." And for the secretary typing away all the time on this machine, this typewriter is a bit of a girlfriend, so he decided to give her a name, and christened it Valentine. And what does a girl do with a friend? She walks around. Well then! He designed a cover and a handle to carry it around. In other words, he invented the portable typewriter! Ironically though, the Valentine did not do very well at the time.

B.L. On the platform to catch a train, the clever ones arrive two minutes early, not half an hour.

C.D. I'd now like to talk about Bertrand's show at the Galerie kreo in 2017. This exhibition results from a pile-up between your two worlds, between art and design. That's the powerful notion behind its title *Didier Lavier*, which acts like a graft, one that has deep roots. You've known each other for more than thirty years.

B.L. A great mutual friend, Christophe Durand-Ruel, an art connoisseur and collector, introduced us in the 1980s. We quickly hit it off.

D.K. I'd been familiar with Bertrand's work before meeting him, thanks in particular to the exhibitions organized in 1976 by the gallery owner Éric Fabre, another mutual friend. In a way, we haven't really come very far! *Cinq pièces faciles*, Bertrand's fourth exhibition in Éric's gallery, which, for many people, established him on the scene, took place in 1981 in rue du Pont-de-Lodi, right near our current gallery. My interest in his work dates from this period. We then got to know each other and our first collaboration was the Embryo experience in 2002.

B.L. It was really Didier's idea. Three years after opening his gallery with Clémence, they did an exhibition project with the Australian designer Marc Newson, who was already very well known at the time for iconic pieces like the Lockheed Lounge Chair (1988), the Alufelt Chair (1993), and the Ford 021C Concept Car (1999). I had started the "pedestal objects" in the middle of the 1990s. When Didier showed me Marc's Embryo Chair, I immediately said to myself: "If I turn it around, it becomes a Picasso!" An instant trigger. I turned it around mentally at first, then we had the idea of physically turning it around, and my pedestal maker did the rest.

View of the "Design Department" room in the exhibition *Bertrand Lavier*, Musée d'Art Moderne de la Ville de Paris, Paris, 2002

With Marc, we got along well right away because we are both great car enthusiasts. I remember lengthy conversations about Italian sports cars!

D.K. Bertrand's action really amused Marc. *Embryo* was exhibited among Marc's pieces; it was even the image used for the invitation. It's in the current exhibition, alongside a painting from the Walt Disney Productions series.

C.D. Bertrand, this relationship to design and, more globally, to the object runs throughout your work. But, for you, it isn't just a question of considering the object in itself but also in terms of exhibition, displaying it, associating it with other objects, its transition in the field of art. I'm sure that this dimension was also one of the forces that grabbed Didier's attention.

D.K. Of course! I remember really clearly the first of Bertrand's painted objects I saw: the spray gun, the camera, the electric drill. I liked the fact that he painted ordinary objects, that his work targeted art objects as much as everyday consumer objects that kept their operating function. The *Steinway & Sons* (1987) painted piano works; we can turn on the painted transistor *Solid State* (1980). This reminds me of what the designer Jasper Morrison theorized with his "Super Normal objects": the idea of creating objects whose principal quality was their ability to be adapted for domestic, everyday life, and not their wide media-appeal properties. Moreover, as a collector, Bertrand's work fits into my personal "puzzle." I'm interested in artists like Haim Steinbach, Claude Lévêque, Hassan Sharif, and Richard Artschwager, who share this thinking about the object, about and beyond the readymade.

B.L. Design is a discipline that I look at as a hobby and as an enthusiast, but also as an inexhaustible source of forms and objects to manipulate and graft. I'm interested in anonymous objects—farm machinery, a motorbike helmet, a car door—as much as in created artworks. For the exhibition at the Musée d'Art Moderne de la Ville de Paris in 2002, I'd created a "Design Department," placed at the end of the building's curved wall, in the space that vaguely resembles a theater. Here there was *Bertoia/Eames* (2001), a graft of a Harry Bertoia Diamond armchair with an Eames Rocking Armchair Rod, *Eames/Panton* (2001), *Panton/Fagor* (1989), and *Paulin/Planokind* (1992). My first work really initiated by design was *Panton/Zanussi* (1989), a plastic chair

by Vernon Panton placed on a fridge. It was closely linked to the thinking that motivated me then and continues to do so now: thinking about the infra-thin space that exists between the desire to make a sculpture and the desire to make a truly utilitarian object. That's the wonderful challenge facing the designer, which is obviously not mine. At the time, I shared this interest in design in relation to art with a group of people. In 2001, I created *Eames/Panton*, being the Panton Chair pierced through with the hole of Eames's chair, for Cyrille Putman's Coopérateur, a structure he established to allow artists to create and produce furniture. Putman also worked with Fabrice Hyber to create his *Fauteuil couteau suisse* (2006).

D.K. It's good to put this period back into its context. We were in fact a group of enthusiasts and amateurs driven by these questions.

B.L. Yes, a kind of club. Today the art world instead resembles a Western! When I think back to the 1970s and 1980s, everything took place in this neighborhood, between the Seine and boulevard Saint-Germain. At least for me! My first encounter with so-called "contemporary" art took place during my studies at the national horticultural school in Versailles. I lived in an attic room in this area and spent every morning in front of the Galerie Daniel Templon in rue Bonaparte; that's how everything began. When I look at this photograph of the opening of *Cinq pièces faciles*, I feel as though it's a montage. There weren't really many of us who'd go to each other's openings.

To come back to my "use" of design pieces in my work, it's obvious that I choose creations because of their plastic qualities. When Pierre Paulin or Verner Panton designs a chair, they obviously have a knowledge of sculpture. Therein lies all the ambiguity of this question. And when I intervene, I make use of this ambiguity; I take advantage of the dynamic of these objects and offer them something more. As they appear to be sculpture, without touching them too much, just by manipulating them, I will satisfy their dreams of becoming sculptures. It's very simple. I make their dreams come true, and I believe that they're happy!

C.D. Instead of talking about the dichotomies of use/non-use, commission/freedom, or your relationship with the readymade (issues about which you have already spoken a lot), I'd like to hear about your relationship between equivocation and univocity, which is another way of approaching the relationship between art and design. What interests you, it seems to me, is that when the artwork is equivocal it escapes any exhaustive analysis.

B.L.   This question is central to what I do. I often say that I work by short-circuit, that I graft one thing to another, in order to stir up trouble. To perturb what we see: is it a pedestal or a safe? But also to disrupt the academic categories: is it painting or sculpture? Or trouble between the techniques: taking an object and playing with it again in a material not natural to it. Producing "gaps," like when I transpose Frank Stella's paintings into neon or Paul Signac's *Le Château des Papes* into ceramics. I like it when the work slips away slightly from what it is physically; we come back to this question of dreams, the potential of objects and forms. When I created *Brandt/Haffner* in 1984, I was above all interested in aesthetic questions like the pedestal. I had in fact noticed that safes possessed formal characteristics identical to those of classical pedestals. Afterwards, I read a whole lot of very knowledgeable critical analyses of this artwork focusing on the relationships between food and money, the question of conservation, etc. I was really pleased, but these issues were far from my mind when I created the piece.

D.K.   That is because you often work with everyday objects and references common to everyone (Walt Disney, the world of sport, the Eiffel Tower). They carry a lot of energy within themselves. The capacity for interpretation is almost infinite.

To complement what we were saying about the relationship between art and design and this question of use, I would like to mention Pierre Charpins's Ignotus Nomen collection from 2011. For this furniture series, Pierre was interested in something that is rarely taken into account in design: the relationship between use and affect. We work better on a desk with which we maintain an emotional relationship. This may be related to the desk's history, the place where it was acquired, but also thanks to the extra bit of soul brought by this apparently non-functional form placed on top of it by Pierre. By introducing an emotional use to his furniture, he shifts the usual questions.

B.L.   When I exhibited, in my retrospective at the Centre Pompidou in 2012, the repainted Langres highway sign, Jean Widmer, the graphic designer who created it, was very amused and flattered to be thus adapted to the "Lavier style." For our exhibition, I've created

a new work in this series: a magnificent panel, again by Widmer, promoting Sainte-Victoire. We've associated it with Naoto Fukasawa's Drilling Table, because both carry the idea of landscape, nature, and material. The legs of Naoto's table were made out of rocks excavated from the site where the table will be installed. It's as tautological as a Saint-Victoire repainted with "my" Van Gogh touch. For me, this "couple" is maybe the most successful, in any case the most straightforward: we practically had the impression of ripping off the Sainte-Victoire! One thing we shouldn't forget about this exhibition is its playful side. This is something that I strive for, that I feel is nice to offer to the public. Jubilation was the effect produced by the *Merci Raymond* exhibition that I organized, in tribute to Raymond Hains, with Chiara Parisi in 2016 at the Monnaie de Paris. Bringing visual and spiritual pleasure is very important to me.

C.D.   Let's talk about an emblematic group of works in the exhibition, the "Ferrari set."

B.L.   This involves the Chop Top Table (2006) by Marc Newson—him again!—a diptych of readymade paintings—*Rouge Ferrari 1956–2004* (2017)—and *Ferrari/Curtiss* (1992), which is the fender of a damaged Ferrari 308 on a fridge. The group is closely linked to my taste for Ferraris. To be a snob and ridiculous, I often say that I got my first Ferrari when I was four years old. Since then, I've always fetishized this object. At certain times in my life, I've owned one; at other moments, I've had none. For me, the Ferrari is not a work of art, it's a very beautiful applied art object, a living object and, perhaps paradoxically, a popular object that makes you dream. I don't think that a Bentley produces the same effect on people. It's the whole Ferrari legend. I'm fascinated, moreover, by the evolution of Ferrari red, which comes back to my interest in language and designations. Ferrari red doesn't exist; there are multiple interpretations, as there are for all colors. I've had the chance to visit the historical headquarters in Maranello, where all the Ferrari models are stored. Well, the red is never the same! In the 1950s, the red was rather purple, very deep. And the more the years went by, the more it got lighter to become this tomato red that we know today. There are several reasons for this: to have a color that works better on screen with the development of televised advertisements, to be in harmony with the red of cigarette packets, and so on.

C.D. I think that red is truly the color of this exhibition, and of this publication. There is red of every hue, from those of Ferrari to those of the group combining your most recent work, *Colonne Lancia* (2017), with two lights from Pierre Paulin's Élysée series. If Didier Lavier were an artist, I'm sure he would paint many red monochromes.

Now the exhibition's been set up and the elements of each "couple" are there—before they were just working hypotheses—what are your feelings?

B.L. I reckon this exhibition has confirmed my intuition and my approach to the "Design Department" where I worked as a "bachelor." Here, we worked with the designers and I could compare my vision with Didier's. I liked to imagine more or less complex or self-evident relationships between my works and the design pieces, playing with the rigidity of the classification and freedom of viewpoint, between order and disorder—a little like what I'm doing in Montpellier with the Jardin-atlas in the Hôtel des collections at MOCO Montpellier Contemporain, my first garden, fifty years after studying in Versailles! In addition, being able to do something new relating to Marc's design is an echo of our very first collaboration twenty years ago that cheers me greatly.

D.K. What interests me is the reaction of visitors, of collectors—both at this exhibition and at those we organized with Marcel Brient, where design sets up a dialogue with art and poetry. Lots of people have realized that, although art and design are obviously not the same thing, the ways of thinking and asking questions about them can be related. Personally, I really like these exhibitions because they throw up other meanings for me, open new horizons. To be able to look together at Arthur Rimbaud's manuscript with its crossings out that Marcel brought us in a shoebox, at design pieces produced by the gallery, and at works by Bruce Nauman and Michel Majerus starts me dreaming. I wonder whether museums shouldn't be more creative and set up this kind of encounter, of emotion.

B.L. I too think that showing art in such a context makes the atmosphere around the works feel more intimate. They escape, as it were, from the white cube; they leave off their "ungrounded" side and revert to something more familiar. "On an equal footing" with everyday objects, a table or an armchair, they are not domesticated, but enter into a new relationship of proximity. They emit a different wavelength.

C.D. To a point this squares with what Didier said at the beginning of this conversation about the best environment for exhibiting design. You make it sound like art and design gain a lot from such encounters. Bertrand, I suppose you've been to Clémence and Didier's. How would you describe how the space is organized in their home?

B.L. As soon as I walk in, I immediately feel that I'm in the home of people who are not spectators of but players in the art and design of their time. The manner in which the works are hung, installed, speaks of an empathy, a dialogue, a selection that is theirs and theirs alone. You immediately feel that this is their home and nowhere else. It's heartwarming.

D.K. A house is a portrait. Unfortunately, for 95 percent of people, they're in a hotel. Depending on their income, they can hire a decorator to fit out their home, look at pictures in magazines, mimic the spaces in a furniture store. Even without massive resources, without being a collector, anyone can do something extraordinary. It's all a question of the eye, of personality.

1. *Bertrand Lavier/Didier Krzentowski*, Éric Troncy (ed.), collection "Pratiques contemporaines" (Saint-Étienne: Éditions du Musée d'Art Moderne de Saint-Étienne Métropole, 2013). Our thanks go to Jeanne Brun and Éric Troncy for authorizing reproduction.

2. France possesses four large-scale public design collections: the Musée National d'Art Moderne/Centre de Création Industrielle, Centre Pompidou, Paris; the FNAC–Fonds National d'Art Contemporain, Paris-La Défense; the MAD–Musée des Arts Décoratifs, Paris; and the Musée d'Art Moderne de Saint-Étienne Métropole, Saint-Étienne.

ALEX COLES

Design writer and editor; Professor of
Transdisciplinary Studies at the University
of Huddersfield, United Kingdom

GALERIE KREO: A NEW SYSTEM FOR DESIGN

1. See Harrison White, Cynthia White, *Canvases and Careers: Institutional Change in the French Painting World* (Chicago University Press, 1965).

2. For an early discussion of "designart," see Alex Coles, "Art Décor," *Art Monthly* (Issue 253, February 2002). With emphasis on the art side of the economy, this was developed in Alex Coles, *DesignArt: On Art's Romance with Design* (London: Tate Publishing, 2005), and Alex Coles (ed.), *Design and Art* (Cambridge, MA: MIT Press, 2007).

3. For an extended discussion of Grcic and his tactical response to "designart," plus extensive interviews with him and his design team regarding the design process, see Alex Coles, "Konstantin Grcic Industrial Design," *The Transdisciplinary Studio* Vol. 1 (Berlin: Sternberg Press, 2012).

The dealer-critic system established in Paris in the last quarter of the nineteenth century introduced the gallerist and dealer into the economic and creative equation of art production and distribution.[1] Not only was the dealer-critic system crucial to the development of a market for modern art—beginning with the impressionists and their first exhibition in 1874—but also to providing artists with the space and resources to continually experiment and innovate. While Paul Durand-Ruel established a market for the work of Claude Monet and his contemporaries, crucially he also encouraged Monet to experiment within the spatial parameters of his commercial gallery. In one infamous instance, this led to Monet painting both the walls of Durand-Ruel's gallery and the frames surrounding his artworks in an attempt to create a more immersive experience for the viewer—fully realized many years later with the enveloping widescreen-like installation of his Water Lily paintings in the Musée de l'Orangerie, Paris. Without the former opportunity, the latter breakthrough may never have occurred. In this sense, Durand-Ruel was essential to not only supporting Monet fiscally but also to the actual aesthetic and conceptual maturation of his art. This relationship between Durand-Ruel and Monet perpetrated a system that, with changes and updates, is still in place in the art world today. The rise of the art fair and the art biennial in the meantime have impinged little on it.

No comparable support network was developed for design either in the nineteenth or twentieth centuries. In part, this was to do with the ubiquitous denigration of design in contrast with art in the modern era—a condition that continued, with brief interruptions, until very recently. While there were numerous opportunities for designers to exhibit, seldom was their creative development nurtured by a commercial gallery with any degree of conviction, partly because individual design objects were deemed to be worth relatively little in contrast to artworks. Ironically, the historical avant-garde's embrace of design did little to change this. So while Marcel Duchamp could transform an example of vernacular design into an actual artwork (*Porte-bouteilles*, 1914), and El Lissitzky could collapse the distinction between art and design by innovatively working across both, the hierarchy remained unchanged. As a result, designers predominantly relied on commissions from manufacturers, obliging them to remain within the often-limiting parameters of set briefs. If the modernist credo of "form follows function" derives from this condition, then the notion that "form follows finance" surely explains it: with few or often no galleries to work with, designers produced industrial designs subservient to the functional requirements of manufacturers' existing home and corporate client base. For the most part this condition prevailed, structuring the design world for decades. Perhaps only figures in Italy such as Gio Ponti, Achille Castiglioni, and Carlo Mollino—either through finding wealthy patrons or generating their own independent exhibition and publishing platforms and so writing their own briefs—pioneered a more dynamic and independent form of practice in the modern era that only partly relied on the backing of manufacturers. Added to this, the postwar rise of modestly sized and often family-owned manufacturers in Italy like Kartell and Artemide meant that the manufacturer could develop more complex briefs from an intimate relationship with designers. This was not mirrored outside of Italy.

When commercial design galleries eventually rose in number and established a unique role for themselves, they did it differently from both the auction houses and the design fairs. Phillips, Design Miami, and the Pavilion of Art and Design accelerated the market for design and even established the key themes and issues underpinning the discourse around it. In order to reduce the supply of select designs and so increase their price, a rarefied form of limited edition design— so-called "designart"—was devised.[2] This meant that the design market was largely brought to fruition by institutions with little direct creative relationship with designers and little if any proximity to the complexity of the design and production process.

Working both in unison with the historical backdrop created by the dealer-critic system in the art world and independently from the fiscal maturation of the design market by the auction houses and fairs, for two decades Galerie kreo has provided a vital incubator for design practice. With the gallery's exhibition history, dating back to 1999, of working across the contexts of design and art—in 2002, for instance, bringing Bertrand Lavier together with the designer Marc Newson—Galerie kreo chose to continue working with designers in the same way as they had been for more than a decade, without paying attention to the "designart" trend that boomed in 2005. That is to say, Galerie kreo felt no need to employ divisive labels.

Detailing just one of the myriad examples of this dialogue between designer and gallerist suffices to give a sense of the mutual benefits of this relationship. In 2004, Konstantin Grcic conceived a brick-like object fashioned from solid wood with a single recess for Galerie kreo's "Missing Object" project. It was a mute object, making no attempt to reach out and caress the viewer with aesthetic flourish.[3] In its place, *The Missing Object* provided a meta-commentary on the at-times antagonistic relationship between design and art, utility and the aesthetic. For although it was clearly based on the application of utility, in no way did it readily lend itself to a specific instance of utility. To a large degree, with *The Missing Object*, Grcic—for many, the industrial designer par excellence—toyed with and eventually thwarted utility. This type of conceptual ingenuity would perhaps only have been possible by gallerist and designer working closely together, a relationship that is fortunately set to continue.

CHRISTIAN SCHLATTER

Philosopher

MISSING OBJECT AND OBJECT GRAMMAR

For this latest return to the context of the missing object, first of all, a plea from me addressed from the Galerie kreo to about ten of its protagonists in the year 2004. The request to "design me a table, a chair, or any other piece of furnishing—portable, storage, or other object," would have been trivial: would it even have been legitimate to ask it of them? Absolutely not! For such a production each decides independently, just as one can choose to respond to a prescriptive demand or not. As for the gallery, this reminder—and it is a badge of honor—Clémence and Didier Krzentowski never go to your workshop to choose their exhibits from among existing pieces. The hallmark of the Galerie kreo is that, not only does it produce what it shows, but also, for every protagonist, it has always offered and remains a potential space for experimentation. This approach underwrites the future of a gallery that still leads the way today, just as it did twenty years ago. To neglect what is the gallery's key characteristic is to fail to understand both its production and the help it provides for all those involved in it.

The missing object. How can such an utterance be unpacked? The title has the advantage of being unconstrained; the object is general, it does not bend the statement, does not stop at any particular request. That said, the sphere of attention and its ensuing framework mutate the statement and turn the object into a terrific oxymoron. The Latin etymology of the lexical unit "object" ob-jicere states: an object is what is thrown before; the object is what is thrown in front (of us), and, thus thrown, the object bears within it a certain violence, imposing itself in all its alterity, in all its presence—but the adjective here determining it declares just the opposite; it is absent, it's not there—do we miss it? A less is observed, there, where it should be.

And yet similarly, the real object is one whose starting point stems from a necessity that is lacking, so that it is, precisely in this sense, initially a missing object; such an absence can be thought of as an impediment—that of the actions previously impossible prior to such an object, as if, by this

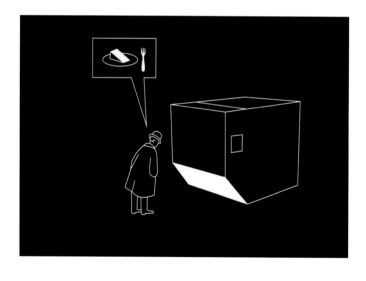

Konstantin Grcic
Illustration for
The Missing Object
(2004), 2009

object, certain gestures become possible, unfolding in distinct yet repeatable instances, so that, owing to this object, certain habits arise. It can therefore be said that here the object itself says something and that this something—this invitation to use it—is not to be sought outside the object.

"That the word BUILD is one of the most beautiful in the language!" and how could construction not be saddled with the uncontrollable plural of corrections? This is what Thomas Bernhard says in his novel *Correction*.[1] Build? Yes, but with corrections pushed to the limit—this is the prologue to the missing object.

Konstantin Grcic has provided two versions of this note on the missing object; the first in 2004 accompanied the exhibition at the Galerie kreo, which saw the unveiling of a copy of his *The Missing Object*; the second can be found in the book *KGID, Konstantin Grcic Industrial Design*, on pages 121–22 devoted to the "Missing Object." Let's hear what he has to say:

> In 2004 curator Didier Krzentowski invited me to make a work for "Missing Object".... A short text by Christian Schlatter provided the creative framework for the project. According to Schlatter, the Latin root of the word "object" means something that is thrown in one's way—a definition containing an inherent violence that I found intriguing. The "missing object" would thus be something that had a strong physical presence, while at the same time being absent (missing). I was immediately attracted by this beautiful thought, but paralysed by what it would mean actually to design such an ambitious object.... The result is a solid block of oak with two excavated handles. The purity of the wood, its weight and raw beauty, define its intense physical power. The carefully thought-out proportions of the wooden block and its two handles give the object the enigmatic charm of something that appears legible but whose purpose remains mysterious.

Object Grammar

"Grammar tells us what kind of object anything is." Ludwig Wittgenstein, *Philosophical Investigations*, §373.[2]

The idea is pursued further with greater precision and extension as to the thing, all the while noting an insurmountable limit concerning grammar, which "only describes and in no way explains the use of signs." In this context, each object possesses its own grammar and this grammar does not take shape, the grammar of the object regulates exchanges with the object, so the meaning of an object depends on the uses it makes possible, a form of life that, through it, can come into being.

Faced with an object, it is possible to say: 1) "I know what I see," and 2) "what I see leaves me calm": this is the essence of the familiar—an object is familiar to me if I know what it is, if I see exactly what it is; here we are simply rehearsing what Wittgenstein states in the *Philosophical Grammar*.[3] The example in the present paragraph was a table; that this object is familiar to me signifies that this object has its grammar, which itself means: I know it is a table, I know how it is used, I know that it looks like a table, I know it is called a table, etc. This in turn entails that the form of the table is predetermined by habits or actions that demonstrate that the table is well constructed and that this table is presented so that certain behaviors become possible. One asks: how is the object to be used? What does one do with it? And in these actions, through this gesture, we learn how to understand this object. The grammar of the object is no more and no less than the "ledger" of the object (Wittgenstein): in this book are shown the effective transactions with the object, those it allows to be effected. These reminders from Wittgenstein, the restatement of questions and determinations derived from the imperatives of object grammar, provide, in the context of a so-called design of today, elements for devastating criticism and the brazen demonstration that most objects of this type have no grammar and that some objects even claim to rise to the dignity (*sic*) of works of art!

If possible, may we suggest that the reader glance again at the reproduction of the two sides presented of the abovementioned Missing Object. The order of the structive is no mere structural principle; it is a principle governing the construction and articulation of every element; it is not limited to the internal cohesion of an object. This economic principle of the object is not far from the nexus, from the nodal point—it shows that the visual configurations of this object derive with great rigor from a construction with which they are in complete accord. Within such an organic arrangement each component refers conceptually to all the others.

The importance, both for Mies van der Rohe's work and for understanding him as an architect, of his reading of §188 ("Every morality is, as opposed to laisser-aller"[4]) in Friedrich Nietzsche's *Beyond Good and Evil* (1886) is a matter of record. Something else that gives the work on Missing Object its character lies in the fact that it is, according to another expression of Nietzsche's in the same paragraph, "a protracted constraint." This Object orders, arranges, measures out, lays down, informs its material; and with what precision!

Thus it obeys a plethora of laws whose rigor and precision defy any purely programmatic formulation. The most important thing is to execute the law for a protracted time and solely in one direction; in the long run, thanks to this uncompromising and wary constraint, something always arises and has always arisen—that something, that Missing Object which alone is worth all the effort. Just start in the right place and everything else will follow suit.

In keeping with Wittgenstein's injunction: "Don't think—look!" the construction of each object must not and does not leave anything to chance; every step has to keep in mind the previous step, with effort; it is the result of accumulated work. One should undoubtedly push this argument further and recognize in construction the traces of significant corrections made in the name of the desiderata of an exclusive principle of selection. Rule number one: "No laisser-aller." Construction comes at this price. We should be committed to living exclusively with beings and things that do not let themselves go, so as to become, ourselves, consequential and distinguished. It is here surely that comes forth a speculative anthropology, by which we designate a technique for systematically inventing imaginary life forms as different as possible from our own.

1. Thomas Bernhard, *Correction* [1975], trans. S. Wilkins (London: Vintage, 2003), 6.

2. Ludwig Wittgenstein, *Philosophical Investigations* [1953], trans. G. E. Anscombe (Oxford: Basil Blackwell, 1963), 166.

3. Ludwig Wittgenstein, *Philosophical Grammar*, IX, §115, ed. R. Rees, trans. A. Kenny (Berkeley and Los Angeles: University of California Press, 1976), 165.

4. F. Nietzsche, *Beyond Good and Evil* [1886], trans. R. J. Hollingdale (Harmondsworth: Penguin, 1973), 92.

Konstantin Grcic
The Missing Object,
2004
Structure made of nine
elements in oiled oak,
h. 15 ¾ × w. 15 ¾ ×
d. 8 in. (h. 40 × w. 40 ×
d. 20 cm)

MARCO ROMANELLI

Design writer and coauthor with Sandra Severi Sarfatti
of *Gino Sarfatti: Selected Works (1938–1973)*
(Milan: Silvana Editorale, 2012)

GINO SARFATTI:
A LIFE DEDICATED
TO LIGHT

Can one begin telling a story from the end? I believe so, as long as the end allows us to understand the beginning. And so we have to wonder how it's possible that, for so many years, Gino Sarfatti and his work were all but forgotten. Since he's now widely recognized as one of the greatest lighting designers the world has ever known, this *damnatio memoriae* seems incomprehensible. And yet there are precise reasons for it.

The first reason lies in his double talent, as both designer and entrepreneur. As the founder of Arteluce, Sarfatti and his business were considered one and the same. But it wasn't just others who saw him this way—it wasn't a case of "external attribution," as happened with Osvaldo Borsani and Tecno or Gastone Rinaldi and RIMA, to name just a few Italian examples; rather, it was a veritable psychological internalization. Sarfatti "was" his company: he lived for his company and oversaw every detail, every day. But Italian design back then struggled—and, to some extent, still struggles today—to accept personalities who didn't fit into the "normal" range of master designers. That's the first reason Sarfatti didn't immediately gain the historic position that was his due: ambiguities (viewed as compromises) are intimidating.

The second reason also has to do with the deep ties between Sarfatti and Arteluce: the moment Sarfatti sold Arteluce to Flos, in December 1973, when he was sixty-one years old, marked a clean break; he turned his back on it as absolutely as he had devoted his life to it up to that point. He opts to "no longer exist" as a designer: for him, his involvement with design died alongside his involvement with his company. He abruptly moved to Lake Como, opened up a stamp-collecting store, and gave up virtually all contact with the world he'd left behind. For a few years he was utterly forgotten. That first changed in 1978, with an exhibition on the 1950s at the Centro Kappa, Milan, and again in 1984, with the major exhibition *Lumières je pense à vous* at the Centre Pompidou in Paris (the rare interview he granted François Grunfeld on that occasion remains an invaluable record). In fact, well before his full critical

Clockwise,
from top left:

Gino Sarfatti/
Arteluce
Table lights 600/P,
600/G, and 600/C,
1966; table light 539,
1968

Lights by Arteluce,
1950s–1960s

Gino Sarfatti/
Arteluce
Reading light 1082,
1962; wall light
232/P, 1961; table
light 591, 1962;
table light 540/G,
1968; table light 586,
1962; wall/ceiling
light 232, 1961

Following page:

Clockwise,
from top left:

Lights by Arteluce,
1960s–1970s

Gino Sarfatti/
Arteluce
Wall light 238/3,
1960; ceiling light
2042/9, 1963; floor
light 1094, 1966;
table/floor light 543,
1965; wall lights
238/2, 1960

Gino Sarfatti/
Arteluce
Floor light 1076/N,
1957

Gianfranco Frattini/
Arteluce
Table light 597, 1961

Massimo Vignelli/
Arteluce
Ceiling light 2049/4,
1964

Gino Sarfatti/Arteluce
Floor light 1091, 1963

Gino Sarfatti/Arteluce
Floor light 1076/FG,
c. 1963

Gino Sarfatti/Arteluce
Tripod floor lights,
1950s–1970s

All lamps: Clémence
and Didier Krzentowski
Collection

rediscovery, especially by design museums, private collectors were the first to realize the importance (and value) of Gino Sarfatti. It is impossible not to mention, in this respect, Didier Krzentowski.

But these parallel entities of "individual/company" weren't the only factors to harm Sarfatti's legacy; at least two others affected it as well. The first is, again, autobiographical: postwar Milan, as it was being rebuilt and during the ensuing economic boom, gave rise to an entire generation of ingenious designers, marking a unique historic phenomenon we are unlikely to see again (from the already elderly Ponti to Gardella, Albini, Viganò, Frattini, Zanuso, the Castiglioni brothers, Munari, Aulenti, and Parisi); within that milieu, Sarfatti stood apart not only as designer-entrepreneur, but also as a singularly focused (dare I say "one-object-only") designer. The overused phrase coined by Ernesto Rogers, "from spoon to city," applicable to his peers, doesn't fit Sarfatti in the least. Sarfatti thought only about light. Between 1939 and 1973 he designed over six hundred lights. (Somehow, from the very beginning, he must have intuited he'd make a whole lot of lamps—why else, instead of naming them, would he have chosen to sequentially number them?) His other, non-lamp design objects can be counted on the fingers of one hand.

The final reason he was forgotten is only partially autobiographical, and fairly "circumstantial": as already mentioned, he withdrew from public life in 1973, just a year after Italian design had garnered worldwide media attention thanks to the New York exhibition *Italy: New Domestic Landscape*. But within that year he'd already moved on to other pursuits while others—many others—were going full speed ahead with press and PR, supported by Italy's extraordinarily rich magazine market. He, however, was no longer interested in any of it.

So, now that we're aware of the peculiarities of his story—including those related to his personality— let's go back and tell it from the beginning. Here we need only touch upon the part of Sarfatti's biography that directly relates to his design work. Born to an upper-class Venetian Jewish family in 1912, Gino

enjoyed a privileged childhood. He chose to study aeronautical engineering in Genoa, but the political situation soon took a nosedive: the closure of Italian ports bankrupted the family business in shipping. He left his studies behind and found work as a commercial agent with the Milan-based company Lumen. Thus lamps and lighting became a part of his life, and by 1939 he had founded a small-scale workshop called Arte-Luce (literally "Art-Light": the words were separated at first, placing prophetic emphasis on the two components he strove for in his entire oeuvre). From then on his journey appeared to be all smooth sailing: the new super-central store on the Corso Littorio (later renamed Corso Matteotti), designed by Marco Zanuso, became one of Milan's first real design boutiques, as well as a regular gathering place for a circle of "designer-intellectual" friends. But fate was once again lurking around the corner: the bombardment of Milan and the passing of antisemitic racial laws forced him to flee the SS by making the perilous border crossing into Switzerland. In October 1945, a few months after Liberation, the Sarfatti family returned to Milan, only to find everything destroyed—the exception being Gino's indomitable will. As the city began rebuilding, Gino's architect friends (Viganò, the partners of BBPR, Zanuso, Albini, Frattini, Latis, and Parisi) asked him to make new, urgently needed lamps for their new buildings. From that moment on, "Modern Milan" became inextricably bound up with Arteluce's lighting designs. Meanwhile, Ponti and his magazine *Domus* became unparalleled international champions of the nascent Italian design movement. In 1962 an extraordinary new store designed by Gino's friend Vittoriano Viganò opened on the Via Spiga, marking Arteluce's acme. Sarfatti received project after project and, unfortunately, remained staunch in his refusal to delegate. Perhaps this was the turning point, unnoticed at the time, which led him to sell Arteluce less than ten years later: demand grew ever higher, work piled up, he had to go from being designer-entrepreneur to entrepreneur-designer, he was incapable of delegating certain aspects of the business (even to his son Riccardo who, as would later become clear in the work of Luceplan, would have been perfectly capable of assisting and then succeeding his father), and his neurotic perfectionism took its toll. Ultimately, the many other "major designs" of that particularly fertile period turned Arteluce's incredible success into a double-edged sword. Sarfatti felt constricted by his own creation and chose to abandon it.

What story, on the other hand, can be told about his working methods and creative practice? His ultra-strong commitment to the workshop came before all else. He designed "by prototype" (more often than not, the drawing phase came later), and worked alongside the company's laborers, with whom he established a close bond. He was a lot like an inventor: experimentation was a key part of the process. The lamps and other lights began as a "dreamlike" vision of the whole, and were then built empirically, "by components," evaluating the available materials on hand and making on-the-spot design decisions. Hence the company's early years were particularly challenging, as Italy was still under authoritarian rule, steep economic sanctions targeted the regime, and resources were scarce. But Sarfatti managed to remain positive: you had to do *well and good* with what there was (he saw this as a moral imperative). Then, when the war finally ended, new paths were paved, making way for daring experimentation, new light bulbs (more on this later), and new materials. This was when Sarfatti was happiest—the entire city came alive with an unmistakeable energy. Everyone sought out *the new*, preferring to forget the trauma of the recent past. New opportunities and materials were everywhere: consider, for example, model 2072 (1953), a.k.a. Jo-Jo, born by chance when Sarfatti simply grouped together a bunch of brand-new, colorful Plexiglas samples. And then there was his ability to spot new possibilities in some of the most overlooked, misunderstood, and problematic elements of lighting design, like the cord, and highlight it in uninhibited designs like model 2097 (1958), an absolute masterpiece.

The new "components" that successively became available also included new light sources. Sarfatti was quick as lightning to take up all the latest bulb innovations, for which he strove to construct, as swiftly as possible, the "ideal shell." (That he viewed lamps as "shells" or "wrappings" for light bulbs was also clear from the very start, beginning in the days of the incandescent bulb.) The same held true when tubular fluorescent bulbs came along: he simply surrounded them with rotatable sheet-metal screens and, voilà—it's the famous model 559, winner of the 1954 Compasso d'Oro award. Similar inventions followed with the advent of the Cornalux or "hammerhead" bulb (see model 566, from 1956), and also with the low-voltage halogen bulb (see model 607, from 1971, where Sarfatti salvaged an automobile headlight and turned it into his final marvel). The powerful, slanted base simultaneously houses the power supply and "leans" toward the reader, with a reflector clipped on and a hole in back that doubles as a handle: every element has clearly been studied and designed to fulfill a specific function but, formal restraint reigns supreme, resulting in a remarkably rare overall vision. (Just consider the bold, risky, yet successful choice of setting that thin top onto that thick base!)

But if we were to stop here, we'd still only have a rather "mechanistic" view of Sarfatti. At least two more points are worth clarifying. The first has to do not with the lights themselves, but the space for which they were created. From the start—before World War II, in an era when light was still considered a "fixed" element in space, usually set right in the center of the ceiling—Sarfatti dreamt of (and designed) lights that would follow people as they moved. Whereas previously the lights in middle-class homes were considered immobile parts of the homes themselves, now the focus was being shifted to the homes' residents and their needs (as Sarfatti said in 1940, a rare and relevant article in *Domus* magazine: "What does it mean to light something up? Certainly it doesn't just mean casting light *everywhere*, but rather *everywhere we are*"). This idea can be seen in his multi-armed, adjustable ceiling lights, which can banish shadows from even the darkest corner of a room; in his floor lamps that cast reflected light upward; and also in the light sources that "lean over" the reader.

The second aspect could be called his "visionaryness": Sarfatti might have been a taciturn and fundamentally melancholic man, but he continually "lifted his eyes to the sky," where he found infinite design inspiration. The planets' movement around the sun inspired the complex and kinetic model 191 (1951), a large wall-mounted "composition" with spatially alternating arms holding out various points of light. Years later, in 1969, the first moonwalk inspired model 604, Moon, a table lamp with a large, colorful methacrylate dome protecting a concave base dotted with tiny three-watt bulbs—a lamp that makes sci-fi look outdated! But it was the full moon that truly became a joyous obsession. Sarfatti transformed the perfection of that luminous sphere into a veritable system (a propensity for "systemic" phenomena was another constant in his work, visible in his awareness of how repeated elements as a whole are worth much more than the sum of the their individual parts): a "moon" set onto a ring became model 237 (1959); two "moons" set onto two rings (model 238); and all the way up to twenty-four "moons" (model 2109) in one immense lamp-sky. The latter is an unforgettable masterpiece that swiftly showed up everywhere, from "high" to "low" places: it lit up Turin's Teatro Regio, designed by Carlo Mollino, as well as large steamships and the atriums of condo buildings on the outskirts of major cities. It was only with Gino Sarfatti's model 237 that early 1960s Milan came to finally, really, broadly understand the meaning of the word *design*.

Gino Sarfatti/Arteluce
Wall light 237/1, 1959
Lacquered metal
mount and frame,
frosted glass diffusers,
diam. 7 in. (diam.
18 cm)

Gino Sarfatti/Arteluce
Table light 607, 1971
Lacquered crackled
aluminum base
and reflector, h. 12 ½ ×
diam. 15 ¼ in. (h. 31 ×
diam. 39 cm)

MARCEL BRIENT

Art and design collector

"NO WIND IS SET FAIR FOR THOSE WHO DON'T KNOW WHERE TO GO"

Recorded during summer 2019, Marcel Brient's remarks testify to his long-held affinity with the Galerie kreo, which, in 2012 and 2013, took the form of two exhibitions at the gallery. A man of few words and a collector of visionary tastes, Marcel Brient, a well-known figure on the contemporary art scene since the 1990s, looks back over his career, his method of collecting, his encounter with Didier Krzentowski, and his relationship to contemporary design.

Arthur Rimbaud, *Lettre du voyant*, "Le Cœur supplicié," 1871

"Today, my tribulations in the art world no longer occupy my mind much. Nevertheless, one little anecdote does come back to me. Alerted by the latest gossip, one day my friend Louis [Clayeux] visited one of my store rooms, strongly suggesting that I cease this 'absurd activity.' 'Where are you going with this?' he asked me. A week later I was off shopping again. At that time I lived in a little house in Nanterre. Not a work of art on the walls. 'An odd sort of collector.' Just piling stuff up!

"In Jean Fournier's gallery on rue du Bac, Joan Mitchell and Sam Francis welcomed me with open arms. Jean Fournier, so attractive. Gerhard Richter, Joseph Beuys, Mario Merz, François Morellet, Giuseppe Penone, and Yan Pei Ming, with the couple Liliane and Michel Durand-Dessert, rue de Lappe. Ghislaine Hussenot's gallery on rue des Haudriettes: Félix González-Torres, Ed Ruscha, Raymond Pettibon, Carl Andre, Richard Serra. Unforgettable Ghislaine! And also Darthea Speyer with Ed Paschke.

"Moored there, cast anchor; hoist sails again, depending on the wind and money. Then came my meeting with Didier—the master of design—at a fair abroad. Unfortunately I can no longer recollect exactly what the Galerie kreo was doing when it started out in 1999. I needed furniture that would go with modern and contemporary art, something that over time they created with enthusiasm. I was going to discover, love, and possess: Donald Judd, Jorge Pardo, Marc Newson, Konstantin Grcic, Franz West, Hella Jongerius, Ron Arad, Mattia Bonetti, Andrea Branzi, Naoto Fukasawa, and many others besides. Thank you to the artists; thank you, Didier.

"I used to go regularly to Diego Giacometti's studio on rue Hippolyte-Maindron to buy and sell his bronze furniture. Louis had something to do with it, too. I imagined that one of these days, in a private space I'd have in the future, I'd place a piece of furniture next to artworks on the walls. I purchased Charlotte Perriand and Jean Prouvé. Then Didier appeared, discreetly opening the door to contemporary design,

Le Cœur supplicié.

Mon triste cœur bave à la poupe.....
Mon cœur est plein de caporal !
Ils y lancent des jets de soupe,
Mon triste cœur bave à la poupe ...
Sous les quolibets de la troupe
Qui lance un rire général ,
Mon triste cœur bave à la poupe,
Mon cœur est plein de caporal !

Ithyphalliques et pioupiesques
Leurs insultes l'ont dépravé ;
A la vesprée, ils font des fresques
Ithyphalliques et pioupiesques ;
Ô flots abracadabrantesques,
Prenez mon cœur, qu'il soit sauvé !
Ithyphalliques et pioupiesques
Leurs insultes l'ont dépravé !

Quand ils auront tari leurs chiques,
Comment agir, ô cœur volé ?
Ce seront des refrains bachiques
Quand ils auront tari leurs chiques !
J'aurai des sursauts stomachiques
Si mon cœur triste est ravalé !
Quand ils auront tari leurs chiques
Comment agir, ô cœur volé ?

Ça ne veut pas rien dire . — Répondez-moi : chez
M. Deverrière pour A.R...
Bonjour de cœur,   Ar. Rimbaud

the one that suits the artwork of today. A fantastic character, simple and understated, armed with a breviary. I followed him about with curiosity and passion. For example, I collected Donald Judd who sometimes 'flirted' with furniture. Then, from there, I encountered Félix González-Torres and his magical oeuvre. Ineffable object! I'd already found my feet among the 'new designers': Marc Newson, Ron Arad, Jorge Pardo, Konstantin Grcic, Hella Jongerius. The list's at Didier's. The right store, the right place!

"Today, there's a stereotype of the 'perfect collector.' As a child, I used to collect candy wrappers, gluing them into a school notebook. My meeting with Félix González-Torres in Paris concluded this singular adventure. My portrait, my weight, 200 lb. (90 kg) of candy of a turquoise blue—the color of my eyes—with the word 'passion' written on those candies, delivered up to desires that gradually disappeared, then reappeared [*Untitled (Portrait of Marcel Brient)*, 1992]. Fellowship—and then, before his tragic death, the project to record the last bars of an opera, followed by applause. I suggested Richard Strauss's *Rosenkavalier* conducted by Herbert von Karajan. Always this obsession with communing through desire, the ultimate work. Félix: extraordinary, an heir to American minimalism and conceptualism. He threw open the gates to the new challenges of contemporary art with adventurous art lovers on his heels!

"One of my first journeys with Louis: Athens, the Parthenon, a masterpiece of antiquity. He took me there around noon, just as the 'marble caught fire.' One of my last trips: the Galerie kreo in Paris. Marc Newson: the Lockheed Lounge Chair. I immediately thought of the portrait of Madame Récamier painted by Jacques-Louis David. Visionaries, two stubborn passions.

"Formal inventiveness: yes, because the very essence of design is surely the originality of a new concept—left-field, but ahead of the game. Usefulness: no, that's too like a hardware store! Materials: they're limitless. My most recent purchase: a cement bench with

holes and tagged by a 'curious Indian' [see p. 22]. An evocative world: the list of designers worth studying are fascinating, from such diverse backgrounds, different cultures, creative opportunities, encounters with the world of art, money, and so on! 'Art is permanent revolution,' to quote Jean Dubuffet. And to end—from Andrei Rublev to Kasimir Malevich—it's always been a *Black Square* on a white ground.

"Our two exhibitions: *Ensemble* in 2012 and *Ce Passant Considérable* [This Estimable Passerby] in 2013 were attempts to combine modern and contemporary art, modern and contemporary design, books and manuscripts, poetry, the idea of the couple, love, friendship. 'This Estimable Passerby' is about meeting on place Denfert-Rochereau in Paris, in 1959, the man who would show me Athens.

"The epigraph to the *Ensemble* catalog is a maxim of Seneca's: 'No wind is set fair for those who don't know where to go.' On windy nights my mother couldn't sleep; Armorica—land of gales. That's where I was born. Fishermen would often come back empty-handed due to poor weather. That was something we all had to put up with. Since then I've always been wary of it, wherever I am—for me the wind is set fair."

Feliz Gonzalez-Torres
Untitled (Portrait of Marcel Brient), 1992
Candies, weight: 200 lb.
(90 kg), variable dimensions
Private collection

Nineteen designers were invited to present an iconic project of theirs produced by the Galerie kreo, accompanied by their comments. The facing page reproduces an influential or inspiring image that throws an unexpected light on their creative universe.

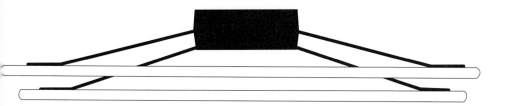

THE DESIGNERS' WORLD

VIRGIL ABLOH
EDWARD BARBER AND JAY OSGERBY
FRANÇOIS BAUCHET
RONAN & ERWAN BOUROULLEC
PIERRE CHARPIN
FRONT DESIGN
NAOTO FUKASAWA
KONSTANTIN GRCIC
JAIME HAYON
HELLA JONGERIUS
JASPER MORRISON
FIEN MULLER & HANNES VAN SEVEREN
MARC NEWSON
JERSZY SEYMOUR
BRYNJAR SIGURÐARSON
STUDIO WIEKI SOMERS

VIRGIL ABLOH

Above
Virgil Abloh creating
pieces for the
Efflorescence
collection, exhibited
at Galerie kreo in 2020

Facing page
Left: Highway
underpass
transportation
infrastructure, USA
Right: Page excerpted
from *Subway Art* by
Martha Cooper and
Henry Chalfant (New
York: Holt, Rinehart
and Winston, 1984)

"I aim to produce a human connection through the showcasing of my works, which facilitates an exchange of societal commentary. The use of graffiti designs brings to light a conceptualization of interdisciplinary knowledge. The works themselves are an embodiment of the creative process, both physically and figuratively. This notion, in turn, gives the artworks the power to create organic human emotions and expressions. The foundational thought behind these works was to intertwine the concept of graffiti with the way botanical ivy exists and its purpose. Similar to how ivy wraps around its surroundings, this graffiti wraps around the viewer's mind and produces a naturally growing texture of modern communication in the world's high-density urban climate. Furthermore, analyzing the forms of the work, the viewer starts to recognize that these are concrete foundations creating a necessary bridge between chic and street environments. In conclusion, it's about constructing a language that adverts to the norm that both a purist and a tourist alike can comprehend."

"Exploring the art form of graffiti naturally leads to an inquiry into urban architecture—specifically typologies that graffiti artists gravitate to and consider as prime canvases.

The architectural underpass, which often takes the form language of brutalist architecture, was a key investigative typology when considering the dialogue between form and graffiti, which in its essence is the relationship of architecture to people: people seeing themselves within their urban condition and wanting to express themselves out of plain sight.

This icon, as well as others, informed the formal language of many of the architectural elements applied in the visual and practical research for this Efflorescence collection."

"Published in 1984, *Subway Art* by photographers Martha Cooper and Henry Chalfant was my art school. Studying graffiti from New York in the 1980s as an extension of hip-hop culture is where, in my mind, I first gained a good hand-eye coordination and point of view. In engineering class, all I was ultimately doing was filling these books up with graffiti."

EDWARD BARBER AND JAY OSGERBY

Above and right
Hakone table, 2016
Solid natural oak,
h. 2 ft. 5 in. × w. 9 ft.
6 in. × d. 3 ft. 7 in.
(h. 73 × w. 290 ×
d. 110 cm)

Facing page
Top, left: Adze head,
undated
Top, right: Stool,
undated
Bottom: Shinto Shrine,
Hakone

"We have always appreciated the skill, precision, and effort required in Japanese joinery. These details, seen during our travels to Japan, have been a longstanding influence on our work.

The Hakone table is such an example, with its generous sweeping curved top and monolithic legs, reminiscent of the Hakone Shinto Shrine on Lake Ashi. The table is constructed from three generously proportioned and tactile forms; two legs and the top. Concave and convex geometries give the impression that the table is floating just above the ground. The visual interplay between these curves animates the table as you move around it. Made in France, each element is produced from the finest quarter-sawn European oak."

"Objects that have been fashioned by hand and have been aged through long-time use give us great pleasure and reassurance. Unpretentious and devoid of non-essential details, they exude the essence of the materials they are made from. We keep a number of these objects around the studio and we often return to them for navigation when lost in the depths of projects."

FRANÇOIS BAUCHET

Above
Cellae, Cellae
collection, 2013
Special commission
Private collection
Technical felt,
fiberglass, polyester
Collection particulière
w. 17 ft. 8 in. × d. 1 ft.
3 ¾ in. (h. 240 ×
w. 540 × d. 40 cm)

Facing page
Windmill, c. 1988
Metal, diam. 13 ft.
(4 m)

"The principle of Cellae is identical to that of cell development. The cells agglomerate together as soap bubbles do, so that there is no free space between them. A skin surrounds them to constitute a homogeneous whole. The difficulty is in defining cell sizes and shapes that allow coherent furniture design, such as a table, shelf, console, etc.

One of the particularities of the cells is that they are not parallelograms, which allows each piece to be naturally braced, in order to avoid any deformation. The cells can be agglomerated illimitably, which allows a large number of possibilities, as we can see here with this private commission.

This project is part of a more general investigation to establish structural systems that are less mechanistic than conventional assemblies. It is not built as an assembly of plans, but rather as the development of a living organism."

"Conceived of at the end of the 1980s as an artistic commission for the Université Jean-Monnet in Saint-Étienne, this 'structure-signal' was installed on the roof of a new building dedicated to research. It was a kind of allegory: the production of energy by the wind as a metaphor for the production of thought—elusive, inexhaustible, and always renewed. This sculpture was not intended to produce electricity but to evoke movement.

It is no longer in place today, but its memory remains as an object designed to meet the demand for artistic production. This idea resulted from broader research into nature and living things, subjects I have always been interested in (I had, for example, developed a method for the cultivation of morels, which had been deemed impossible).

It was an object nearly 13 ft. (4 m) in diameter, a kind of UFO on a roof. It was built around a vertical axis, which had the advantage of always catching the wind, without having to be oriented to pick it up. This type of windmill therefore requires less space than the large horizontal-axis ones that we see in our fields today. More compact, it naturally makes more sense on a rooftop, and is now a solution that is under development."

ERWAN BOUROULLEC

"Choosing this photograph in which Didier is looking at Black Light was an obvious choice for us. In addition to recalling his passion—his obsession, even—for lights, it is also a way of paying tribute to him, as well as to Clémence, whose gallery is an essential driving force for our practice. Since the beginning of our collaboration, Galerie kreo has been a place where we can produce and exhibit pieces that we could not make elsewhere; and the design of lights constitute a thread through all of our exhibitions at kreo.

Creating lamps offers the possibility to propose something formal, with a strong symbolic value, and which, in the case of ceiling lights, occupies a space that is not visually filled in. Our lights at kreo always have a particular presence; they inhabit spaces as if they were sculptures, as well as being the result of real typological research, which has often been developed subsequently in our industrial design."

"The digital drawings I have been making for the past few months allow me to explore the notion of protocol, of an *a priori* method, while rediscovering a certain freedom of expression. I have always been interested in artists like Sol LeWitt, for whom the interplay between seriousness and difference is essential. These drawings combine the rigor and precision of the coding that is at the origin of their creation, with a pictorial joy linked to the colors and the feeling of movement they radiate."

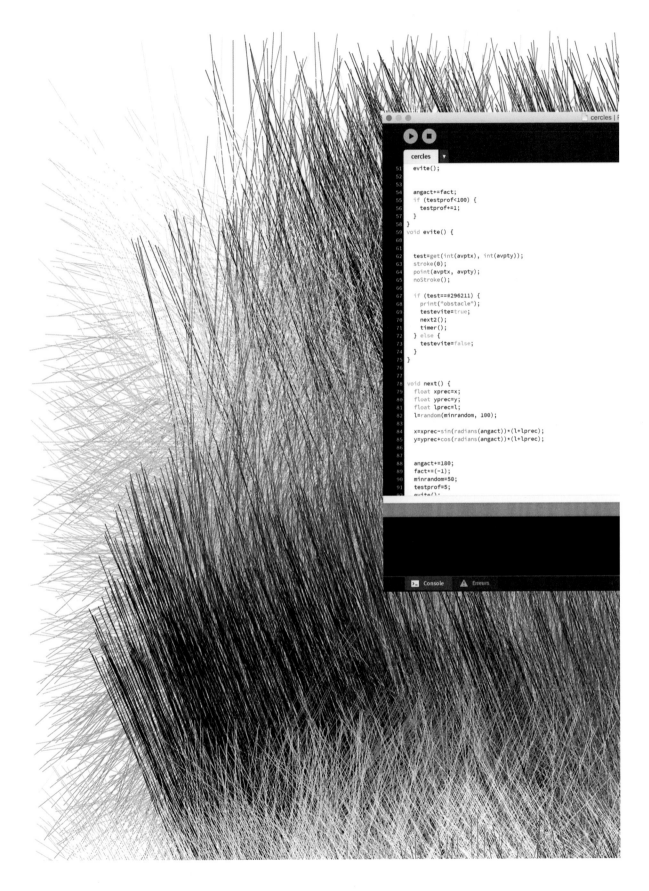

```
51    evite();
52
53
54    angact+=fact;
55    if (testprof<100) {
56      testprof+=1;
57    }
58  }
59  void evite() {
60
61
62    test=get(int(avptx), int(avpty));
63    stroke(0);
64    point(avptx, avpty);
65    noStroke();
66
67    if (test==#296211) {
68      print("obstacle");
69      testevite=true;
70      next2();
71      timer();
72    } else {
73      testevite=false;
74    }
75  }
76
77
78  void next() {
79    float xprec=x;
80    float yprec=y;
81    float lprec=l;
82    l=random(minrandom, 100);
83
84    x=xprec-sin(radians(angact))*(l+lprec);
85    y=yprec+cos(radians(angact))*(l+lprec);
86
87
88    angact+=180;
89    fact*=(-1);
90    minrandom=50;
91    testprof=5;
92    evite();
```

cercles | P

cercles ▼

Console   Erreurs
```
```

RONAN BOUROULLEC

"For almost twenty years we've collaborated with Galerie kreo, a place where we have had the freedom to regularly show-case our research. Without doubt, the lamp is the type of object that we have worked on the most, from the *Luminous Object* (2004) to the lamps of the Wajima collection (2009) and the *Lianes* (2010), first made in leather for the gallery, then produced by Flos in an industrial version.

With its combinatory principle and its wonderful char-acter, the *Chaînes* series (2017) is the result of our lat-est research in lighting. We like the way it creates an atmo-sphere—a radiance—from a simple accumulated module. Here, too, it is a question of occupying the space in a renewed and, all in all, rather delicate way, from the ceiling."

Right
Ronan & Erwan
Bouroullec
Chaînes, 2016
Plaster, metal, LEDs,
various dimensions
Exhibition view, Galerie
kreo, Paris, 2016

Facing page
Ronan Bouroullec
Malachappe, 2018
Felt pen on paper,
h. 29 ¾ × w. 29 ¾ in.
(h. 76 × w. 76 cm)

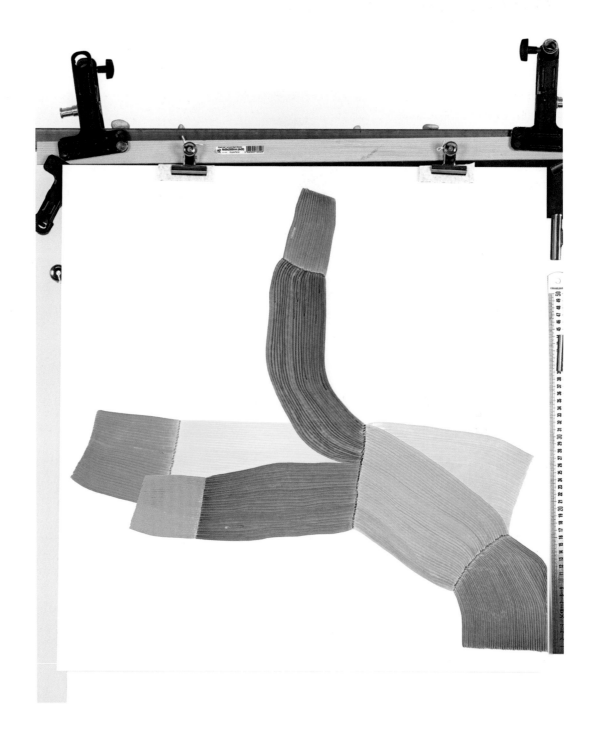

"I draw daily, as if I were keeping a diary. I remember drawing in class on the blank backs of wallpaper samples that our teacher gave us. These drawings express colorful, formal sensations, without any direct relationship with my work as a designer. They allow me to experience the slowness or speed of a gesture, the fluidity of a line, the alliances between colors."

PIERRE CHARPIN

"*Ignotus Nomen* is undoubtedly the series of objects that is the most representative of my research tackling the notion of presence. These objects require no explanation, no justification. They are there; they stand before us and confront us with their strong power of evocation. If we had to do it all over again, it'd be the same!"

"When I feel threatened by current mediocrity, or tired of the insignificant invasiveness of the millions of stylized forms, my cure is called Carl Andre. (I have a few other remedies available.)"

FRONT DESIGN
ANNA LINDGREN AND SOFIA LAGERKVIST

Above
Large Reflection
Cupboard, 2007
Printed MDF, car
paint, h. 2 ft. 9 in. ×
w. 6 ft. 7 in. × d. 1 ft.
5 ¾ in. (h. 84 ×
w. 200 × d. 45 cm)

Facing page
Archaeological
drawing of an obsidian
stone mirror found in
the excavation of
Çatalhöyük, Anatolia,
c. 6000 BCE

"We have long been interested in the different aspects of an object that might not be visible, or in features that you do not necessarily notice at first. We want people who see our design to grow curious and notice qualities in objects that surround us every day. The reflections on the surface of an object are one such element we have worked with.

We created a cupboard with a permanent reflection printed on its surface. The printed and the real reflection blend with each other—one permanent, recounting the history of the object, and one that changes with the context of the object's surroundings. It is also a way to explore time as a quality to work with in an object."

19447.X3

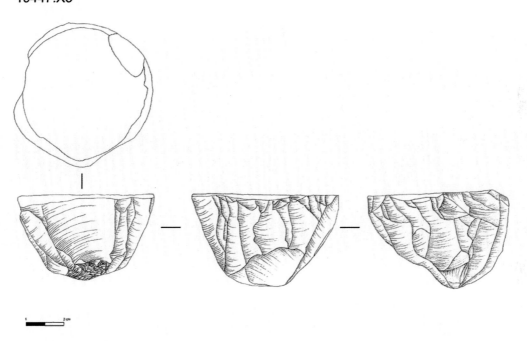

"Mirrors of obsidian stone are the first known, man-made mirrors and were made in 6000 BCE. Historical objects and their use in different cultures are a great source of inspiration for us. Their history and meaning to different civilizations tell a fascinating story that we often try to reflect on in our own work."

NAOTO FUKASAWA

"Noticing the unnotice-
able is the foundation for
my art and design work.
No matter whether a
rich material or highly
skilled, handcrafted
work, I design it as a
silent object until it
becomes noticed."

Top
Chaos, 2012
Black onyx pearls,
diam. 16 ½ in. (diam.
42 cm)

Bottom
Hanger, 2008
Oak, aluminum nails,
h. 3 ½ × w. 25 ¼ ×
d. 2 ¾ in. (h. 9 ×
w. 64 × d. 7 cm)

Facing page, top
Richard Wentworth
Caledonian Road,
London, 2000

Facing page, bottom
Richard Wentworth
Staten Island, New
York, 1975

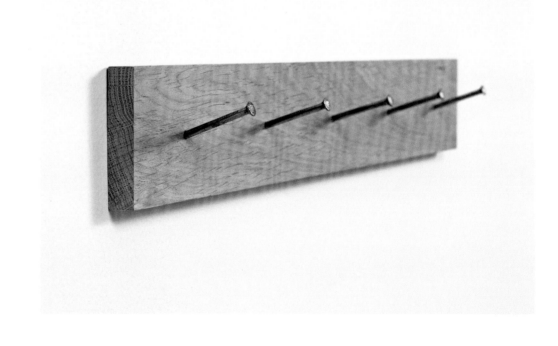

"All humans, plants, and animals unconsciously give value to their environment and everyday circumstances, thanks to their 'affordances,' to sum up James J. Gibson's theory."

KONSTANTIN GRCIC

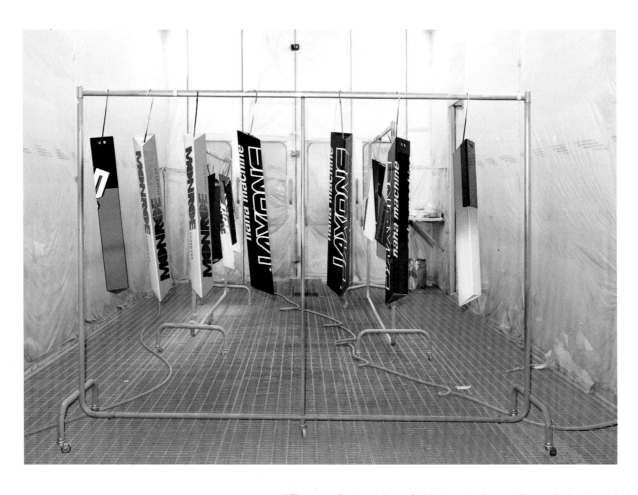

Above
View of Walter
Maurer's paint-shop
during the production
of the CHAMPIONS
collection, 2010

Facing page
Two BMW Art Cars
being reworked
at Walter Maurer's
paint-shop; in the
background: Alexander
Calder's BMW
3.0 CSL (1975); in
the front: Roy
Lichtenstein's BMW
320i Turbo (1977)

"For my first solo exhibition at the gallery, I designed CHAMPIONS, a collection of lacquered tables. They are spray-painted by Walter Maurer, a former racing driver, artist, and master craftsman. Maurer painted BMW's legendary art cars by Calder, Warhol, Stella, Lichtenstein—he also lacquers entire airplanes. His extraordinary skills were crucial for the project, which set out to transform a static table into a speed machine.

I had never before used graphics on furniture, but it was so much fun trying it out. Discovering its enormous potential became one of the exciting parts of this project—like learning a new language. An algorithm helped me create fictional words, which I would turn into fantasy brand names and logos. Developing the first prototypes took nearly a year. During that period, we worked closely with Mr. Maurer at his paint-shop on an ex-army airfield, which gave the project an extra edge."

"As a boy, I spent hours reading sports catalogs, memorizing them page by page. I like sports, but that was not the point. I was fascinated by the beauty of the equipment: skis, bikes, rackets, running shoes, climbing gear. In a way, sports catalogs were my first design teacher. I was completely immersed in this world of things that are designed to perform, through the sheer efficiency of their materials, construction, and shape. On top of it all, there are the go-faster stripes and colorways, the stickers and logos, which add a boost of psychological adrenalin to the users of the equipment.

When I conceived the project for Galerie kreo, I wanted to transpose this phenomenon into the world of furniture. How would the performance of a table change if it were painted with sport-like graphics? Would it radiate speed, self-confidence, and power?"

JAIME HAYON

Above
Pinkoz vase,
ChromaticO collection,
2018
Hand-blown Murano
glass, marble, h. 20 ×
w. 12 ½ × d. 8 ½ in.
(h. 51 × w. 31.6 ×
d. 22 cm)

Facing page
American walnut
elements for the
Twenty-Two handmade
chair, Ceccotti
workshop, Cascina,
Italy, 2019

"I created these vases for the *ChromaticO* exhibition in 2018. They represent an intense collaboration with the legendary glassblowers from the island of Murano, who lent their master skills to bring about these curious objects. The vases combine opacities, colors, and forms springing from my imagination, my cosmos. They are placed on top of solid marble plinths of various colors, and I like the interplay of the delicate with the strong in this mix of noble materials, creating a series that is both fun and sophisticated."

"When working with an artisan, I like to ask, 'What have you never done?' and then I encourage them to do something new. I say, 'Let's try it.' With the industrialization of design, we have lost a bit of the magic of craftsmanship, since 3D printing allows us to push a button and the piece comes out straight away. But touching the material directly and working together with the extraordinary expertise of craftspeople allows us to raise the level of creation. That's how I try to bring craftsmanship to contemporary design, to preserve it for future generations."

HELLA JONGERIUS

"Many of my works deal with the relationship between users and their objects. In Frog Table the frog functions as an intermediary. Having become an almost autonomous 3D figure, which will not be ignored at your table, it plays with the user's imagination. It thus reveals an outspoken view of the power of decoration in design. Although my interest is to work as an industrial designer, I like to explore the borders between art and design.

I am not a modernist, but I do feel that the modernist tradition is still the holy grail in my profession. I believe design now assumes a completely different function than in the modernist era: you no longer formulate function solely in terms of use or comfort. Sometimes it even lies—paradoxically—in its non-functionality, in the extent to which products appeal, above all, to your imagination."

"In 2018–19, I took a sabbatical during which I had the occasion to work at the European Ceramic Work Centre (ECWC) in 's-Hertogenbosch, The Netherlands, where everything started for me almost twenty-five years ago. Once there, I decided to make earthenware pears—considering them as white canvases, and as a metaphor to ask myself what I had reaped and what had I sown in the last decades. I really enjoyed the making of these juicy-looking, irregular pears, and simply coming back to hand-making generally. It gave me a sensation of creative freedom, of liberation, just as when I'm swimming, surfing, crossing the waves."

JASPER MORRISON

"I thought about the missing object—a research topic proposed by Galerie kreo in 2004—and it occurred to me that while the picture frame existed for flat artwork, there was no equivalent for three-dimensional objects. The Object Frame was a simple outward extrusion of a picture frame to provide both a shelf and a frame for the displayed object. It was not a great success."

Above
Object Frame, 2010
Oak, h. 17 ¾ ×
w. 31 ½ × d. 9 ½ in.
(h. 45 × w. 80 ×
d. 24 cm)

Facing page
Photograph by Jasper
Morrison, 2019

"I have often admired the art of displaying objects, not least when it becomes a matter of survival. In this image, we see a somewhat hopeless collection of formerly useful items cleverly arranged to catch the eye. The star-offers—two nearly new bicycle tires—are used to frame some of the less appealing products. The single flipper may have been excluded for its size, or the unlikelihood of a suitable swimmer passing by. The two sizes of blue hammers, needing no extra promotion, are also left out. Design itself, being primarily a service to make life more efficient—and more pleasurable—is the perfect tool to bring to the exercise of display."

FIEN MULLER & HANNES VAN SEVEREN

Above
Bended Mirror #3,
2018
Polished stainless
steel, h. 19 ½ ×
w. 13 ¾ × d. 12 in.
(h. 49.5 × w. 35 ×
d. 30 cm)

"We made three mirrors, all created from a single sheet of metal. Through cutting and folding, openings were created, from which multiple functions can arise."

"A simple cut, or a series of cuts, functions as a powerful drawing and redefines spatial situations and structural units—this is Gordon Matta-Clark's lesson."

Gordon Matta-Clark
Office Baroque, 1977
Site-specific project
realized in Antwerp

MARC NEWSON

"My idea was to take a mundane functional implement—the ladder—and turn it into an esoteric, airy, sculptural object that serves its intended purpose while being exceptionally sturdy and lightweight."

"Sometime in the 1980s, I saw a photo of Gio Ponti's Superleggera chair being held by a child with nothing but his pinky and it has stuck in my mind ever since. I thought the idea behind the design was really cool because it predated high-tech composite materials and was still so lightweight. The traditional wooden library ladder has always appealed to me because, unlike almost every other type of ladder, it's not meant to be hidden when not in use. But because these types of ladders are typically so heavy that they need a rail to be moved back and forth, I wanted to go in the opposite direction and make a ladder so light it could be held with a finger and used anywhere. Carbon fiber, which I had first used for the Black Hole Table fairly early in my career, turned out to be the perfect material for this."

Above, left
Carbon Ladder, 2008
Carbon fiber, h. 6 ft.
7 in. × w. 1 ft. 8 ¾ in. ×
d. 2 ½ in. (h. 201.5 ×
w. 52.5 × d. 6 cm)

Above, right
A traditional library
ladder
Marc Newson
Archives, London

Facing page
Gio Ponti,
Superleggera chair,
1957

JERSZY SEYMOUR

Right
Metal Scum Lamp,
2008
Galvanized metal,
h. 3 ft. 10 ½ in.
(118 cm), base diam.
15 ½ in. (39.5 cm), top
diam. 10 ½ in. (27 cm)

Facing page
Top: *A Dinner for the
End of National
Frontiers and the
Attainment of a Global
Equality of Human
Rights and Welfare—
Part 1: Fuel for
Slogans*, Jerszy
Seymour's studio,
Berlin, 2011

Bottom: *Lucky Larry's
Cosmic Commune*,
10th Saint-Étienne
International Design
Biennale, Saint-
Étienne, 2017

"The Metal Scum Lamp was realized in 2008 as a conclusion to a series of installations. Using free-form polyurethane foam, it is based on the meaning of scum from the Latin definition of 'foaming' or 'bubbling', while having a negative connotation in the vernacular, meaning the lowest of all things; my intention was to create a series of primordial 'zero' situations and a design that has no relation to anything—ethics, politics, use, taste, production—but still is. It could be seen as both a manifestation of the psychological underbelly of existence and an illumination to discuss it."

"I have always understood my practice as the creation of situations, and this is what fuels my work. The images here are from two of my projects.

The first, entitled *A Dinner for the End of National Frontiers and the Attainment of a Global Equality of Human Rights and Welfare–Part 1: Fuel for Slogans* was made in 2011 at my studio in Berlin. It started off with a group of artist friends and people from the local Occupy movement. At the beginning of the evening I served pasta arrabiata and the discussion was quite political, but as the evening progressed, words were not enough and it became something very primordial. The next day, we took part in the Occupy protests, with the banners we had made as part two of the dinner. The third part of the dinner would have been the celebration for when the goals were achieved.

The second project is from a morning yoga session at the Disco Farm at Lucky Larry's Cosmic Commune, made in 2017—a living social sculpture and a model towards a possible society. It looked at alternative forms of economy, organization, and collectivity, always under the gaze of Lucky Larry, a quasi-deity/non-deity—totally unbelievable and therefore maybe just believable, not there but omnipresent. 'Lucky Larry was around at the beginning of time before the first molecules started to replicate, he's lucky and he wants to share it with you.'"

BRYNJAR SIGURÐARSON

Right
Entrance Table,
The Silent Village
collection, 2013
Ash wood, metal, Krion,
rope, nylon string, and
various materials
including feathers, fur,
leather, printed fabrics,
chains, and hooks,
h. 4 ft. 8 in. × w. 4 ft.
10 ½ in. × d. 4 ft. 2 in.
(h. 1.43 × w. 1.46 ×
d. 1.27 m)

Facing page
Photograph by Brynjar
Sigurðarson

"A visual vocabulary speaking the language of an Icelandic fishing village. That is what The Silent Village collection for Galerie kreo is to me. An attempt to translate the atmosphere of a place and its cultural scenery into objects.

What if one day an unknown wooden structure were to get caught in a fishing net in the ocean outside Iceland? How would that structure look? That is what I asked myself when I designed this object."

"There is something visually striking about nets. There is depth, transparency, texture, and a variety of colors. There is a sense of function, although a net lying around at a netting workshop looks nothing like it does when it is floating around the depths of the ocean looking for fish.

Taking photographs is one of the most important parts of my practice: a constant exercise in looking at things, in defining what I am drawn to. From these observations, ideas start to emerge."

STUDIO WIEKI SOMERS
DYLAN VAN DEN BERG AND WIEKI SOMERS

"The Frozen in Time collection was inspired by images collected in the *IJzelboek* ('Icebook') which I found at a flea market. It shows how a blizzard brought the Netherlands to a standstill on March 2, 1987. The entire country was covered in a thick layer of ice. Fascinated by this silence and how ice preserves, conserves, protects, and at the same time eternalizes, we started thinking about a 'durable ice' applied to products and had the idea to dip things in it for a certain time. So we set up a workshop with large baths for dipping and ultraviolet lighting fixtures. The vases, carafes, tables, and even lights gained in strength through the repeated dippings. After a few months we managed to finally 'freeze' the material into a solid yet transparent layer—one that connected all the individual components. It was a playful and very intuitive process.

We believe in the value of research and long-term partnerships with clients and collaborators who are willing to face the challenge of imagining another reality. It is an ideal combination to design industrial products for companies and more artisanal small series for a gallery like Galerie kreo. We envision it as a laboratory where there is the time and freedom for research, and for which we make collections that serve as experimental trials with materials or special themes that could eventually lead to large-scale productions."

"We always like to look at reality a little bit differently, in a similar way to Elspeth Diederix's way of working. For our book *Out of the Ordinary* (2014), she made this photograph titled *Reflection*: a non-photoshopped image of a mirror in the sea.

Perhaps this 'looking with different eyes' also explains our fascination with Magical Realism: the art movement characterized by its fantastic scenes that are depicted in a very detailed, realistic way, which makes reality strange and mysterious. In our work it is more about transforming the ordinary. We ask ourselves what the things around us are and what they could be. We observe ordinary situations and customs, how people relate to things and the associations things have for people. We let our imagination run free. We make the ordinary extraordinary, in a subtle way."

This chronology, which is not exhaustive, lists the main exhibitions of the Galerie kreo designers since 1999, as well as their various awards, exhibition designs, and public projects. Other events (major thematic exhibitions, creation of design spaces, etc.) are also mentioned to contextualize Galerie kreo's activities in the contemporary design landscape of the past twenty years.

A CHRONOLOGY OF CONTEMPORARY DESIGN

GALERIE KREO: A MAJOR PLAYER IN THE 2000S AND 2010S

1999

Opening of the Galerie kreo at 11, rue Louise Weiss, in the 13th *arrondissement* in Paris

Exhibition *Radi Designers: Fabulation*, Fondation Cartier pour l'art contemporain, Paris

Maarten Van Severen designs the interior architecture of the Maison Lemoine, Floirac, Bordeaux (architect: Rem Koolhaas/OMA), and the exterior furniture of the Pont du Gard, Vers-Pont-du-Gard

2000

Galerie kreo moves to 22, rue Duchefdelaville, still in the 13th *arrondissement*. They temporarily program a second space located nearby at 1, rue Zadkine

Exhibition *François Bauchet: Mobilier et objets, 1980–2000*, Musée des Arts Décoratifs, Paris

Exhibition *Marc Newson: Ford 021C*, Design Museum, London

Ronan & Erwan Bouroullec design the A-POC Store, Issey Miyake concept store, Paris

Opening of the MUDAC–Museum of Contemporary Design and Applied Arts, Lausanne

Second edition of the International Design Biennale, Saint-Étienne, France, created in 1998

2001

Exhibition *Élisabeth Garouste & Mattia Bonetti/1981–2001*, Grand-Hornu Images, Grand-Hornu, Hornu (Belgium)

Exhibition *Jasper Morrison: A World Without Words*, Design Museum, London

Exhibition *Marc Newson: Design Works*, Powerhouse Museum, Sydney

Konstantin Grcic receives the Triennale di Milano's Compasso d'Oro for his May Day light for Flos

Closing of the Galerie Néotù, founded in Paris in 1985 by Gérard Dalmon and Pierre Staudenmeyer

2002

Exhibition *Ronan & Erwan Bouroullec*, Design Museum, London

Exhibition *Jerszy Seymour*, Design Museum, London

2003

Exhibition *Hella Jongerius*, Design Museum, London

Jaime Hayon resigns as director of the Design Department of La Fabrica—the academy of design and communication founded by Benetton in Treviso, Italy—to found his own studio

Ronan & Erwan Bouroullec are named "Designers of the Year," Salon du Meuble, Paris

Exhibition *Philippe Starck*, Musée National d'Art Moderne/ Centre de Création Industrielle, Centre Pompidou, Paris

2006

Exhibition *Konstantin Grcic*, Museum Boijmans van Beuningen, Rotterdam; Haus der Kunst, Munich

Exhibition *Super Normal*, curated by Naoto Fukasawa and Jasper Morrison, Axis Gallery, Tokyo; Triennale di Milano, Milan; touring to Helsinki, London, and New York

Exhibition *Ettore Sottsass: Contre-design*, Fonds régional d'art contemporain–Frac Centre, Orléans

Adrien Rovero, recipient of the Jury Prize, Design Parade, Villa Noailles, Hyères, France

Reopening of the Musée des Arts Décoratifs, Paris

2007

For Design Miami/Basel, Galerie kreo presents Front Design's Magic collection on the occasion of their Designer of the Future award

Exhibition *Jerszy Seymour: Living Systems*, Vitra Design Museum, Weil am Rhein, Germany

Exhibition *Ettore Sottsass: Work in Progress*, Design Museum, London

Konstantin Grcic is named "Designer of the Year," Maison & Objet, Paris

Hella Jongerius is named Art Director for Colors and Materials for the furniture company Vitra

Opening in Tokyo of the museum 21_21 Design Sight—the first Japanese museum dedicated to design—founded by Issey Miyake, Taku Satoh, and Naoto Fukasawa, and designed by architect Tadao Ando

Exhibition *Design contre Design*, curated by Jean-Louis Gaillemin, Grand Palais, Paris

2004

Exhibition *Andrea Branzi*, Fonds régional d'art contemporain–Frac Centre, Orléans

Exhibition *Ronan & Erwan Bouroullec*, Museum of Contemporary Art, Los Angeles

Exhibition *Zest for Life: Humberto and Fernando Campana*, Design Museum, London

Exhibition *Marc Newson: Kelvin 40*, Fondation Cartier pour l'art contemporain, Paris; Design Museum, London; Groninger Museum, Groningen, Netherlands

Pierre Charpin designs a water bottle for Eau de Paris, in an edition of 10,000 pieces

Konstantin Grcic designs the exhibition *Design en stock: 2000 objets du Fonds national d'art contemporain*, curated by Christine Colin, Palais de la Porte Dorée, Paris

2005

Marc Newson is named one of *Time* magazine's "World's Most Influential People"

First edition of Design Miami, founded by Craig Robins and Ambra Medda, one year prior to the inception of Design Miami/Basel

Exhibition *SAFE: Design Takes On Risk*, curated by Paola Antonelli, Museum of Modern Art, New York

View of the exhibition *Super Normal*, curated by Naoto Fukasawa and Jasper Morrison, Axis Gallery, Tokyo, 2006

Wieki Somers, *Merry-Go-Round Coat Rack*, 2008, permanent installation in the entrance area of the Museum Boijmans van Beuningen, Rotterdam

View of the exhibition *Quali Cose Siamo (The Things We Are)*, Triennale di Milano, curated by Alessandro Mendini, exhibition design by Pierre Charpin, Triennale di Milano, Milan, 2010

View of the exhibition *Pierre Charpin: vingt années de travail*, Centre d'innovation et de design, Grand-Hornu, Hornu, 2011

View of the exhibition *Marc Newson: At Home*, Philadelphia Museum of Art, Philadelphia, PA, 2013–14

2008

Galerie kreo moves to 31, rue Dauphine, in the 6th *arrondissement* in Paris

Exhibition *Ron Arad: No Discipline*, Musée National d'Art Moderne/Centre de Création Industrielle, Centre Pompidou, Paris; Museum of Modern Art, New York

Exhibition *Andrea Branzi: Open Enclosures*, Fondation Cartier pour l'art contemporain, Paris

Exhibition *BIG-GAME: Overview*, Grand-Hornu Images, Grand-Hornu, Hornu, Belgium

Exhibition *Jerszy Seymour: Being There*, Villa Noailles, Hyères, France

Exhibition *Ettore Sottsass*, Musée National d'Art Moderne/Centre de Création Industrielle, Centre Pompidou, Paris

Merry-Go-Round Coat Rack, permanent installation designed by Studio Wieki Somers for the entrance hall at the Museum Boijmans van Beuningen, Rotterdam

Ron Arad receives the Triennale di Milano's Compasso d'Oro for his Rocking Chair MT3 for Driade

Exhibition *Design and the Elastic Mind*, curated by Paola Antonelli, Museum of Modern Art, New York

2009

Exhibition *Aujourd'hui plus qu'hier et moins que demain: La Collection de design de Clémence et Didier Krzentowski*, Galerie des Galeries, Galeries Lafayette, Paris

Exhibition *Antibodies: The Work of Humberto & Fernando Campana 1989–2009*, Vitra Design Museum, Weil am Rhein, Germany

Exhibition *Pierre Charpin: Entre les vases*, MUDAC–Museum of Contemporary Design and Applied Arts, Lausanne

Exhibition *Konstantin Grcic*, The Art Institute of Chicago, Chicago

Exhibition *Design Real*, curated by Konstantin Grcic, Serpentine Gallery, London

Exhibition *Jasper Morrison: Take A Seat!*, Musée des Arts Décoratifs, Paris

Exhibition *Jasper Morrison*, Musée des Arts Décoratifs et du Design, Bordeaux; on this occasion, the exhibition *Super Normal*, curated by Naoto Fukasawa and Jasper Morrison, is also displayed

Exhibition *Wieki Somers: Thinking Hands, Speaking Things*, Stedelijk Museum 's-Hertogenbosch, Den Bosch, Netherlands

Installation *Jaime Hayon: The Tournament*, London Design Festival, London

François Bauchet designs the exhibition *Dessiner le design*, featuring Ronan & Erwan Bouroullec, Pierre Charpin, Marc Newson, Jasper Morrison, Konstantin Grcic, and Naoto Fukasawa, Musée des Arts Décoratifs, Paris

Opening of the Cité du Design, Saint-Étienne, France

2011

Exhibition *Ronan & Erwan Bouroullec: Bivouac*, Centre Pompidou-Metz, Metz, France; Museum of Contemporary Art, Chicago

Exhibition *Pierre Charpin: Vingt années de travail*, Centre d'innovation et de design, Grand-Hornu, Hornu, Belgium

Exhibition *Pierre Charpin et Ettore Sottsass: En verre et contre tout*, MUDAC–Museum of Contemporary Design and Applied Arts, Lausanne

Exhibition *Martin Szekely: Ne plus dessiner*, curated by Françoise Guichon, Musée National d'Art Moderne/Centre de Création Industrielle, Centre Pompidou, Paris

Ronan & Erwan Bouroullec receive the Triennale di Milano's Compasso d'Oro for their Steelwood chair for Magis

Ronan & Erwan Bouroullec are named "Designers of the Year," Maison & Objet, Paris

Konstantin Grcic recieves the Triennale di Milano's Compasso d'Oro for his Myto chair for Plank

Jean-Baptiste Fastrez and Brynjar Sigurðarson are joint winners of the Grand Prize, Design Parade, Villa Noailles, Hyères, France

Jerszy Seymour founds "The Dirty Art Department" program for the Applied Art and Design Masters, Sandberg/Rietveld Academy, Amsterdam, with Catherine Geel, Stéphane Barbier Bouvet, and Clémence Seilles

Publication of *The Complete Designers' Lights 1950–1990*, edited by Clémence and Didier Krzentowski (JRP|Ringier); revised and expanded edition in 2014

2010

Exhibition *Hella Jongerius: Misfit*, Museum Boijmans van Beuningen, Rotterdam

Exhibition *Confort*, curated by Konstantin Grcic in the context of the 7th International Design Biennale, Saint-Étienne, France

Exhibition *Quali Cose Siamo (The Things We Are)*, curated by Alessandro Mendini, exhibition design by Pierre Charpin, Triennale di Milano, Milan

Studio Wieki Somers participates in the exhibition *elles@pompidou*, Musée National d'Art Moderne/Centre de Creation Industrielle, Centre Pompidou, Paris

Pierre Charpin designs the exhibition *Mobi Boom: L'explosion du design en France, 1945–1975*, Musée des Arts Décoratifs, Paris

Opening of the Design Museum, Holon—the first museum dedicated to design in Israel—designed by architects Ron Arad and Bruno Asa

2012

Exhibition *Galerie kreo à Monaco*, the first exhibition held off the gallery's premises, Galerie Art & Rapy, Monaco

Exhibition *François Azambourg: 127 pièces*, Villa Noailles, Hyères, France

Exhibition *Guillaume Bardet: L'usage des jours*, Cité de la céramique, Sèvres; Centre d'innovation et de design, Grand-Hornu, Hornu, Belgium; Château des Adhémar–Centre d'Art Contemporain, Montélimar, France; MUDAC–Museum of Contemporary Design and Applied Arts, Lausanne

Exhibition *Ronan & Erwan Bouroullec: Album*, Vitra Design Museum, Weil am Rhein, Germany

Exhibition *Adrien Rovero: Landscale*, MUDAC–Museum of Contemporary Design and Applied Arts, Lausanne

Exhibition *Gino Sarfatti: Il design della luce*, curated by Marco Romanelli and Sandra Severi Sarfatti, Triennale di Milano, Milan

Publication of *Gino Sarfatti: Opere scelte, 1938–1973*, edited by Marco Romanelli and Sandra Severi Sarfatti (Silvana Editoriale)

Exhibition *La Naissance d'une icône du design: La chaise .03 de Maarten Van Severen*, Centre d'innovation et de design, Grand-Hornu, Hornu, Belgium

Julie Richoz receives the Grand Prize, Design Parade, Villa Noailles, Hyères, France

Edward Barber and Jay Osgerby design the torch for the London Olympic Games

First edition of the Istanbul Design Biennale, Istanbul

2013

Exhibition *Humberto and Fernando Campana: Barocco Rococo*, Musée des Arts Décoratifs, Paris

Exhibition *Ronan & Erwan Bouroullec: Momentané*, Musée des Arts Décoratifs, Paris

Exhibition *Jaime Hayon: Funtastico*, Groninger Museum, Groningen, Netherlands; touring in 2016–18 to the Shanghai Modern Art Museum, Shanghai; Songshan Cultural Park, Taipei, China; Design Museum, Holon, Israel

Exhibition *Julia Lohmann: The Department of Seaweed*, Victoria & Albert Museum, London

Exhibition *Marc Newson: At Home*, Philadelphia Museum of Art, Philadelphia

Exhibition *Living Objects—Made for India*, curated by Doshi Levien (Nipa Doshi and Jonathan Levien), Centre d'innovation et de design, Grand-Hornu, Hornu, Belgium

Hella Jongerius designs the interior of the North Delegates' Lounge, United Nations Headquarters, New York

Ronan & Erwan Bouroullec design the Gabriel chandelier, in collaboration with Swarovski, Gabriel staircase, Château de Versailles

View of the interior
for the United Nations
North Delegates'
Lounge designed
by Hella Jongerius,
United Nations
Headquarters,
New York, NY, 2013

View of the exhibition
*Konstantin Grcic:
Panorama*, Vitra
Design Museum,
Weil am Rhein,
Germany, 2014

View of the Nuage
Promenade,
conceived by Ronan
& Erwan Bouroullec
for the Miami Design
District, Miami, 2017

View of the exhibition
*Virgil Abloh: Figures
of Speech*, Museum
of Contemporary Art,
Chicago, IL, 2019

2015

Exhibition *Light Reflection*, the second exhibition held off the gallery's premises, Espace 11 Columbia, Monaco

Exhibition *Ronan & Erwan Bouroullec: 17 Screens*, Tel Aviv Museum of Art, Tel Aviv

Exhibition *Pierre Charpin: Villégiature*, Villa Noailles, Hyères, France

Exhibition *Olivier Gagnère*, Musée de Vallauris, Vallauris, France

Exhibition *Konstantin Grcic: The Good, the Bad, the Ugly*, Pinakothek Der Moderne Die Neue Sammlung–Design Museum, Munich

Exhibition *Jasper Morrison: Thingness*, Centre d'innovation et de design, Grand-Hornu, Hornu, Belgium

Exhibition *Muller Van Severen: Designers of the Year*, Bozar, Brussels

Exhibition *Maarten Van Severen & Co. Designers, Artists, and Makers*, Maarten Van Severen Foundation; Design Museum, Ghent

Exhibition *Lightopia*, Vitra Design Museum, Weil am Rhein, Germany; Fundação EDP, Lisbon; Design Museum, Ghent

Samy Rio receives the Grand Prize, Design Parade, Villa Noailles, Hyères, France

Ronan & Erwan Bouroullec design Le Kiosque, commissionned by the Groupe Emerige, Paris

2014

Galerie kreo opens at 14A Hay Hill, Mayfair, London

Exhibition *In the Making*, curated by Edward Barber and Jay Osgerby, Design Museum, London; Vitra Design Museum, Weil am Rhein, Germany

Exhibition *Konstantin Grcic: Panorama*, Vitra Design Museum, Weil am Rhein, Germany

Exhibition *Studio Wieki Somers: Out of the Ordinary*, Museum Boijmans van Beuningen, Rotterdam; touring in 2017 to MUDAC–Museum of Contemporary Design and Applied Arts, Lausanne

Marc Newson designs the Apple Watch as Apple's Designer for Special Projects

Alessandro Mendini receives the European Prize for Architecture

Daniel Rybakken receives the Triennale di Milano's Compasso d'Oro for his Counterbalance light for Luceplan

Exhibition *Fundamentals: 14th Venice Architecture Biennale*, curated by Rem Koolhaas, Venice

"After Ronan, who thought I was a fool, I received Erwan who wanted to check the possibility and seriousness of the 'Bouroullec House' project. Together, they finally gave me their approval for this project. We went to Nantes with Clémence, Didier, and Ronan, and the construction started. 'The machine' and its 'Gyro Gearloose' did the rest, under the technical and aesthetic supervision of the Bouroullec brothers. It is not only a marvel of design: it is a contemporary vision of architecture, of the intelligence of design, and above all, the testimony of the trust that can be built between artists, their worthy representatives, and their humble sponsor."
Laurent Dumas, friend of Clémence & Didier Krzentowski, 2019

View of Le Kiosque, modular and nomad pavilion conceived by Ronan & Erwan Bouroullec for Emerige, here located in the Jardin des Tuileries, Paris, 2015

2016

Exhibition *Ronan & Erwan Bouroullec: Rêveries urbaines*, Les Champs Libres, Rennes; in parallel, exhibitions at the Frac Bretagne (retrospective exhibition and *17 Screens*) and installation of Le Kiosque in the courtyard of the Parlement de Bretagne

Exhibition *Jasper Morrison: Thingness*, Tate Modern, London

Exhibition *Al(I)–Projects in Aluminum by Michael Young*, Centre d'innovation et de design, Grand-Hornu, Hornu, Belgium

Konstantin Grcic receives the Triennale di Milano's Compasso d'Oro for his OK chair for Flos

Daniel Rybakken receives the Triennale di Milano's Compasso d'Oro for his Ascent chair for Luceplan

Exhibition *21st Century: Design After Design*, Triennale di Milano, Milan

2017

Exhibition *Guillaume Bardet: La fabrique du présent. Premier chapitre: La Cène*, Couvent Sainte-Marie de la Tourette, Éveux, Lyon

Exhibition *Dan Friedman: Radical Modernist*, Design Museum, Chicago

Exhibition *Hella Jongerius: Breathing Color*, Design Museum, London; Museum Boijmans van Beuningen, Rotterdam

Exhibition *Hella Jongerius & Louise Schouwenberg: Beyond the New*, Pinakothek der Moderne Die Neue Sammlung–Design Museum, Munich

Exhibition *Ettore Sottsass: There Is a Planet*, Triennale di Milano, Milan

Exhibition *Ettore Sottsass: Rebel and Poet*, Vitra Design Museum, Weil am Rhein, Germany

Ronan & Erwan Bouroullec design the Nuage Promenade, Miami Design District, Miami

Pierre Charpin is named "Designer of the Year," Maison & Objet, Paris

Marc Newson is awarded The Design Prize: Lifetime Achievement Award, Salone del Mobile, Milan

2018

Exhibition *Ron Arad: Yes to the Uncommon*, Vitra Design Museum, Weil am Rhein, Germany

Exhibition *Daniel Rybakken: Daylights and Objects,* The Torsten and Wanja Söderberg Prize Exhibition, Helsinki Design Museum, Helsinki

Naoto Fukasawa receives the Isamu Noguchi Award

Exhibition *Azzedine Alaïa: The Couturier*, Design Museum, London, with the participation of Ronan & Erwan Bouroullec, Konstantin Grcic, and Marc Newson

2019

Exhibition *Virgil Abloh: Figures of Speech*, Museum of Contemporary Art, Chicago

Exhibition *BIG-GAME: Everyday Objects*, MUDAC–Museum of Contemporary Design and Applied Arts Lausanne

Exhibition *Jaime Hayon: Serious Fun*, Daelim Museum, Seoul

Exhibition *Hella Jongerius: Interlaces*, Lafayette Anticipations–Fondation d'entreprise Galeries Lafayette, Paris

Exhibition *Mondo Mendini: The World of Alessandro Mendini*, Groninger Museum, Groningen, Netherlands

Exhibition *Brynjar Sigurðarson*, The Torsten & Wanja Söderberg Prize Exhibition, Helsinki Design Museum, Helsinki

The Circle Flute (2015)—a collaboration between Brynjar Sigurðarson and singer Björk—is used for her *Cornucopia* world tour

Ronan & Erwan Bouroullec design the *Champs-Élysées Fountains*, rond-point des Champs-Élysées, commissioned by the Fonds pour Paris, Paris

Exhibition *Broken Nature: Design Takes On Human Survival,* curated by Paola Antonelli, Triennale de Milan, Milan

First edition of the Porto Design Biennale, Porto

This book is published to coincide with the twentieth anniversary of Galerie kreo, Paris and London. A French edition is also available.

Acknowledgments

Clément Dirié would like to extend his thanks to all the collaborators at Galerie kreo for their unstinting assistance during the preparation of the present volume, as well as to Clémence and Didier Krzentowski for the trust they have shown.

Clémence and Didier Krzentowski would like to express their gratitude to the gallery's designers and to all those appearing in this book, to the public and private partners who place their trust in the gallery, to all the collectors who share in their enthusiasm, to all the collaborators since 1999, as well as to Azzedine Alaïa, Alessandro Mendini, and Marcel Brient for their support—past, present, and future; and of course to their daughters, Victoire and Clara.

Finally, all three would like to thank all of the contributors to this book, as well as Julie Rouart, Kate Mascaro, and their teams at Flammarion for their assistance and eagerness while preparing this book for publication.

General Editor
Clément Dirié

Design
Amélie Boutry

Editorial Director
Julie Rouart

Editor
Marion Doublet

Administration Manager
Delphine Montagne

English Edition

Editorial Director
Kate Mascaro

Editor
Helen Adedotun

Translation from the French
David Radzinowicz

Translation from the Italian
(pages 314–19)
Alta L. Price

Copyediting
Lindsay Porter

Typesetting
Alice Leroy

Proofreading
Nicole Foster

Production
Corinne Trovarelli

Color Separation
Ilan Weiss, Brussels

Printed in Barcelona, Spain by Indice

Simultaneously published in French as *Made in kreo: Le laboratoire du design contemporain*

© Flammarion, S.A., Paris, 2019

English-language edition
© Flammarion, S.A., Paris, 2019

19 20 21 3 2 1

ISBN: 978-2-08-020419-6

Legal Deposit: 11/2019

Facing page
Ronan & Erwan
Bouroullec
Chaîne Mineral Simple,
2016
Special commission
Private collection
Plaster, metal, and
LEDs, h. 40 ft.
(h. 12 m)

Facing page
Studio Wieki Somers
Frozen Cabinet, Frozen in Time collection, 2010
Marcel Brient Collection
Plexiglas and brass hinges, h. 3 ft. 1 in. × w. 3 ft. 9 in. × d. 1 ft. 7 in. (h. 94 × w. 115 × d. 49 cm)

Page 376
Alessandro Mendini
Proust Armchair, All'Aperto collection, 2008
Private collection
Polyurethane structure, Bisazza mosaic tiles, h. 4 ft. × w. 5 ft. × d. 3 ft. 1 in. (h. 120 × w. 152 × d. 100 cm)